WELL-BEING IN AMSTERDAM'S GOLDEN AGE

WELL-BEING IN AMSTERDAM'S GOLDEN AGE

Derek Phillips

PALLAS PUBLICATIONS

Cover: Geert de Koning, Ten Post
Lay-out: ProGrafici, Goes

ISBN 978 90 8555 042 6
NUR 685/694

© Derek Phillips / Amsterdam University Press /
Pallas Publications, Amsterdam 2008

ONCE AGAIN, FOR KLASKE

CONTENTS

ACKNOWLEDGEMENTS

Authors of scholarly books inevitably incur debts, and acknowledgements are regularly made to those who helped them. Various foundations, funding agencies, and academic institutions are thanked for the financial support which made the study possible. Appreciation is expressed for leave time, and teachers, students, and research assistants are thanked as well. There are words of gratitude for scholarly colleagues and friends who carefully read different versions of various chapters. Thanks are given to academic audiences to whom portions of the work were presented in seminars and forums.

Authors nowadays often compete to outdo one another in listing their accumulated debts. Pulling down a few books from my shelves, I see that one author lists travels to twenty libraries and archives, and dutifully thanks staff members in each. Another thanks academic audiences at more than a dozen distinguished universities for helpful remarks and comments, and then goes on to expresses gratitude to a long list of hosts and hostesses, mentioning the food and drink they shared as well.

One author lists eight different sources of financial support. Another is eternally grateful for the help of twenty colleagues who read versions of different chapters, and is especially indebted to the seven scholars who read the final manuscript. All too often, these acknowledgements strike me as self-promoting and as offering (perhaps unintentionally) a self-portrait of the author as a seasoned networker and academic entrepreneur.

Virtually everyone thanks partners and family members. Not only spouse, children, and parents are mentioned by name, but sometimes siblings, nieces and nephews, and in-laws as well. So, too, are long-time friends. Increasingly, gratitude is also expressed to a helpful neighbor, the guys and gals at the gym, a jogging group, a hairdresser, and even a wonderful dog, cat, or, in a book I just opened, a parrot. In many books, an author's list of effusive acknowledgments seems endless.

This book has been largely a solitary labor, and I have accumulated few debts. I would like to thank the following persons for helping me: Lionel Lewis, Robert Loudon, Maurice Punch, and, most especially, my wife, Klaske Muizelaar.

INTRODUCTION

A s human beings, we have an innate disposition to care about the wellness of our being. This is evidenced in legends and literature throughout the world, in everything from fairy tales of the past to contemporary novels. Granted the difficulties of articulating a timeless ideal of well-being, it obviously bears upon the most important features of our common humanity. In most respects, after all, human beings are the same across time and space.[1]

We all care about staying alive, as well as about avoiding disease, physical pain, bodily harm, disability, and assaults on our dignity. Adequate nourishment, water, shelter, security, satisfying work, autonomy, and self-esteem are everywhere essential to human life and functioning. So, too, are relationships with others. These include giving and receiving care, loving and being loved. Our well-being matters for its own sake.

In recent years, philosophers, economists, demographers, sociologists, psychologists, epidemiologists, medical investigators, students of welfare, and policy-makers have become preoccupied with the subject. Whether termed well-being, quality of life, standard of living, or given some other designation, it is a topic of widespread scholarly interest today.

Some scholars are concerned with defending a particular concept of well-being, justifying its central and universal features, specifying its various dimensions or components, and locating the most adequate ways of assessing the wellness of people's being.[2]

Others are involved in empirical studies assessing the level of well-being in different times and places.[3] Most of these studies focus on people in one society or another at a given time. Sometimes, however, attention is given to people's well-being at different times or to comparing two or more societies during the same period.

Far less common are assessments of the well-being of different categories of people *within* a particular society.[4] Even rarer are such comparisons within a society retrospectively, that is to say, in historical perspective.[5] Rarest of all are historical comparisons within a specific city. The present study constitutes just such a retrospective assessment, focusing on well-being in Amsterdam's golden age.[6]

This book has two aims. Its major aim is to assess the well-being of Amsterdam's inhabitants, comparing people differentially located in the city's most important systems of inequality. Towards that end, I conceptualize well-being in terms of human functionings: biological, physical, social, and emotional. I identify its most relevant dimensions, specify various indicators relevant to assessing those dimensions, and examine the historical evidence concerning people's well-being.

The second aim is to identify, describe, and explain the mechanisms linking people's positions in the different systems of inequality to the wellness of their being. By so doing, I hope to deepen our understanding of the processes underlying differences in people's well-being not only in seventeenth-century Amsterdam but in other times and places as well.[7]

The book is a backward-looking exploration of well-being in a city where, as elsewhere in early modern Europe, inequality pervaded the lives of everyone. The word inequality is, however, too weak and virtually a euphemism when considered in terms of its *human cost* for many of Amsterdam's inhabitants.

The word understates and conceals power differentials among groups and within households, as well as what they meant for the quality of people's lives. This book describes these inequalities, most especially in the spheres of work and the domestic household, and examines their consequences for well-being.

Although emphasizing the equality of all in the eyes of God in the great hereafter, seventeenth-century religious authorities considered hierarchy and subordination as the very core of life on earth. So, too, did political and social commentators, the authors of books on good conduct, poets, playwrights, teachers, and almost everyone else who took pen to paper. Virtually all were men. Inequalities were viewed as reflecting the natural hierarchy of social distinctions, with privilege and authority for some and submission and obedience for others.[8]

In fact, a variety of inequalities structured people's everyday relations and well-being. Three, often overlapping, systems of inequality were especially significant: they were associated with civic status, economic standing, and gender. Dominance and subordination characterized each and played a large role in determining who got what and why. Apart and in combination, the three sources of inequality had an enormous impact on the wellness of people's being.

Consider, first, civic status. The Dutch Republic was by far the most decentralized state in early modern Europe. In the absence of a powerful central government, cities were semi-autonomous units, each with its own constitution, civil laws, administrative arrangements, rules, practices, and unwritten customs.[9] In a formal sense, there was no such thing as Dutch citizenship.

A city was physically distinguished from the countryside surrounding it by means of walls and gateways.[10] People living inside the walls regarded themselves as belonging to that city, rather than to an abstract Dutch Republic. Some people had the legal status of citizen, but most did not. Difference in civic status had a profound influence on the well-being of a city's inhabitants.

Citizenship was a crucial aspect of institutional arrangements everywhere, penetrating into virtually every aspect of life.[11] We are accustomed today to thinking of citizenship in terms of political equality and full membership in the polity. All citizens enjoy certain rights and privileges in common, most fundamentally the right to vote and to participate in government. Although the conception of citizenship in the Dutch Republic also involved having various rights and privileges, these basic rights were not among them. Citizenship referred to a formal relationship between the individual and the local community.[12] Though it excluded the right of every citizen to vote and participate in government, the relationship ensured that all citizens did have legal rights not enjoyed by non-citizens. It also provided citizens with various political, economic, and social privileges and advantages. These differed somewhat from one city to another.

Wherever people lived, however, the vast majority lacked the rights and privileges connected with citizenship. This was certainly true in Amsterdam with its civic hierarchy of regents (*regenten*) or the ruling elite, common citizens, non-citizen residents, and temporary inhabitants.

Membership in the governing elite was, in practice, restricted to a handful of rich patrician families. Through their power of patronage, the city governors wielded great political and economic influence.[13] Their jurisdiction included virtually everything that occurred in Amsterdam, and penetrated far beyond the political sphere into economic, educational, religious, and even familial arrangements in Amsterdam.[14]

The regents had enormous power. Their duties included making by-laws (*keuren*) that affected the well-being of everyone. A mass of detailed legal regulations specified people's entitlements, constrained their behavior, and stipulated sanctions for misconduct. They touched on both the private and the public sphere: marriage, the rights and obligations of husbands and wives, births and deaths, employment opportunities, wages and hours of work, education and vocational training, housing, poor relief, and even the clothing people were permitted to wear.

Membership in the other civic categories had an impact on people's work and earnings, as well as on the social benefits and charitable assistance to which they were entitled. That membership was, to a considerable extent, associated with the city's large immigrant population. During the seventeenth century, tens of thousands of migrants traveled to Amsterdam from other parts of the Dutch Republic, the southern Netherlands, Germany, the Scandinavian countries, Spain, Portugal, England, France, and elsewhere. At mid-century, roughly half of Amsterdam's inhabitants had come from somewhere else.[15]

A second major inequality among people in seventeenth-century Amsterdam was in their economic standing, with dramatic differences among the city's households.[16] Though not constituting a system of distinct classes as such, the wealthy elite, the middling group, the lower orders, and the poor occupied different positions within the city's economic, social, political, educational, and religious arrangements. By international standards of the time, inequalities in wealth and income in the city were extreme.[17] Over the course of the century, these inequalities increased.[18]

The major division was between the rich and everyone else, for the rich were set apart from all ordinary people who worked with their hands and earned a living by the sweat of their brows. Even so, differences in the economic standing dividing the middling group, the lower orders, and the poor also had an impact on people's well-being.

They had direct consequences for the ability of household members to meet their basic needs for housing, food, clothing, health care, and other subsistence needs, and thus for their survival and general well-being. These commodities were the *means* to help assure that individuals were physically secure, adequately nourished, warm, in decent health, and able to avoid escapable morbidity and premature mortality.

Economic inequalities were accompanied by feelings of intense superiority on the part of the wealthy elite. They viewed the poor and the many people who made up the lower orders as inferior creatures, variously calling them the rabble, the mob, the riffraff, and other pejorative names.[19] The wealthy and privileged used the expression "*het gemeen*" (the common people) in referring condescendingly either to the lowest orders or to the public in general.

The third major source of inequality was gender. The Dutch Republic was a male-dominated society, and inequality between the sexes existed everywhere. The two sexes were widely believed to be different sorts of beings, a belief with roots in the Christian tradition and in medical understanding of the biological differences between males and females. A woman's fundamental inferiority was thought to date from creation: weak and sexually innocent, she was thus in need of masculine guidance.

At the same time, a woman was believed to have an insatiable sexual appetite that derived from her physiology. Both popular stereotypes and the law regarded women as the more lustful sex, lying in wait to devour vulnerable males. She was, after all, the daughter of Eve. Such beliefs were a common theme in jokes, songs, books, the theatre, and works of art – all produced by men.[20] A woman clearly needed protecting from herself.

Much of a woman's life was spent in a position of dependence on a man: her father, another male relative, or, in the case of domestic servants, the head of the household that employed her; and then, if she married, on her husband. In general, a woman was expected to submit to the authority of a man. This is not to say, however, that every woman did so.

Women had less autonomy and less control over their lives than men. And although they were not prohibited from holding citizenship, women had fewer rights and privileges. This was true whatever their economic situation. The dominant ideology emphasized women's innate inferiority to men. Some women may have accepted this ideology, at least in part, but others did not. One reason is that many were actively engaged in making their own living.

Until relatively recently, historians of early modern Europe have identified "work" almost exclusively with the paid activities of men. But it has become clear that at some point in their lives the majority of women supported themselves, either fully or in part, by paid work.[21] This was particularly true of single young women.

In fact, domestic servants (*dienstmeisjes*) were the largest group of wage earners in seventeenth-century Amsterdam. Of the 200,000 residents in the last decades of the century, an estimated 12,000 worked as household servants, a number approaching the total membership of the city's fifty or so guilds.[22] Other adolescent girls and young women also left the parental home to labor at various kinds of poorly paid work.

Many spent a decade or so earning their own living before getting married in their mid or late twenties. Other women never married and continued to support themselves. Some were involved in paid work after marriage. Having been free of parental control for several years and earned their own living, it was difficult for these women to accept subjection to men. Not surprisingly, some men saw them as threatening the existing social order.

As with civic status and economic standing, the inequalities associated with gender were viewed by the privileged and powerful as right and proper. By God's ordinance, it was claimed, human beings are unequal: some will always occupy the highest positions, others somewhat lower positions, others still lower, and so on. This natural and perfect order must be maintained.

It is striking how often the literature at the time emphasized the need for individuals to know their place, recognize their limitations, and conduct themselves accordingly. Various Dutch writers called upon the of-ten-told tale of the fall of Icarus in this regard.[23]

The Icarus myth was a warning to those who aspired too high, aped the conduct of their betters, or strained against their proper position as assigned by an all-knowing God. With such behavior, wrote Jacob Cats and other authors of manuals for proper conduct, people risked sinking beneath their station. An individual who climbs higher than he ought, wrote Jacob Cats, will fall further than he had ever expected.[24] All should remain in their proper place.

It was in the scheme of things, then, for the governing elite to wield authority over common citizens, common citizens over non-citizens, non-citizen residents over temporary inhabitants, men over women, husbands over wives, parents over children, masters over apprentices, employers over employees, mistresses over servants. This authority was maintained and reinforced by both formal and informal mechanisms, many of them benefiting the privileged and powerful.[25]

People's face-to-face involvements with others reflected the dynamics of power: how it was exercised, accommodated, and resisted. Relationships were governed by norms and expectations of obedience, deference, respect, and other acknowledgements of superiority and subordination. The vast majority of individuals were, in fact, subject to the will of others. Humiliation and other unpleasant emotions would have been familiar to most people.

Interpersonal and institutionalized inequalities imposed material, physical, social, and psychological harms on the less advantaged. These harms were not always fully intended or willfully malicious. In fact, they were often unintended and unrecognized, as with paternalism and benevolent sexism in the relationships of men and women ("it's for your own good, dear").[26] Such inequalities affected the wellness of people's being.[27]

Similarly, vulnerable subordinates suffered harms in the absence of force, intimidation, manipulation, or explicit threats. Such harms are, in fact, a routine and often inconspicuous feature of unequal relations in every society.[28] So it has been through the ages. And so it was in seventeenth-century Amsterdam.

I will show that inequalities in civic status, economic standing, and gender had an impact on everything that enhanced or reflected people's well-being: their personal autonomy, the size and quality of their homes, what they ate, what they wore, their ability to read and write, the availability and conditions of work, their education and training, their susceptibility to disease, injury, and disability, and their life expectancy.

As regards life expectancy, nothing is more crucial to the wellness of our being than staying alive. Death is the final arbiter of my ability to attain the things I need and want. It eliminates my ability to function and my freedom to pursue life-enriching activities. Nothing is more comprehensive than the loss of my life, since it includes everything I care about and hold dear. The same holds, of course, for you and the loss of your life. Much writing about both well-being and early modern Europe forgets this simple fact. In this book, death and its disruptions occupy a prominent place.

-II-

For the most part, I focus on Amsterdam during the second half of the seventeenth century. My reasons for this choice of place and time are threefold. One is that differences between the urban and rural parts of the Dutch Republic, between the maritime and the inland provinces, and between the first and second half of the century, are too great to allow me to examine "the whole" of seventeenth-century Dutch society. Amsterdam, the Republic's largest and most important city, is an appropriate unit of analysis for a study like mine.

The second is that it allows me to draw upon archival data about Amsterdam families and their household goods gathered for other purposes. Supplemented by additional information about the people involved, Klaske Muizelaar and I used some of these inventories of household goods in a book about paintings in the domestic and imaginative lives of Amsterdam families.[29] Most of the men and women in these families were born in the period 1640-1660, and thus lived in the city during the second half of the seventeenth century.

A third reason is more personal, yet relates directly to the content of this book. In July 1971, I moved from New York City to Amsterdam. When I arrived, home was the place I left behind. For months and even years, that remained the case. From the beginning, however, I felt comfortable here. Over the years, I have come to embrace the city, to have strong feelings of belonging and attachment. In short, Amsterdam is now my home.

But "home" is not only a state of mind or a matter of sentiment. It can also be a physical structure, a place with walls and a roof, a place of shelter and security, a specific domicile. Here, too, my home is relevant to my focus on Amsterdam during the second half of the seventeenth-century.

For more than twenty years, I have been living in the kind of house in which most ordinary families lived in the city's golden age. My home consists of a basement and four floors above, each measuring about 4 x 7 meters. Today, my wife and I occupy the whole house. Three centuries ago, it was a multi-family dwelling lived in by three laboring families. They lined up behind the house to use the privy.

Much of my thinking about people's domestic lives, daily activities, and personal relationships has been informed by the place I call home. Knowing that it was once shared by three families has influenced my thinking about everyday routines, intimacy, and privacy within and amongst Amsterdam households. It has given me inside knowledge, as it were, about the size, internal division, heating, light, and comfort of the city's multi-family dwellings, as well as a sense of what people would have seen, heard, and smelled.

Home, as both a state of mind and a physical structure, features throughout this book. Both being at home and having a home are, I believe, central to people's well-being. In a city of immigrants, the sense of being at home differed within families coming from elsewhere. For many adults, home was the place they came from: if not a specific village, town, or city, then Germany, Norway, Spain, or wherever. Other immigrants lived in Amsterdam long enough to come to think of it as home. For their children who were born here, Amsterdam was home from the beginning.

Home as a physical structure had a direct and profound impact on the functioning and welfare of everyone. Its size, location, division of space, standard of hygiene, amount of light, ventilation, state of repair, and density of inhabitants had life and death consequences for household members. For some people, home was a large mansion on one of the city's main canals. For many more, home was a single room.

-III-

Since I conceive of well-being in terms of people's functioning in the widest sense, it is necessary to assess a plurality of distinct areas of human life in comparing the affects of civic, economic, and gender inequalities on the wellness of people's being. Given the nature of the human animal, certain things have importance for everyone.

Staying alive is the most crucial dimension of our well-being. In this connection, we care about food, water, rest, sleep, shelter and security (housing), and about avoiding disease, physical pain, and bodily harm. We care about them not only for their own sake but because they bear upon our interest in survival. Life has intrinsic value for all of us and (normally) a longer life is desirable in its own right.

Access to economic resources is a second important dimension of well-being. Economic resources are the means for satisfying our most basic subsistence needs and avoiding misery. Such resources may come from our own earnings, those of other household members, accumulated wealth, charitable or welfare arrangements, or other sources. Much human suffering arises from a lack of adequate economic resources.[30] Nothing has a greater impact on the length of our lives.[31] Some minimum level of financial security is essential for well-being.

Relatedness to others is a third dimension.[32] Each of us is some mother's child, and we have all experienced the relational character of human life. From birth onwards, social relationships are an inescapable given: at home with the family, at work, in the spheres of love and sex, and in a wide variety of other settings.

Such relationships may be intrinsically rewarding, as well as being sources of social support, solidarity, and identity.[33] They may also involve unhealthy dependence and vulnerability. Dependence and interdependence are central features of human life, and our emotional life is usually anchored in our involvement with other people.

Self-esteem, a secure sense of one's own worth, is a fourth important dimension of well-being. We all care about avoiding assaults on our honor or dignity: being humiliated, treated with cruelty, condescension, contempt, or as if we were invisible.[34] But it is difficult to maintain self-esteem in relationships characterized by hierarchy, domination, dependency, and subordination. This is particularly true of relationships from which it is difficult to withdraw.

Autonomy is a fifth dimension of well-being that everyone cares about.[35] Having autonomy means being able to do things for one's own reasons rather than simply responding to the needs, wishes, interests, or threats of others. Being autonomous contrasts with being a dependent, passive recipient of the actions of other persons. Autonomy can be only imperfectly realized in oppressive social relationships.

These five dimensions of well-being are to some extent intertwined and overlapping, and are anything but mutually exclusive. They are obviously not the only ones pertinent to people's functionings. I will be considering other dimensions of well-being in later chapters. In any case, we can generate a list of the things that people care about simply by considering what we must have and be able to do if we are to live and function in human society.

Just as it is difficult to provide an exhaustive list of the dimensions of well-being, it is also difficult to choose the most appropriate empirical indicators. This is a problem even when data are collected for the express aim of assessing well-being, as with studies of people in societies today.[36] It is a far greater problem in retrospective studies like mine.

I have chosen a variety of indicators for the different dimensions of well-being. Among them are housing conditions, diet, and infant mortality for the survival dimension; literacy, training, work, and charitable assistance for the economic resources dimension; relationships between husbands and wives, parents and children, and among siblings for the social relatedness dimension; and the character of work and family arrangements for the dimensions of self-esteem and autonomy.

Any investigator's choice of indicators is obviously limited by the availability of relevant evidence.[37] The necessary information is often lacking, partial, fragmented, or pertains to only a limited section of the population. This is one reason that retrospective assessments of well-being are so rare.

Retrospective assessments are also limited by the availability of the *type* of evidence relied on by most economists, economic historians, demographers, historically-oriented sociologists, and regional specialists: systematically collected data found in birth, marriage, death, and tax registers, and in databases containing information about rent, food prices, and the like. In the absence of this data, such scholars are reluctant to use other sources.

My approach is different. I take it for granted that there is often a lack of systematic data concerning the things that interest me. While I would prefer that such evidence were available, I assume that I can only approximate the empirical requirements of an ideal study design. This is certainly the case when assessing people's well-being more than three centuries ago. I consequently cast my net wide in seeking evidence about the different dimensions of well-being and their association with civic, economic, and gender inequalities.

As with my multidimensional approach to the dimensions of well-being, the use of multiple indicators has particular strengths. It allows for a more comprehensive and accurate assessment of differences in the wellness of people's being, and it increases the opportunities for uncovering the mechanisms linking these differences to people's positions in the city's main systems of inequality.

Although I utilize original sources as well, this book is based largely on recent research by other investigators. Some of it specifically concerns Amsterdam, some the Dutch Republic, and some early modern Europe. Most of the studies are by historians, many of whom are Dutch, and many are published in specialist journals (often in Dutch).

As well as historical research, I draw on studies by biologists, economists, demographers, psychologists, sociologists, specialists in public health, and other investigators that have relevance for the wellness of people's being. I use, for example, evidence about the impact of the disease environment (including air pollution, hygiene and sanitary conditions, sewage and waste disposal, crowding, and housing quality) on infant, child, and adult mortality.

Since I am concerned with the ways that inequalities affected people's well-being across the entire lifespan, I consider their impact during infancy, childhood, adolescence, adulthood, and old age, for the unmarried, the never-married, the married, the widowed, and the orphaned. With this lifespan approach, different dimensions of well-being emerge in my discussion and analysis. Throughout, my analysis is driven by the question "What was it like to...?"

Well-being concerns people's functionings: biological, physical, social, and emotional. We cannot, of course, recover the emotional lives of people long dead. How, then, can we gauge their feelings and emotions?[38] Archives, which occupy a privileged position in writings about the past, are the most logical place to look for evidence about what it was like to relate to others on the basis of civic, economic, or gender inequality, to be an immigrant in the city, to be sexually harassed, to have a child die in infancy, to lose a spouse, or to have both parents die.

While thousands of personal letters, diaries, memoirs, and autobiographical writings must have once existed, few survive today. Those that do come mainly from the well-placed.[39] Few of the writers were women.[40] Whatever their position in society, individuals indicated little about "what it was like to..."

Notable exceptions are the writings of a few wealthy men, expressing grief about the death of a loved one, pride in having secured a lucrative position, or anger about a child's failure to heed parental advice.[41] But little is revealed about personal setbacks, disappointments, or their own shortcomings. Perhaps a belief in their own superior rectitude prevented these men from even considering such subjects.[42]

Most individuals set little down on paper and almost nothing for introspective ends.[43] The silence of women in the historical record is especially apparent, though understandable.[44] Since they had a lower level of literacy than men, they were less often involved in keeping account books and family records. And they may have had less time and opportunity to record their thoughts. In any case, testimony from ordinary men and women about their private lives, social relationships, and personal feelings is generally absent from the written record.[45]

This does not mean, however, that we are totally ignorant about the emotions and feelings of people three or four centuries ago. After all, "ways of knowing" include more than an appeal to written documentation, data, facts, and other types of information. Insight, awareness, wisdom, the ability to empathize with historical actors, understanding, and explanation are also forms of knowing.[46]

Although I try to be as accurate as possible in drawing conclusions from the available evidence, precision is not the sole criterion for the adequacy of evidence. Relevance also plays a role, especially with regard to the emotional lives of people long dead. Consider the death of a husband or wife. Nothing can be inferred about a survivor's feelings from registers of death or studies based on such registers. Yet, loving and being loved are central to the goodness of our lives.

In discussing how the loss of a husband or wife would have affected an individual's well-being, I draw on contemporary research regarding the feelings and emotions. I draw as well upon insights and understandings acquired in a lifetime of reading. Novels, memoirs, and autobiographies are crucial in this regard.

Another way of learning about the feelings and emotions of people in other times and places is to examine the conditions that helped shape their emotional experience. The balance of power in their relationships is especially relevant. To the extent that structures of power operate in comparable ways, they give rise to similar emotional responses.

These responses are more than "merely personal"; they are a consequence of the relationships in which people find themselves.[47] Enough is known about the kinds of emotions evoked in certain relationships to make a critically informed inference about what people in other times and places would have felt in similar circumstances.

Consider, for example, someone who is under constant surveillance at work for signs of sloth or theft and is subjected to demeaning comments as well. It is easy to imagine him feeling anger or even rage. When intrusive supervision and negative comments occur in the presence of other people, feelings of embarrassment and humiliation are likely. Keeping the job may require him to keep his mouth shut. In such a situation, he may even act in a servile, obsequious, sycophantic, or fawning manner. A loss of self-esteem is the result.

It would, of course, be completely inappropriate for someone in this relationship of subordination to respond with feelings of pride. Sincere praise for a job well done, on the other hand, might very well give rise to feelings of pride.[48] In any case, humiliation and pride have nothing in common. Nor do, for example, fear, grief, envy, and affection.

Specific sorts of emotional feelings are rational and appropriate reactions to particular situations.[49] Our emotional responses sometimes give rise to other emotions, as when we are ashamed of feeling jealous. Emotions do not occur without reason, and we can usually describe them in terms of what they are about: an assault on one's dignity, a sense of loss, invidious comparison, remorse, or the violation of internalized moral standards.[50] This was as true in the Dutch Golden Age as it is today.

-IV-

In the remainder of this book I want to accomplish the two aims specified earlier: to assess the impact of inequalities in civic status, economic standing, and gender on people's well-being in seventeenth-century Amsterdam; and to identify, describe, and explain the mechanisms linking those inequalities to the wellness of their being.

I hope to accomplish something else as well: to remind readers of the extraordinary sameness of human beings throughout the ages. All too often, people in the past are presented as if they were quite different from the way we are today. But our shared humanity makes for an undeniable similarity among individuals everywhere. We begin as hungry babies. We eat and drink. We sleep. We get sick. We suffer. We love. We grieve. We die. So it is with all of us, and so it was in Amsterdam's golden age.

CHAPTER 1

IN THEIR PROPER PLACE: THE CIVIC HIERARCHY

I t is Thursday, July 29, 1655. Amsterdam's Town Hall is being inaugurated. Following a sermon in the New Church, the members of the city government leave the church and walk to the impressive new structure. Proceeding across the city's central square and then entering the Town Hall, they are led by the mounted guard and the city messengers. The rest of the procession takes the following order:

> My Lord Sheriff, going alone, with his aides at his side, of whom the first carried the rod of justice
> The Burgomasters
> Judges
> Ex-burgomasters
> Treasurers
> Trustees of the city orphans
> The council, without any distinction as to whether they
> were ex-magistrates or not
> The secretaries
> The clerks...

All are in their proper place.[1] The same rules of hierarchical order determined the assignment of various offices and chambers within the Town Hall itself, allotting the smaller quarters of lesser city functionaries on the basis of rank and seniority.[2]

Ceremonial precedence was operative on all official occasions in Amsterdam: as, for instance, with the position of a man's chair in meetings of the city governors, in swearing-in ceremonies, in criminal proceedings, and even in the funeral cortèges of high city officials. It reflected and embodied the centrality of inequality. Harmony or social order required hierarchy and subordination; all were expected to know their place.

The account of the inauguration is concerned with the hierarchical ranking of the members of the city government. But these men constituted only a small percentage of people who held Amsterdam citizenship, and a vastly smaller percentage of the total population of the city. The city had around 175,000 inhabitants at the time that the Town Hall was inaugurated in 1655 and more than 200,000 inhabitants by 1680. Let us consider, then, civic status in seventeenth-century Amsterdam.

-I-

The city's civic hierarchy consisted of regents (*regenten*) or the ruling elite, common citizens, non-citizen residents, and temporary inhabitants. Not all scholars, however, agree about these categories. Prak, for instances, speaks of regents, ordinary citizens, and the rest of the city's inhabitants. Elsewhere, he and Kuijpers collapse the distinction between the ruling elite and rest of the citizenry. In doing so, they downplay the vast distance between the regents and ordinary citizens.[3]

Although the distinctions were less finely calibrated than the rankings of the members of the city government, these hierarchical differences nevertheless had consequences for people's relationships to the urban community and to each other, their rights and obligations, the kinds of work they did, and their economic standing. Civic status affected the well-being of all concerned.

Regents: The Ruling Elite
The regents, that small group of prominent citizens holding office in city government, were at the top.[4] As elsewhere in the Dutch Republic, the city was governed by two bodies of men (women were excluded from public office): the *magistraat* or magistracy and the *Vroedschap* or Council. The magistracy had responsibility for administrative, legislative, and juridical matters. The Council's main responsibility was the yearly election of the magistrates.

In Amsterdam, the magistracy was made up of four burgomasters (mayors), a *schout* or sheriff, and nine *schepenen* or judges. This group wielded the political power in the city, although all matters of importance were supposed to be discussed with the council. The latter consisted of thirty-six men with life tenure, who themselves chose a new colleague whenever a vacancy occurred. But the council had little political power.

The office of sheriff was nominally the highest in the city. In practice, however, the burgomasters were the most important and powerful members of the government. It was they who were responsible for the day-to-day running of the city. Each of the four held the position for a term of two years and was then ineligible for a period of one year, being eligible after that for another term. During the intervals, the ex-burgomasters occupied other high positions in the city government. At any given time, there were usually fewer than a dozen men in this inner circle of reigning and ex-burgomasters.[5]

Amsterdam's form of government was oligarchic, with a few wealthy citizens exercising authority over the rest of the city's inhabitants.[6] In theory, any man who was 40 years of age and had been a citizen for at least seven years was eligible for the office of burgomaster. In reality, burgomasters were chosen from among a tiny group of the wealthy elite.

The city governors were elected from their own ranks, essentially by one another. Such elections took place within a circle consisting of only a few dozen regent families.[7] In no other country of Europe did regents acquire as much political and economic power as they did in the Dutch Republic.[8]

The same men served over and over again, controlling the patronage of virtually all the highest positions in the city and many of the lower posts as well: directors of the East and West India Companies, commissioners of the Exchange Bank, trustees of orphanages, directors of charities, heads of guilds, school teachers, and even the cobbler on the market.[9] Essentially, notes Van Nierop, the regents ran things for their own benefit.[10] Ordinary citizens were virtually powerless.

In both theory and law, the power of these men verged on the absolute. The Amsterdam regents, in fact, saw it as God's will that they should rule. If nothing else, they viewed their wealth as a sign of his intentions. Free from the burden of material want, from having to work with their hands or be dependent on others, the regents argued, they were able to devote themselves to ensuring the common good of all the city's inhabitants.[11]

Needless to say perhaps, the regents did work that was interesting, challenging, complex, allowed for a sense of accomplishment, and provided satisfaction. It took place inside, was clean, safe, involved little bending, and required no heavy lifting. These were men who never got dirt under their fingernails.

Along with setting the hours of work for others, the regents had the freedom to work whatever hours they liked: for the most part, it appears, a few half days a week. The four burgomasters, for example, ordinarily met four days a week in the morning from 10:00-12:00.[12] During the long summer months, the city fathers were often absent from the city for weeks at a time.

Common Citizens
Common citizens had no political involvement in the affairs that were important to their lives. Although powerless politically, they nevertheless enjoyed many advantages in comparison to non-citizen residents and tem-

porary inhabitants. Civic status was, in fact, the main way of identifying individuals in official documents.

Citizens were excused from paying certain tolls and could not be tried by courts outside Amsterdam. Within the city, they had to appear before the court only when called and had the right to present written documents in their defense. Non-citizens, on the other hand, could be incarcerated for interrogation and had no right to legal assistance.

More importantly, citizens had a privileged position in regard to eligibility for poor relief. And only their children were entitled to a place in the Burgerweeshuis (municipal orphanage) when they died, thus assuring that the children received superior care to that available in the city's other orphanages.

Lucrative professional and administrative positions and offices in the city were open exclusively to citizens. Only they were entitled to exercise a trade or market their commodities. In addition, citizenship conveyed a measure of social status and served as evidence of an individual's honor and good reputation.[13] While the regents generally saw everyone else as *gemeente* or common folk, ordinary citizens attempted to distance themselves from those they considered their inferiors: people lacking citizenship.[14]

In principle, every male citizen between the ages of 18 and 60 was expected to serve in one of Amsterdam's militia companies (*schutterijen*). But militiamen had to buy their own equipment, thus effectively excluding many ordinary citizens. The militia's officers were appointed by the burgomasters. Without exception, these officers were from regent families. Leadership functions were too important to be left to common citizens. The militia companies were one of the few places where at least some common citizens came into direct contact with the regent elite.[15]

Only citizens could belong to Amsterdam's craft guilds. Entry to the city's fifty or so guilds was undoubtedly the greatest advantage of citizenship, as it had direct consequences for an individual's ability to earn a living. Belonging to a guild had a considerable impact on the well-being of guild members and their families.

A guild functioned to serve the interests of its members in several ways: by excluding outsiders, setting the length of training, limiting the size of workshops, regulating the hours of work and other working conditions, fixing output quotas, and doing whatever else was necessary to ensure a monopoly in the production and sale of its products. Many of these measures were justified in terms of ensuring the high quality of guild members' work.

Along with the advantages that guilds provided for earning a living, they offered other benefits affecting the well-being of members and their families. Social insurance did not yet exist. But guilds were a source of mutual aid to minimize the effects of illness, invalidism, old age, widowhood, and death. Through their members' contributions, they provided funeral expenses, sick care, and pensions for members, their wives, and widows.[16] Craft guilds had, in fact, enormous control over the lives of their members.

Most guilds had no women members. The seamstresses had their own guild. And a few women belonged to the guild for peat carriers. Although requiring citizenship, it was a poor-paying job of low status. Carrying peat (turf) was dirty work involving heavy lifting and being outside in all kinds of weather.

This makes it clear that the general absence of women in Amsterdam' guilds was not the result of a paternalistic concern that artisan activities were too physically strenuous and demanding for members of the fairer sex. Instead, it reflected the judgment that women should be kept in their appropriate position as subordinates to men. This meant keeping them out of most guilds. In general, women's citizenship constituted a sort of "secondary" citizenship.

An individual could become a citizen (*poorter*) in four ways: through birth, marriage, purchase, or special dispensation. The children of Amsterdam citizens automatically acquired citizenship, and this was the usual way that people became citizens. Every generation was required to reconfirm its citizenship by swearing the citizens' oath before a local official.[17]

Although women were not excluded from citizenship, housekeeping and raising children were seen as the real business of a woman's life. But having citizenship gave the daughters of citizens a privileged position in the marriage market, since a man without citizenship could acquire it by marrying a citizen's daughter.

During the second half of the century, marrying an Amsterdam woman was the most common way of becoming a citizen for those who had not acquired it by birth.[18] Obtaining citizenship through special dispensation from the city government, as some religious refugees from elsewhere and a few public figures did, was unusual.[19]

Purchasing citizenship was expensive, costing 50 guilders after 1650. Of that amount, 22 guilders were designated as funds for people in need.[20] Given an average yearly income of 300-350 guilders, 50 guilders was the equivalent of two or three months' wages. Such an amount was beyond the means of most people. More than 90 percent of migrants to the city never acquired citizenship.[21] Some became non-citizen residents, while others remained in the city only temporarily or traveled back and forth for seasonal work. All were second-class townspeople.

In fact, only a minority of Amsterdam inhabitants held citizenship. The regents were, of course, citizens. They made up less than one percent of the city's families.[22] Even this figure may be too high, since many of the same men held office over and over again in seventeenth-century Amsterdam.

The powerful regent, Andries Bicker, for example, served ten times as burgomaster between 1627 and 1649; and Johannes Hudde served twenty-one times between 1672 and 1703. Men filling other official and professional positions in the city were also citizens. Soltow and van Zanden estimate their number at less than 3 percent of the total number of heads of households in the city.[23]

Members of the city's guilds constituted the largest number of Amsterdam citizens. Guilds are known to have had 11,000 members in 1688, although the actual number may have been as high as 13,000. They accounted for roughly 25 percent of all adult males in the city.[24] Assuming that each guild member headed a household, these men provided the advantages of citizenship to 25 percent of the city's population.

Beyond the regents, guild members, and high officials and professionals, it is difficult to determine the number of Amsterdammers holding citizenship. Jews could become citizens, but were generally excluded from guild membership. As with women and non-citizens, they were apparently viewed by guild masters as possible competitors. Perhaps for the same reason, retailing and manufacturing also excluded Jews. Some were employed in the tobacco, sugar, chocolate, silk, diamond, and publishing industries, which were not organized as guilds, and others worked as small-scale merchants.

Jews made up less than three percent of the population around 1650 and perhaps six percent at the end of the seventeenth century. Few were citizens.[25] Among those who were, citizenship did not automatically pass from parents to children as with Christians in the city. Each generation had to purchase citizenship anew.[26]

Another small proportion of citizens consisted of wage-earners outside the guilds. Kuijpers and Prak found that almost one-third of the men purchasing citizenship in the period 1636-1652 earned their wages as soldiers, seafaring men, and ordinary laborers, occupations for which citizenship was not required.[27]

Citizenship was attractive for these men, the authors suggest, because it provided their families with a privileged position in obtaining poor relief and entitled their children to admission to the municipal orphanage if both parents died. But relatively few men outside the guilds purchased citizenship.

The total number of men purchasing citizenship was, in fact, quite small: in the period 1636-1652, around four hundred a year. By 1690, the number had dropped to fewer than two hundred a year. The total acquiring citizenship through purchase, marriage, or special dispensation in that year was roughly six hundred.[28]

The proportion of the population holding citizenship consisted, then, of regents, professionals and the occupants of high positions in the city who received a salary, the members of Amsterdam guilds, some male citizens working outside the guilds, a small number of Jews, and an unknown number of female citizens heading households. Taken together, no more than a third of Amsterdam families enjoyed the benefits of citizenship.[29]

In the hierarchy of civic status, the regents made up the ruling elite. Below the regents was the much larger number of people entitled to the many advantages of citizenship, but lacking political power. Most of the common citizens (but few women) were guild members. And below the common citizens were the two-thirds of the populace *without* the privileges associated with membership in the Amsterdam community: non-citizen residents and temporary inhabitants.

According to Van Nierop, pamphlets and diaries from the time agreed on a threefold division of "rulers, common citizens, and 'the mob' (*regenten*, *burgers*, and *gemeen* or *grauw*)...." The mob, he says, consisted of all those below the level of economically independent citizens. But, he notes, "most of our information comes from individuals with a high social status, who regarded the lower orders with feelings of suspicion and disdain."[30] Let me consider, then, the so-called lower orders.

Non-Citizen Residents and Temporary Inhabitants
Throughout the seventeenth century, the number of deaths exceeded the number of births in Amsterdam. Infant mortality was high, and bubonic plague and other epidemics of communicable disease took many lives. Epidemics of the plague in Amsterdam in 1655, 1663, and 1664 exacted a high toll.[31] The impact on people's physical well-being was considerable.

Tens of thousands more men died at sea and while working abroad. Among men employed by the VOC (Dutch East India Company), unhealthy living conditions on board ship and in Java and other colonial posts were responsible for a particularly high death rate. Of the 300,000 people who left for the East Indies in the service of the VOC during the seventeenth century, only a third ever returned to the Netherlands.[32]

Even more men were involved in seafaring activities other than the VOC, but no figures are available for the death rate among men serving in the West India Company, in the navy, and in the whaling and fishing industries.[33] In any case, the high mortality rate among seamen resulted in a large surplus of women in Amsterdam during the last decades of the century.

The city was able to grow and maintain its labor force only because of a huge influx of people from elsewhere.[34] As emphasized by Erika Kuijpers in her recent book, *Migrantenstad (Migration City)*, Amsterdam was a multicultural city. She estimates that a minimum of 425,000 immigrants came to Amsterdam during the period 1600-1700, with more coming during the first than the second half of the century. This was an average of 4,000-5,000 people a year.[35] Family migration was more common earlier in the century, with unmarried men and women being more common later on.

Roughly 40 percent of the immigrants came to Amsterdam from somewhere else in the Dutch Republic, a third from Germany, 10 percent from the Scandinavian lands, and the remainder (around 17 percent) from elsewhere in Europe.[36] Among them were some wealthy families from the Southern Netherlands. At mid-century, half of the city's population had been born outside the borders of the present-day Netherlands.

Migrants had a variety of reasons for leaving the places and people they knew best and becoming strangers, aliens, and outsiders in a foreign city. Most migrated because of poor economic conditions, often to escape poverty. They were "subsistence migrants," searching for a means to maintain themselves rather than social betterment.[37] Like most people at the time, survival was their major concern.

Others left to escape religious persecution. Runaways, fleeing to escape unsatisfactory relationships, unwanted responsibilities, and unpaid debts, also migrated. Amsterdam offered the possibility of religious freedom and, more importantly, opportunities for semi- and unskilled wage work. Some came for reasons of curiosity, novelty, or were attracted by the lure of the big city. Although the "pull" factors were important, the "push" factors of escaping poverty and economic misery were more so.

Some migrants were just passing through, coming to do a particular kind of seasonal work, staying a night or two in Amsterdam, and then traveling on to the countryside to do haying, work on the dikes, or labor in the peat bogs. These seasonal migrants arrived in the early spring and worked until November, when they returned to wherever they had come from.[38]

Other migrants intended to stay a few years in Amsterdam, perhaps acquiring some sort of training, accumulating savings, and then returning to their place of birth.[39] They were likely to be young, unmarried, and without children. Many were young women who sought work as household servants. These were temporary migrants. No one knows exactly how many there actually were. There was no counting or registration of migrants leaving their home towns, arriving in Amsterdam, or leaving Amsterdam to return whence they came.

Then there were the so-called permanent migrants, individuals who came to Amsterdam with the intention of remaining there. Among them were people unable to return home, for economic, religious, or political reasons, or because of bad debts, troubles with the law, or the like. Others may have hoped to acquire citizenship, become a member of a guild, and build a career in Amsterdam. Whatever their intentions, it is difficult to imagine a more important decision than to immigrate.

This three-fold division of seasonal migrants, temporary migrants, and permanent residents is obviously schematic.[40] Some people who came as seasonal workers remained several years in Amsterdam, a few even permanently. Some temporary migrants married, had children, and then spent the rest of their lives in the city. Most became non-citizen residents. Others intending to remain permanently gave up and returned home. And some migrants, many of them poor women, were ready to move to wherever they might make a living.[41]

In what has long been considered the definitive research into the composition of Amsterdam's population in the seventeenth and eighteenth centuries, Simon Hart counted more than 2,000 different occupations or job-designations in the city.[42] Far and away the largest group consisted of seafaring men, employed by the Dutch East India and West India Companies, in the navy, and working in the whaling and fishing industries.

According to Hart's estimate, they made up 22 percent of the Amsterdam work force. One in five was a citizen of the city, one in five was from elsewhere in the Dutch Republic, and three in five were from elsewhere in Europe.[43] In the second half of the century, more seamen came from the coastal areas of Norway than anywhere else.[44]

Although Hart found that seamen were the largest occupational group in the city, some scholars writing about Amsterdam virtually ignore them. It is easy to understand why. Even though seafaring men crowded into the city in the spring and autumn, when ships came and went, they were otherwise absent for months or even years at a time. Many, because of the high mortality rate, never came back.

Even when not physically present in the city, some seamen maintained a household in Amsterdam. Their wives and children were thus non-citizen residents. We know this because Hart based the percentage of seafaring men in Amsterdam on the occupations of bridegrooms listed in the declarations of intent to marry (*banns*). Although the occupations of brides were never recorded, a high percentage were probably domestic servants.

Like Hart, other historians have used declarations of intent to marry as evidence about people's age at marriage, the occupations of bridegrooms, their places of birth, and, based on whether or not they could sign their name, the literacy of brides and bridegrooms. But these registers, argues Kuijpers, have serious weaknesses as evidence.

For one thing, some people married clandestinely. More importantly, migrants are severely underrepresented in the marriage registers. This is because the evidence relates only to those migrants who married *in* Amsterdam. It ignores men and women who were already married when they arrived, those who moved on to marry elsewhere, and those who never married (more often women than men).

By Kuijper's estimate, in the first quarter of the seventeenth century only one in five immigrants in Amsterdam married. This rose to perhaps two in five during the course of the century. Thus, the majority of immigrants are completely left out of calculations based on marriage registers.[45] The implications of this are enormous. With seamen, the largest occupational group represented in the registers, there were probably five times as many foreign-born as is indicated by the registers.[46]

Whatever their actual number, only a minority of the households headed by seamen enjoyed the benefits connected with citizenship. The wives and children of seafaring men were non-citizen residents rather than temporary inhabitants. Their husbands may have intended to settle ashore after just a few years of seafaring.[47] Most, however, did not do so. In any case, non-citizen residents were sometimes entitled to receive charitable assistance not available to temporary inhabitants.[48]

-III-

Strangers in the City
Most immigrants arrived in Amsterdam by ship, having traveled with friends, relatives, or other trusted companions. Travel was uncomfortable and often took several days or even longer. Typically, an immigrant had no savings and little in the way of possessions: perhaps some extra clothing, a few tools, and food to eat on the way.

For those planning to stay, whether temporarily or permanently, starting life over in a strange city was often a terrifying prospect. Contacts with people already living in Amsterdam were crucial. Many immigrants entered the city with an address in their pocket: for a relative, an acquaintance, a friend, a friend of a friend, or perhaps a cheap lodging. Those lacking contacts or connections must have been especially apprehensive about their future in a new place. They were, I imagine, homesick and lonely. But we have no record of how they felt.

An immigrant's first concern was to find a job and a place to sleep for the night. For most, finding somewhere to stay was probably most crucial. It was important that the lodgings were affordable in terms of expected earnings. This might mean sharing a room or even a bed with one or more other people in a cheap room in the harbor area.[49]

Newcomers were forced to take whatever work they could get. More often than not, this meant bottom-of-the-heap jobs. Most jobs required little or no training or special skills.[50] Thus men who came with some specialized training were unlikely to find the kind of employment they wanted. Few, however, had such training. Women, too, encountered uncertain employment, bad working conditions, and low pay. They often ended up as domestic servants.

Many immigrants found employment in unskilled and poorly paid jobs in the textile and building industries, the shipyards, breweries, sugar refineries, and elsewhere, toiling as ordinary day-laborers, dock hands, sailors, soldiers, and in other types of physically demanding and disagreeable work.

With 1,000-1,200 men working in the Oostenburg shipyards, the East India Company (VOC) was far and away the city's largest employer.[51] Employment at the VOC's wharves and warehouses meant steady work, and was thus highly prized, but only a small percentage of VOC employees worked in the city.

Every year the VOC recruited thousands of young men as sailors and soldiers. Amsterdam was its main recruitment center. "It is hardly an exaggeration," write De Vries and Van der Woude, "to say that the Company [VOC] swept the city streets of beggars and the unemployed."[52] The majority had been born elsewhere and were desperate for work. As Lucassen points out, "It was the worst imaginable alternative for someone seeking employment: low wages, years of separation from home, a good chance of dying en route or in the Far East."[53]

It was work done out of necessity, in which men had little autonomy and toiled in relationships of domination and subordination. In such circumstances, their self-esteem must have been severely undercut. On board ship, Dutch-speaking men had higher positions than the seamen from Scandinavia. With ships sailing from Amsterdam, the ranks of officers were made up mainly of the sons of regents and of high-ranking officers.[54]

A similar pattern existed with soldiers: large numbers of foreign-born men in the lower ranks were commanded by Dutch-speaking officers from a regent background.[55] What was it like, I wonder, for these foreign-born seamen and soldiers to hear orders barked in a language they could barely understand?

Some migrants ended up doing the same sort of work friends, acquaintances, and fellow-countrymen – their first contacts in Amsterdam – were doing. We can see this from the overrepresentation of men from the same regions of the Dutch Republic, Germany, and Scandinavia in particular kinds of work: for example, as tailors, cobblers, bakers, and seamen.[56]

Virtually nothing is known about the men's backgrounds and possible training in their countries of origin. Some probably arrived in the city with experience in these occupations. But it is more likely that they were drawn to the occupations by way of contacts with acquaintances in Amsterdam coming from the same regions as they did.[57]

Although men and women in subordinate positions usually understood enough Dutch to follow orders, language was a problem for many. Immigrants from different areas of the Dutch Republic were generally able to understand one another, albeit sometimes with difficulty. Those from Germany could usually get by. But the Dutch language would not have been fully comprehensible to people from Scandinavia, and even less so for those from England, France, Spain, and Portugal.

Learning to speak *Hollands* (the official name for Dutch) was a problem.[58] There is a critical period around age thirteen after which most people learning a foreign language are unable to pronounce words like a native-born speaker.[59] People older than that often speak with thick accents and in broken sentences, making the same mistakes over and over. This would have been the case with many immigrants from the countries above.[60] Few people are fluent in a language learned during adulthood.

In any case, language served to "place" the city's inhabitants, both in terms of where they came from and where they belonged in the civic hierarchy. It also served as an important means of describing people. This can be seen in notices appearing in the city's oldest newspaper: the *Amsterdamse Courant*.

Published three times a week, the paper contained local, national, and international news, much of it concerning wars, business, and general affairs. From around 1625, it also contained what were termed *advertisse-menten* or advertisements. These were usually reports or notices rather than advertisements as we know them today. They concerned positions offered and sought, announcements of sales, auctions, and the like, and notices about missing persons, runaways, and thefts or other crimes.[61] Consider some examples.[62]

A notice in the issue of August 8, 1690, reports that a servant, employed in the houschold of Simon Koeslager, has stolen a large sum of money and valuable household goods. Her name is given as Elisabet or Lysbet, she is 26-30 years of age, was born in Brabant or Luyk, and speaks only limited French (the language often spoken in the homes of the rich at the end of the century).

The servant's employers are uncertain as to her first name, her age, or where she came from. It is unlikely that they knew her last name, since a servant was usually referred to either by her first name or simply as "the servant girl." Servants were often viewed as a means to satisfy the needs of the family employing her and not as people in their own right.

A notice on September 29, 1693, seeks information about a missing boy: Joan Hendrik, eleven years of age, who is described as speaking only high German (*Hoogduyts*). This was apparently his mother tongue, suggesting that the boy was newly arrived and had not yet learned to speak Dutch.

A notice appearing on October 3, 1690, places the emphasis on someone's proficiency with Dutch and other languages. It concerns an Englishman, Barener Randolph, born in Kent, and forty-five years of age. Described as speaking through his nose, he is said to speak good Dutch, along with good English, some French, good Italian, and "Turks" as well. He seems to have been missing in connection with some sort of financial transaction.[63]

With a high level of migration to Amsterdam throughout the seventeenth century, generational differences in linguistic assimilation were significant: the usual pattern with immigrants.[64] The first, or immigrant, generation arrived speaking their native tongue (or dialect) and probably learned just enough Dutch to get by.

People who stayed in the city spoke their native tongue to their children: the second generation. Many a mother must have told her children about life *before*: before she came to Amsterdam, before she was a wife, before she was a mother. Fathers probably did the same. Inevitably, this must have raised questions in the children's minds about what might have been.

Although they were raised hearing German, Norwegian, Swedish, Spanish, French, English, or another language or dialect at home, the children learned Dutch: on the streets, in school, in apprenticeships, and at work. It is likely that most were bilingual, speaking an immigrant language with their parents and Dutch in other situations.

When people from the second generation married, Dutch was the language spoken to their own children: the third generation. Born and raised in the city, second and third generation immigrants probably considered Amsterdam their home. For people of the first generation, home was the place they came from.

At the same time, linguistic assimilation and feelings about home differed in many ways: depending, for example, on where people in the first immigrant generation had come from, on whether both of a child's parents had the same native tongue, and on whether there was back-and-forth travel between Amsterdam and a migrant's original home.

So far as I am aware, these differences have never been a subject of scholarly inquiry. In fact, little attention has been given to the significance of language differences in the Dutch Golden Age.[65] But the ability to speak Dutch would have enhanced an individual's sense of being at home in Amsterdam.

The same was true about being able to read and write the language. As measured by the ability to sign one's name on a marriage certificate or other legal document, the Dutch Republic had the highest level of literacy in Europe. Late in the seventeenth century, 75 percent of Amsterdam-born bridegrooms and 53 percent of Amsterdam-born brides could sign their own names.

The proportions were smaller for men and women born abroad, with only 30 percent of the women being able to sign.[66] A higher percentage could read. It took between one and three years to learn to read, and a further three years to learn to write. Fewer people could write than read since many families could not afford to keep their children in school long enough to acquire writing skills.

Still, most people were able to attach their signature to a document. But this is only the most basic element of literacy.[67] It indicates nothing about the ability to write a letter or maintain a personal diary or notebook. The vast majority of people were unable to write with ease.[68]

Learning to speak the language and to read and write were problems for many first generation immigrants. Their general lack of autonomy was another. Even more than their children and grandchildren, members of the first generation experienced a lifetime of dependence on the better-situated. Disproportionately, they did the city's dirty work.

These immigrants had come to the city because of poverty and limited prospects for work in their place of origin. It is likely that they did earn more in Amsterdam than they had at home. But the city was also more expensive than most other places in Europe.[69]

Wages remained generally stable over the century, while the cost of such necessities as food and rent increased.[70] This had, of course, a deleterious affect on the well-being of ordinary wage-earners. They were, in fact, worse off at the end than at the beginning of the seventeenth century. While the rich got richer, the poor got poorer.

Kuijpers attempted to trace a sample of immigrants from Germany back to the places they came from so as to compare their work and earnings there and in Amsterdam. But her attempt at "record-linking" proved unsuccessful.[71]

For one thing, numerous individuals in both places had the same names. For another, men's names in the Amsterdam marriage registers were translated into Dutch variations of German names. The German Heinrich, for instance, became Hendrik or, sometimes, Dirk. Moreover, several German villages had identical names, and the names of many villages had multiple spellings.

Whatever their situation at home, Kuijpers is surely correct in referring to those immigrants from Germany, Scandinavia, the east of the Republic, and elsewhere as the "guest workers" (*gastarbeiders*) of seventeenth-century Amsterdam.[72] They did the heavy, dirty, dangerous, and lowly-paid work shunned by Amsterdam citizens, toiling twelve or thirteen hours a day, usually outside, whatever the weather. No more than today, were they integrated with the native population. Their well-being left much to be desired.

Chapter 2

GRADIENTS OF WEALTH AND INCOME: THE ECONOMIC HIERARCHY

T he year is 1682. Adriaen de Waert, a wealthy regent, is appointed *schout* or sheriff for the city of Amsterdam. De Waert, his wife, and children are living in a large house on the Keizersgracht, located between the Leidsestraat and the Spiegelstraat. They own a country estate as well. Domestic servants in both houses see to their daily needs.[1]

The position of sheriff is the most lucrative in the city government: the man occupying it receives half of the fines that people are sentenced to pay for misconduct.[2] His activities are largely uncontrolled, and the reputation of the office of sheriff is far from spotless. During the 1669-1732 period, Amsterdam sheriffs earned roughly 6,000 to 9,000 guilder per annum. De Waert earns more than 7,000 guilders during his year in office. At the time of his death in 1695, De Waert's wealth was estimated at 275,000 guilders.[3]

-I-

In terms of both wealth and income, the rich and the rest lived in different worlds. Wealth means such assets as land, houses, horses, carriages, boats, cash, stocks, bonds, gold and silver, jewelry, paintings, porcelain, tapestries, furniture, etc. Many rich families had wealth exceeding 100,000 guilders.[4] The wealth of some, like Adriaen de Waert, went far beyond that. These men seem to have devoted their lives to the accumulation of money and whatever it could buy.

In the large and stately mansions that the rich called home, the carpets underfoot, the paintings on the walls, the custom-made beds in which they slept, the fashionable clothing in which they were dressed, and the rest of the expensive furnishings and decorations spread through their homes often represented expenditure of tens of thousands of guilders.

At the other extreme, the total wealth in four out of five Amsterdam households amounted to less than 1,000 guilders.[5] While the wealthy elite may have owned several houses in Amsterdam and elsewhere, few other people owned the roofs over their heads. Most, in fact, lived in buildings owned by the rich. I will be saying much more about the city's housing conditions in Chapter 3.

The differences between the wealth of the rich and the rest were enormous. In 1674 the richest one percent of Amsterdam households owned about 45 percent of the total wealth in the city, and the richest 10 percent 93 percent of the total.[6] Representing an estimate based on taxes for the total wealth of all household members, these figures probably underestimate the extent of wealth inequalities. This is because the vast majority of households had too little wealth to be subject to the wealth tax.[7]

The distribution of household incomes was also highly unequal. Little is known about the incomes and earnings associated with most kinds of work in the seventeenth century or the bases on which they were established. Evidence in this regard is fragmentary and incomplete. But information from surviving tax records for a slightly later period allows us to see the *comparative* earnings of people in the city's workforce.

In 1742 all Amsterdam households – including individuals living alone – were assessed a tax payment on the basis of their yearly earnings. Only those households with an annual income of 600 guilders or more were taxed. The records indicate that 77 percent of the city's households paid no taxes at all.[8] The pattern of earnings fifty or so years earlier would not have differed substantially, since tax inequality is known to have risen until 1700 and then remained the same for almost half a century.[9]

People's incomes were tied to their positions in the civic hierarchy. It was not, however, a one-to-one relationship. Regents generally had the highest incomes, but a small number of other wealthy citizens had similar earnings. Still, regent households had higher earnings than the vast majority of citizens, non-citizen residents, and temporary inhabitants. Similarly, some people without citizenship earned as much or more than some citizens. But again, citizen households had higher earnings than the bulk of people who lacked citizenship.

De Vries and van der Woude provide an estimate of the proportion of households in different income categories among those earning less than 600 guilders a year.[10] I have combined this information with the tax assessment from 1742 in arriving at Table 2.1.[11] It shows what the distribution of incomes in Amsterdam would have looked like around 1700.

The Wealthy Elite
A high position in the Amsterdam government was a sure path to riches, as we saw with the position of sheriff. Regents used their positions to benefit themselves, their families, and their friends.[12] In making decisions about the expansion of the city's canals and the availability of lots for building,

Table 2.1   *Distribution of Incomes in Amsterdam around 1700*

Income Bracket	Percentage of Total
4,000 guilders and more	2 %
2,000-3,999 guilders	3
1,000-1,999 guilders	7
699-999 guilders	10
500-599 guilders	8
400-499 guilders	10
350-399 guilders	15
300-349 guilders	30
less than 300 guilders	15
Total	100 %

for instance, the regents took advantage of privileged information to enrich themselves by speculating in land. Money excused anything done to acquire it.[13]

Burgomasters controlled a large number of positions in the city. They took turns appointing their friends, children, grandchildren, and other relatives to lucrative positions. High offices were traditionally reserved for the eldest sons, and men who had available descendants or relatives were often succeeded by them.[14] This sort of patronage was taken for granted by the members of the political elite.

Joan Corver is an excellent case in point. Corver (1628-1716), who occupied a number of high offices, became burgomaster in 1681. While in office, Corver appointed his grandsons as postmasters in three different cities: Nicolaas at age 12, Gerrit at 10, and Joan at six. A half-brother of his grandsons shared in the spoils; Gerbrand Jan Pancras was appointed at the age of nine as Captain of a regiment of soldiers in Amsterdam. The boy was paid a yearly salary of 1,600 guilders. Corver appointed other relatives to high offices, some paying as much as 4,200 guilders a year.[15]

Many regents had made their money through investments, trade, manufacture, or in other kinds of business activities. Others had inherited a fortune or married into a rich family. Some prospered through the buying and selling of the houses in which most of the city's inhabitants lived. The wealth of some was the result of their earnings on loans to the government. Towards the end of the seventeenth century, most of the political elite were no longer involved in business; they had become full-time politicians.[16]

The salaries of burgomasters and other highly-placed regents made up only a minor part of their incomes. To have begun a political career in the first place, they had to be wealthy. Their wealth generated direct income. Beyond that, as Soltow and van Zanden note, they had "the 'access' which wealth provides to particular social-political networks and the income which flows from them."[17] These networks provided opportunities to eventually occupy highly lucrative positions, such as Director of the Dutch East India Company.[18]

The ruling elite had a degree of autonomy unknown to most other people in the city. They were in a position to set forth and achieve their own aims and to exercise individual initiative and judgment, and they seldom had to respond to the wishes of others. Few external or internal forces undermined their exercise of personal autonomy.

Table 2.1 shows that a small proportion of households – about two percent of the total – had an annual income of 4,000 guilders or more. Roughly half of the households of the ultra-rich were headed by regents. Heading the other half were prosperous merchants, investors, traders, industrialists, businessmen, and other people who made money through entrepreneurial activities. As a group, regents had the highest earnings in Amsterdam. The average income for high government functionaries in sixteen cities in 1742 was more than 7,000 guilders.[19] In Amsterdam, it was even higher.[20]

The city governors were keenly aware of the enormous importance of trade and business for the city's economy and were thus sensitive to the needs of wealthy men outside regent circles. The latter gained informal access to the city fathers at social gatherings and through ties of kinship and marriage.[21] Regents and other wealthy families worked hand in glove.

The top five percent included that small percentage of Amsterdam men who received a salary rather than wages: the occupants of high city office appointed by the burgomasters, and men occupying the top positions in law, medicine, and other professions. The average income of these men has been estimated at 2,639 guilders a year.[22]

The twelve percent of households with a yearly income above 1,000 guilders also included some manufacturers, high-ranking military officers, jewelers, a small number of artisan masters, and a wide variety of successful merchants. Merchants were, in fact, found at every level of Amsterdam society, for the designation "merchant" (*koopman*) was a vague one, then "applicable to hundreds, perhaps thousands of Amsterdammers."[23] Among them were some smaller traders and shopkeepers, as well as men involved in overseas commerce.

It was such rich and well-to-do households that employed most of the city's domestic servants. The presence of one or more servants to perform menial tasks distinguished these privileged households from the common people.

The Middling Group

The eighteen percent of citizen households earning between 500 and 1,000 guilders per year consisted mainly of members of the city's guilds. They made up the largest segment of the working population able to exercise some independence in earning their livelihoods. The training, schooling, skills, or other qualifications of these guild members gave many a degree of autonomy not experienced by the lower orders.

Their artisan activities must have provided a sense of self-esteem as well. Moreover, as we saw in the previous chapter, guild members were in a highly privileged position in that they were entitled to various benefits in case of need: for funerals, sickness, old age, and widowhood.

The largest guilds, with several hundred members each, were those for tailors (including seamstresses), bakers, shoemakers, men in the construction trades, and those connected with ships and shipbuilding.[24] Among the many others were guilds for bricklayers, carpenters, stone masons, glaziers, plasterers, plumbers, brewers, butchers, and tavern keepers.[25] Some guilds included several different trades. The guild for blacksmiths, for example, also included locksmiths, cutlers, gun-makers, and the makers of swords.

A master artisan's earnings depended on the particular guild to which he (or rarely, she) belonged. Men with the highest earnings were members of the more exclusive guilds: for surgeons, goldsmiths, silversmiths, tinsmiths, painters, wine merchants, and bookstore owners. A minority of grocers, tobacconists, tavern keepers, hatters, carpenters, bricklayers, and bakers also had relatively high earnings. So did many merchants.

At the other extreme were the members of the peat-hauler's guild (*turfdragers gilde*), one of the largest guilds in Amsterdam. This physically demanding work was seasonal and very poorly paid. So, too, were the trades of cobbler, wool knitter, and wicker worker.[26] Anyone belonging to a guild was, of course, a citizen of the city.

Throughout the seventeenth century, the burgomasters were deeply involved in the affairs of Amsterdam's guilds. Each year, they appointed the administrators or officials of the city's guilds. Every guild proposed a list of names (usually double the number required) and the burgomasters then appointed administrators from those listed. Ordinarily, these included a dean and two "overmen." This procedure gave guilds a voice in the appointment of their officers, while assuring the burgomasters a final say in the matter.

The same men were appointed again and again, suggesting the social exclusiveness of the members of the official board. But board members had no power as far as the governing of the city was concerned.[27] Like almost everyone else, guild officials were excluded from the political process. It is safe to say that nowhere in early modern Europe did citizens have a lower rate of political participation in the urban community.[28]

The Amsterdam burgomasters were involved in guild activities in other ways as well. Van Tielhof discusses the three guilds connected with grain in this regard. These guilds had responsibility for transporting the grain to where it was to be stored or shipped, sorting the grain, and weighing it. The burgomasters, she says, rarely concerned themselves with the men in the guild transporting the grain.

They were, however, actively involved in deciding how many men would be admitted to the guilds responsible for sorting and weighing grain. In fact, they appointed specific men as protégées. The reason for the burgomasters' active involvement was that weighing and sorting had direct consequences for the city's grain tax, an important source of revenue at the time.[29] More generally, the city fathers involved themselves with guild activities that had direct implications for Amsterdam's economic and tax-related interests.

For families outside the circles of the wealthy elite, membership in one of Amsterdam's many guilds was the major route toward a middling economic position and the way of life accompanying it. Guild masters often prepared their sons for the practice of their own craft, while other families had to pay for a boy's training.

In the latter case, a formal apprenticeship contract was signed with a master craftsman. He was then responsible for providing room and board, clothing, and other essentials, along with the boy's training in the craft. Although the young apprentice became a member of the household, there was usually considerable social distance between the boy and the family of the master who trained him.[30]

A guild master was entrusted with preparing a boy for both the world of work and for functioning in the wider society.[31] For his part, an apprentice was expected to respect and obey his master as he would his father. Apprenticeships were directly overseen by the guilds.

Beginning when a boy was anywhere from ten to fourteen, an apprenticeship normally lasted several years. Guild masters insisted that this long period of formal training was necessary to assure mastery of the necessary skills and protect the public against inferior workmanship and dangerous practices. At the same time, of course, such extended training provided master craftsmen with an assured income.

At the completion of his training, the apprentice was usually required to demonstrate the mastery of his craft with the production of a so-called "masterpiece" and to pay an entrance fee to become a guild member himself. Those coming from outside Amsterdam paid more than other young men. The sons of guild masters often paid a lower fee, and some paid nothing at all. They could also acquire work more easily.[32] An apprentice was bound to his master by contract and needed a letter of recommendation to establish himself in the trade.

The guild for which a boy trained was strongly related to his family's economic standing. The guild for surgeons was highly exclusive, although a surgeon (*chirurg*) did not have the status of a medical doctor. The latter was among the small percentage of men, all from wealthy families, who had had a university education. In the training of a medical doctor, the emphasis was on anatomy and the internal organs of the body. His province was internal medicine.[33]

A surgeon's training was more practical, and dealt with fractures, wounds, and minor injuries. Over the course of the seventeenth century, however, the distinction between the two became somewhat blurred as the training of surgeons came to resemble that of medical doctors. But their social status remained much lower.

Even so, the surgeons' guild was probably the most exclusive of the city's many guilds (there was none for medical doctors). With an entry fee of 250 guilders at a somewhat later period, it attracted young men from comparatively well-off Amsterdam families. Only they were able to afford its long and expensive period of training. Along with the guilds for booksellers and brokers, the surgeons' guild sometimes admitted Jews.

Beginning at the age of fourteen, a boy went to live with a master-surgeon, with the amount of payment determined by the master himself. A master-surgeon was allowed just one apprentice, and the boy's training and work activities differed somewhat from one master to another.

The minimum training period was five years, but it often stretched to ten years or longer.[34] Only the sons of affluent citizens were able to afford the expenses involved in setting up an independent practice. Towards the end of the seventeenth century, Amsterdam had 241 surgeons.[35] Bos estimates their earnings at 850 guilders a year.[36]

Adolescents and young men training to be painters also came from privileged backgrounds. Their training, averaging between four and six years, was longer than that for most other guilds and therefore more expensive.[37] Its total cost of 600-700 guilders was about two year's income for the average Amsterdam family.

On August 27, 1665, the father of Elias van de Broeck signed a contract with the master painter Cornelis Kick for an apprenticeship for his son. The contract specifies that the training was to be for a period of four years, at a cost of 140 guilders per year, with an additional 100 guilders to be paid at the end of the last year.

The boy's father is to assure that his son has proper clothing, while Cornelis Kick will provide lodgings, food, and drink. He will also see that the boy's clothes are washed and ironed. Everything that Elias draws or paints during his apprenticeship shall come to the profit of the master. The contract specifies that in taking the boy into his service Cornelis Kick will prepare him in the practice of drawing and painting as a master is supposed to do.[38] As was typically the case, there is no mention of the specific skills to be acquired.[39]

Although women could become members of the guild for painters (the Guild of St. Luke), few families were able or willing to pay such a high amount for the training of a daughter. Women who became painters were usually the daughters, sisters, or wives of male artists, and were trained within the family circle.

The guild probably had 165-200 painters toward the end of the century.[40] Since the income figures for the guild do not distinguish painters from other members of the guild, it is difficult to estimate their earnings. But few earned as much as surgeons, goldsmiths or silversmiths.

In most guilds, the vast majority of members earned less than 600 guilders per annum.[41] Only about one-fifth of the tailors, the largest guild, had an income of 600 guilders or more. In several guilds, those for shoemakers, weavers, small peddlers, and bargemen, for example, not one member earned more than 600 guilders a year.[42]

Along with being a citizen, an artisan's main source of social identity was his particular occupation: as a surgeon, painter, shoemaker, carpenter, tailor, or whatever, and not as a member of a category of people called artisans.[43] After several years of apprenticeship, an artisan was bound to his occupation. As with his civic status, a man's (but not a woman's) occupation was registered at marriage. Different occupations had different sorts of clothing, and people on the street could place one another on the basis of what they wore.

Around a quarter of all Amsterdam households had an income of between 350 and 500 guilders a year. Many were headed by artisans from guilds characterized by lower earnings. Although this differed from one guild to the other, in the last quarter of the century, the average master craftsman earned a daily wage of about 28 stuivers (there were 20 stuivers in a guilder) or 370 guilders a year.[44]

Those master artisans earning less than the members of the more exclusive guilds were still better off than the majority of non-citizen residents and temporary inhabitants. They also enjoyed guild benefits in case of need. At the bottom of this income category were some households headed by artisan journeymen, small merchants, and men performing various lower functions for the city government. Most would have been Amsterdam citizens.

The Lower Orders and the Poor

The 30 percent of Amsterdam households with an income between 300 and 350 guilders a year consisted mainly of people without citizenship, most of them immigrants. Many worked as common laborers, as seamen or soldiers, and in industries devoid of guilds. The latter included oil-pressing, soap-boiling, breweries, and other kinds of dirty and disagreeable work. If we take into account the room and board they received, the city's 12,000 or so domestic servants can also be included here. Some were Amsterdam citizens.

A large number of immigrants worked as artisans, although they were *not* themselves guild members. Alongside the 20-25 percent of Amsterdam's work force who were guild members towards the end of the seventeenth century, an estimated 50 percent of Amsterdam men earned wages as a journeyman for a guild boss. In other words, as many as three-quarters of the male labor force worked in guild-related occupations.[45]

Theory and reality differed greatly in this regard. In theory, a young man who underwent an apprenticeship and then served a period as a journeyman in his chosen craft could thereafter become a master craftsman. In reality, this was not the pattern for most men who had come to Amsterdam from elsewhere. Many immigrants undertook apprenticeships and became journeymen but never rose to the level of master artisan.

Some were unable to pay for the masterpiece required of apprentices. Others could not afford Amsterdam citizenship and so never became guild members. Except for the guild for ships' carpenters, journeymen were not members of guilds. There were also men who were guild members but lacked the capital, credit, and contacts needed to become an independent craftsman. All ended up performing wage-labor for a master craftsman, often in his shop.[46] An artisan master who owned a shop was distinguished from a merchant by the fact that he was involved in producing what he sold.

Men from elsewhere did different and lower-paying work than native-born Amsterdammers.[47] Typical occupations for the non-Amsterdammers represented in the marriage registers were unschooled laborers in the construction trades (96%), tailors (92%), bakers (92%), shoemakers (81%), and seamen (76%). Tailors, bakers, and shoemakers were overwhelmingly Germans, while a disproportionate percentage of seamen were from Scandinavia or coastal areas of the Dutch Republic.

At the same time, immigrants were underrepresented among ships' carpenters: 69 percent of whom were born in Amsterdam, with another 21 percent coming from elsewhere in the Republic. A high percentage of house carpenters, painters, printers, surgeons, and merchants were native-born Amsterdammers.[48]

Most studies that use information from the Amsterdam marriage registers make no distinction between master artisans and journeymen who worked for individual masters. Throughout the seventeenth century, bridegrooms gave their occupation simply as baker, tailor, shoemaker, or whatever, with no further specification. But in the 1641-1650 period bridegrooms were required, for unknown reasons, to specify their status as either a master or a journeyman.

Examining this information, Kuijpers found that in many occupations bridegrooms from outside Amsterdam were journeymen working for wages under the direction of a guild master: 96 percent of the tailors, 92 percent of the bakers, 82 percent of the cloth-shearers, and 78 percent of the shoemakers.[49] There is no reason to expect the figures to have been much different in other periods.

Consider the example of bakers. As a group they were mostly men from Germany, with journeymen far outnumbering masters. Furthermore, most journeymen worked for an Amsterdam-born master, someone who was an independent baker, owned his own bakery, and employed two or more journeymen.

A journeyman baker worked long hours at physically demanding work for low pay, usually with no prospect of ever becoming a master and owning a bakery himself. In his unequal relationship with and social distance from an Amsterdam-born employer, the German journeyman was in a position of inferiority and dependence.

Similar patterns and relationships existed within other guild-related occupations in which men from outside Amsterdam were overrepresented: tailors, cloth-shearers, shoemakers, blacksmiths, hatters, masons, and coopers. Master artisans were largely Amsterdam-born. Journeymen, who constituted the majority in guild-related crafts, were mostly from elsewhere.

In the second half of the century, a tightening of guild regulations made the master-journeyman relationship more formal and increased the gap between them. The activities of journeymen were constantly monitored in the workshops of master artisans. Noordegraaf writes of the "magnification of the social distance between masters and helpers."

He goes on to say that "the opportunities for helpers to start for themselves diminished as they were required to pay more to be admitted to the guild and to complete a more difficult master's examination than the sons of established master craftsmen – who were sometimes not even required to produce a masterpiece."[50]

What we see, then, is the ability of Dutch master artisans to maintain their own privileged positions and higher earnings at the expense of journeymen who worked for wages. Everywhere in the early modern Low Countries, write Lis and Soly, master artisans were deeply concerned about compulsory guild membership, maintaining the local monopoly, rigid compliance with guild regulations, meticulous quality control, and "ongoing supervision of the labour market to prevent young journeymen from becoming independent producers."[51]

Guild officials had privileged access to municipal authorities.[52] They submitted petitions lobbying the city government for bylaws assuring economic benefits for guild members. Van Nierop suggests that this was a mechanism by which the regents were able to keep ordinary citizens (most of whom belonged to guilds) out of government in exchange for privileges favoring guild masters.[53]

Guild officials worked with the city governors to prevent the establishment of anything like today's labor unions.[54] Overall, workers in the Dutch Republic were much less organized than those in Germany, France, or England. A more repressive climate left little room for such organization. In Amsterdam especially, the large number of foreign workers must have been a factor.[55]

Seventeenth-century Amsterdam was characterized by a segmented labor market: a "primary" market segment with desirable, skilled, well-paid, steady kinds of employment, good working conditions, and a degree of autonomy; a "secondary" segment with dead-end, semi-skilled or unskilled, often temporary, low-paid jobs, bad working conditions, and tight supervision; and what de Vries and van der Woude term an "employer of last resort: the VOC."[56]

The vast majority of men holding citizenship were employed in the primary sector. Immigrants, with little access to primary employment, were confined to the secondary sector or to sailing from Amsterdam with the VOC. Working women, native-born and immigrants alike, were generally in the secondary sector. They earned roughly half of what men earned for the same work.[57] The differences in their economic well-being were considerable.

Most working people in seventeenth-century Amsterdam earned low wages. The majority of men worked 260-270 days a year, with some working 300 days or even more.[58] In the summer months, men toiled between eleven and thirteen hours a day: starting work at 5:00 a.m. and working through until 7:00 in the evening, with an hour's break for a midday meal. In the dark winter months, they worked seven or eight hours a day. Their earnings were correspondingly less.

Ordinary laborers earned about 22 stuivers a day, which amounted to an annual income of around 300 guilders for those able to find work throughout the year.[59] Since it has been estimated that a family of husband, wife, and two children needed about 300 guilders a year to survive, these households barely got by. For most, poverty was just around the corner.

Along with the 30 percent of Amsterdam households with a yearly income between 300-350 guilders, another 15 percent earned less than 300 guilders per year.[60] In total, more than two-fifths of Amsterdam households lived either just above or below the poverty line. Most were people who had come to Amsterdam from elsewhere.

The more unskilled the work someone did, the more tightly it was controlled. Commenting on the work situation of laborers employed by the VOC in Amsterdam, Schijf and van Woerkom note their lack of rights and the fact that they could be fired at any time. VOC regulations were strict, authoritarian in tone, and listed various sorts of forbidden behavior: smoking, drinking, cursing, fighting, blasphemy, and excessive talking.

Anyone late for work would be sent home. Drunkenness or rude behavior resulted in the loss of a day's wages. With these and other rules, the administrators and supervisors of the VOC tightly regulated the conduct of these unskilled workers.[61]

The vast majority of men in Amsterdam did work that was physically demanding and dirty. It was often degrading as well. Most had few opportunities to set their own goals, little room for exercising initiative or choice, and limited space for controlling their behavior. Few were in a position to relate to others on the basis of equality and mutual respect.

Spending much of their work lives responding to the commands and wishes of the better-situated, men (and some women) from the lower orders were subject to close supervision, constant orders, capricious control, contemptuous treatment, and assaults on their self-esteem.

Moreover, their lack of autonomy in the work sphere is likely to have carried over into their lives more generally. For to the extent that people labor at jobs allowing little thought and individual judgment, they are made less capable of coping adequately in other situations.[62] This lack of autonomy had an obvious impact on people's well-being, for all human beings value having control over their lives.[63]

-II-

Responding to Economic Stress

Whatever their economic situation, the city's inhabitants did what they could to assure their survival and that of their loved ones. The culture of credit was of enormous importance in this regard. Many financial transactions involved credit: payment of the rent, the purchase of goods in a neighborhood shop, or, for the well-to-do, having a doctor come to the house.[64] The availability of credit represented access to economic resources, an important dimension of the wellness of being.

Both men and women were involved in the system of debt and credit. Reputation was crucial, not only whether an individual could be trusted to eventually pay for whatever was acquired on credit but also whether he or she was viewed as being *able* to pay what was owed. Newcomers were obviously disadvantaged, since their reputations were not known to potential creditors. Access to credit was, in general, strongly related to people's positions in the economic hierarchy; the higher their position and the greater their assets, the greater their access to credit.

Although paying on credit was common, it seems to have been the rich and powerful who most regularly delayed payment for services rendered. Ordinary people were usually helpless in this regard. A man delivering turf or firewood to a wealthy family was rarely in a position to demand immediate payment, especially if he also wanted the next order placed with him. The same was true for a seamstress, a tailor, or someone else providing services to the wealthy elite and the well-to-do.

Consider, for example, the debts of Jurrian Kramer and Catharina Adriaans at the time of her death.[65] Kramer was a successful wine merchant, and he and his family enjoyed a comfortable existence. An inventory of household possessions made when Catharina died appraised the furniture at 3,137 guilders, the family silver at 1,703 guilders, gold objects at 638 guilders, jewelry at 581 guilders, and paintings at 496 guilders. A horse and sleigh were appraised at 122 guilders and a hundred pounds of lobster at 120 guilders. In addition to the large house where the family lived, Kramer owned several other houses in the city.[66]

Among this wealthy family's debts when Catharina died were the following: Albertus Seba "apotheker" (apothecary) 2:10 (2 guilders and ten stuivers); Meester Willem "Chuirurg" (Surgeon) 14:8; Pieter Cockney "dockter" (doctor) 3 guilders. An apothecary, a surgeon, and a doctor may not have needed the money right away. But Kramer and his wife had other debts as well: Jan van Roma, "cleermaker" (tailor), was owed 110:14; Gerrit Laagman, "schoenmaker" (shoemaker) 23:10; and an unnamed "franse naaijster" (French seamstress) 20:13.

A tailor, a shoemaker, and a seamstress were people who generally had low earnings. They may even have been in urgent need of the money owed them. But the lower down an individual's position in the economic hierarchy, the greater his or her reluctance to insist on a debt being paid.

Delayed payment could, of course, have a chain reaction. It not only affected the creditor to whom an individual was in debt, but also the people whom the creditor owed, and the people they owed, and so on. Delayed payment could make it difficult, if not impossible, for a household to meet the basic needs of its members.

Economic stress was a familiar occurrence in the majority of Amsterdam households. Because of unemployment, irregular work, protracted illness, disability, old age, funeral expenses, or the death of the major bread-winner, household earnings and access to credit were often insufficient to meet basic needs: pay the rent, feed a hungry child, buy fuel in a harsh winter, have a pair of shoes repaired.

In such instances, a limited number of options were available. I sum-marize the principal ones in Table 2.2. The greater a household's vulner-ability to economic stress, the further down the list of options its members had to descend in making ends meet.[67]

Table 2.2   *Responses to Economic Stress*

1. Drawing on savings (if available).
2. Requesting help from a guild, if a member.
3. Turning to help from relatives, friends, or neighbors.
4. Changing living patterns (e.g., cutting consumption, delaying marriage, postponing having children).
5. Getting other family members to work.
6. Requesting charitable help from the church or the city.
7. Turning to illegal sources of income, begging, or theft.

Option 1 was not available to the vast majority of people in Amsterdam, few of whom were in a position to accumulate much in the way of savings. Nor was option 2 available in most households, since only a quarter of the city's adult males were members of a guild. Moreover, guild members who had fallen behind with dues payments or had become ill as a result of drunkenness or consorting with loose women were not eligible for guild benefits. The same was sometimes true for men who had belonged to a guild for less than six years.[68]

Turning to relatives, friends, or neighbors for assistance (option 3) was not a viable alternative for most people. It might result in temporary help, but nothing long term. After all, most households had difficulties as-suring the economic well-being of their own members.

Changing living patterns was the next option for meeting basic needs (option 4). This often meant an even more exclusive concentration on bread as the staple food in a family's diet. Many poorer households spent half a year's income on bread, leaving little for other necessities.[69] Poor families probably cut back on what they ate rather than fall behind with the rent and find themselves out on the street. Married couples would have delayed having children in instances of economic stress. Men or women living alone might have to double up with other people.

If these measures were not sufficient, people turned to option 5: getting other family members to work. In such instances, wives not already employed outside the home took on work as seamstresses, washerwomen, or some other type of work for which they rolled up their sleeves to bring in some meager earnings. Sometimes even six- and seven-year-old children had to seek paid work. Children, like women, earned much less than men doing the same work.[70] So even increasing the number of people in the household who were working often did not guarantee adequate earnings.

When these options proved insufficient, people sought the help of the church to which they belonged or the city of Amsterdam.[71] At any given time, about 13 percent of the city's families received some sort of "poor relief." Old people with no income, widows with young children, individuals too sick to work, tramps, and beggars were worst off.[72]

Throughout the seventeenth and much of the eighteenth century, 10-15 percent of Amsterdammers lived in stable poverty. As much as one-quarter of the population required regular charitable assistance at one time or another.[73] Appreciative as they must have been, such assistance would have brought a sense of inferiority to the recipients and damaged their self-esteem.

The percentage receiving charitable help was higher still during the "hunger years," which occurred thirty-eight times in the period 1595-1715. During those years between 50 and 75 percent of Amsterdam households were dependent on some sort of food distribution.[74] Thousands woke hungry every morning and went to bed hungry every night .

Jacob van Loo's (1614-1670) *Allegory on the Distribution of Bread to the Poor* (Illustration 2.1) shows a group of indigent women. Belonging to different age groups, some are accompanied by small children. Given their clothing, the women and children presumably represent the "deserving" poor rather than beggars or the down-and-out.

Even people who did not, strictly speaking, meet the city's citizenship or residence criteria or those for church membership were sometimes given charitable assistance. But not everyone received help. Men and women considered "undeserving" by the authorities were not helped. These included people who had not paid their debts, the able-bodied who refused to look for work, people fired from their jobs for insubordination or other reasons, and women of dubious reputation.

In desperation, some of these men and women turned to such illegal activities as theft and prostitution to acquire the means to get by (option 7). Others turned to begging. These were, so to speak, the options of last resort. And they were options that most people avoided if at all possible.

-III-

Differences in the conditions and resources that enhanced or reflected the well-being of the wealthy elite, the middling group, the lower orders, and the poor were enormous: in the quality of the relationships, autonomy, self-esteem, in where and how they lived, the food they ate, their physical appearance, the clothes they wore, their education and training, literacy, state of health, and life expectancy. An increase in economic inequalities during the century magnified their impact on people's wellness of being.

As regards life expectancy, nothing is more crucial to the wellness of our being than staying alive. Much writing about seventeenth-century Amsterdam forgets this simple fact. The most attention is given to the high mortality rate among men sailing with the VOC, many of whom were immigrants, and to the many victims of the plague.

Much less is written about those many infants and children, and smaller numbers of adolescents and young adults, who died an early death: human beings who entered the world like everyone else but departed it much too soon. And virtually nothing is said about differences in mortality as a consequence of people's civic and economic status.

In the following chapter, I consider one of the major conditions affecting life expectancy in the early modern period: the quality of the physical environment. Both the areas of the city in which people lived and the housing conditions within those areas were strongly related to people's civic and economic status. The quality of both aspects of the physical environment had life and death consequences for the inhabitants of seventeenth-century Amsterdam.

Chapter 3

AT HOME IN AMSTERDAM: THE PHYSICAL ENVIRONMENT AND EARLY DEATH

S ir William Temple spent 1668 to 1670 as England's ambassador in
The Hague. In a book published in 1673 he notes the presence of
water everywhere in this generally flat country, remarking that water
and land seem to contribute equally to forming the landscape. The province of Holland, he says, is divided between them. Temple notes as well the
density of population in the cities.[1] He then links the two, commenting on
the influence of the country's damp environment and its crowded conditions on people's behavior and health.

"The extreme moisture of the air," writes Temple, "I take to be
the occasion of the great neatness of their Houses, and cleanliness in their
Towns. For without the help of those Customs, their Countrey would not
be habitable by such Crowds of people, but the Air would corrupt upon
every hot season, and expose the Inhabitants to general and infectious Diseases…"

He goes on to add that "The same moisture of Air makes all Metals
apt to rust, and Wood to mould; which forces them by continual pains of
rubbing and scouring, to seek a prevention or cure: This makes the bright-
ness and cleanness that seems affected in their Houses, and is call'd natural
to them, by people who think no further."[2]

Despite their concern with cleanliness, the Dutch are "generally
not so long-lived as in better Airs; and begin to decay early, both man and
woman, especially in Amsterdam." Temple writes that "The Diseases of the
Climate seem to be chiefly the Gout and the Scurvy; but all hot and dry
Summers bring some that are infectious among them, especially in Amsterdam and Leyden."[3] Especially with crowded living conditions, he suggests,
a damp environment has an adverse effect on the most fundamental aspect
of people's well-being: staying alive. What Sir William is referring to, of
course, is escapable and premature mortality. He is pointing to the influence of the physical environment on early death.

Temple, as the historians de Vries and van der Woude note, was "acutely observant."[4] Moreover, his observations about crowds and mortality were largely correct. A strong relation between population density and mortality levels did exist in early modern Europe.[5] In the Dutch Republic, as elsewhere in the period, there was widespread excess mortality in the cities.[6] This is often referred to as "the urban penalty."

Given the much higher level of urbanization and greater presence of water in the Dutch Republic than in neighboring countries,[7] Temple was probably correct in claiming that the Dutch were not so long-lived as people in better airs. This cannot be shown with certainty, however, since there is a general absence of quantitative information about mortality patterns in the Dutch seventeenth century.[8] The same is true for the eighteenth century. In any case, the seventeenth-century English lived longer than any other people for whom systematic evidence is available from the time.[9]

Amsterdam, with a population of 200,000 inhabitants around 1670, was the Republic's largest city.[10] It was a city build on drained land and surrounded by water. From its harbor on the IJ, an inlet of the Zuiderzee, thousands of people entered and left the city by ship every day. Most of the traffic within the city was by way of the canals.

In 1660, the regent Caspar Commelin described Amsterdam as consisting of ninety islands connected to one another by two hundred and eighty wooden and stone bridges.[11] It is thus understandable that Temple singled out Amsterdam for special mention as far as the effects of a damp environment and crowding on death were concerned. More were buried than were born within the city walls.[12]

Temple was not the first to show an interest in the relationship between the environment and health. Such a concern has a long history, beginning perhaps with Hippocrates' writings on *Airs, Waters, and Places* in the fifth century BC. Differences in the air, the water, the place, the season, and other variations, he argued, were associated not only with health or illness but specific types of illness as well.

A resurgence of Hippocratic ideas occurred in early modern Europe, as both medical and non-medical observers asked why mortality varied by locality and why different environments were conducive to different types of disease.[13] Among their concerns was the contrast between rural and urban settings and the influence of each on people's health. Cities, with their density of inhabitants and confined spaces, were viewed as places of a "thousand stinks."[14]

"Noxious vapors," writes Dobson, "were believed to arise from open sewers, churchyards, slaughter houses...burial grounds, cesspools and from every other sort of putrefaction, excrement, decay, human and animal filth." The vapors could arise as well from such closed and crowded spaces as lodging houses, tenements, basements, alehouses, and ships.[15] These miasmas or malign qualities of the air were thought to be the cause of disease.

Although correct in linking disease with a dirty and crowded environment, medical observers were mistaken about the mechanisms involved. It was only with the emergence of germ theory in the nineteenth century that attention was turned from the sources of noxious vapors to germs themselves and the things that carry them: insects and small particles not usually visible to the naked eye.[16]

The focus of early modern observers was on filth, foul air, and stagnant water. More than anything else, it was an aversion to unpleasant odors that sensitized people to trying to combat pollution and improve the air. Little attention was given to human waste as a contaminant. As regards the adverse effects of crowds of people living in cities, it was because crowds created the conditions for noxious vapors that observers were concerned. No one yet recognized the negative impact on people's health of other conditions associated with life in crowded cities.[17]

Although much more is understood today than in earlier centuries about the influence of the physical environment on premature mortality, certain aspects of the relationship receive little attention in studies of early modern Europe. This is particularly true of differing environmental conditions *within* cities.[18] But there are partial exceptions, at least if we assume that people of differing economic status inhabited different areas of a city.[19]

Findings for Geneva in the period 1650-1684 show large differences in the influence of economic status on life expectancy at birth: about 20 years for workers, 26 years for the middle class, and 37 years for the wealthy elite.[20] Similarly, Quakers in London, a largely middle class group, had a life expectancy of just short of 29 years in 1650-1699, an advantage of 6-7 years over the average Londoner at the time.[21] But neither study explicitly considers the effects of the social differentiation of residential areas on life expectancy.

As far as seventeenth-century Amsterdam is concerned, data about life expectancies are meager. In the period 1678-1682, life expectancy has been estimated at 29 years for the wealthy nominees of life annuities.[22] Information about people other than the rich is, however, lacking. But assuming a gradient for economic status similar to Geneva and London, the life expectancies of the middling group, the lower orders, and the poor were correspondingly shorter.

Quantitative evidence about mortality figures for people living in Amsterdam's different residential areas is nonexistent. Given what is now known about the effects of the physical environment on mortality rates, this is unfortunate. But there is no reason to expect things to have been different in seventeenth-century Amsterdam than in other large cities. That is to say: the worse the environmental quality of a residential area, the higher the risks of premature mortality for the people living there.[23]

The vast majority of deaths in early modern Europe were caused by endemic disease, their number far exceeding the number caused by epidemic diseases.[24] Most common were typhoid fever, cholera, dysentery, acute respiratory infections, influenza, diphtheria, measles, and smallpox.[25] Almost all were associated with infancy and childhood. Death was, in fact, most common among infants and children.

The mortality rate among infants was highest during the first year. Although there were differences from one country to another, overall roughly a quarter of infants died before reaching their first birthday.[26] Problems associated with breastfeeding, which I discuss in a later chapter, played a major role in the early months. Thereafter, surviving children were susceptible to infectious diseases.

Between 40 and 50 percent of children died before the age of ten.[27] After age ten, the mortality rate dropped dramatically.[28] Parents were especially concerned that a child should survive its early years. The longer a child survived, the better its chances of reaching adulthood. A child reaching age fifteen could expect to live another thirty to thirty-five years. In the last decade of the seventeenth century, roughly 20 percent of Amsterdammers were age fifty or older.[29]

The diseases of infancy and early childhood were communicable, transmitted from person to person. This could occur directly by air or water, or indirectly, by way of insects, fomites (inanimate objects), or food. Environmental factors promoting the spread of communicable diseases were enormously important in this regard.

The high population density found in cities was especially conducive to the spread of disease, creating more hosts for communicable disease and more opportunities for the transmission of diseases borne by air and water. People crowded together acted as a reservoir for infection. Smallpox and measles were specifically crowd diseases: breath-borne infections. In crowded housing conditions, children transmitted these infections to one another and to their parents through coughing, sneezing, and nose-blowing.

Smallpox was the worst and most feared disease, because it spread quickly, had a high death rate, and permanently disfigured its survivors. "Its effects," writes Crosby, "are terrifying: the fever and pain; the swift appearance of pustules that sometimes destroy the skin and transform the victims into a gory horror; the astonishing death rate, up to one-fourth, one-half, or more by the worst strains."[30]

Dirty housing harbored lice, fleas, and cockroaches, all of which transmitted disease. It was also responsible for internal parasites. Household filth allowed for their multiplication, as it did for the multiplication of mice, rats, houseflies, insects, and worms. Dogs, too, were a breeding ground for intestinal parasites.

Also helping the spread of disease was the enormous problem of disposing of human waste in large cities like Amsterdam. Human waste carries various pathogens that cause disease. So, too, does animal waste. Given the large number of horses in Amsterdam, animal waste would have been found on virtually every street. Because of people living in close proximity, contact with waste would have been common. This was particularly dangerous to people not used to washing their hands after urinating or defecating, or before eating.

-II-

The remainder of this chapter focuses on differing environmental conditions *within* Amsterdam in the period around 1670 when William Temple visited the city. My focus is on two, somewhat overlapping, aspects of the physical environment: the city's major residential areas and the housing conditions within those areas.

The characteristics of both were related to people's positions in Amsterdam's civic and economic hierarchies. In general, the higher people's positions in the hierarchies, the better the quality of the area where they resided and the better the quality of their housing. Knowing this provides the possibility of informed speculation about the impact of each on mortality and well-being.

In principle, several components of the physical environment need to be considered in assessing its impact on health and mortality. With residential areas, they include outdoor air pollution, chemical hazards, sewage and waste disposal, hygiene and sanitation, and the quality of the water supply.

With differing housing conditions within the same residential area, the components include indoor air quality (related to the fuels used for domestic heating and cooking), ventilation, dampness and cold, pest infestation, crowding (including the sharing of beds), and the quality of the housing units themselves. All are aspects of the disease environment.

I can do no more than touch on these components in the following pages. But given the general absence of any systematic exploration at all of the relationship between the physical environment and mortality in seventeenth-century Amsterdam, even my limited discussion expands the narrow vision of most investigators concerned with the quality of life in the Dutch Golden Age.[31]

The Residential Environment

People in seventeenth-century Amsterdam inhabited a number of worlds largely distinct from one another spatially, economically, socially, and with regard to the disease environments that surrounded them. The consequences for their physical well-being were considerable. In illustration 3.1, I show the areas where the vast majority of the city's inhabitants lived in the period when William Temple visited the city.[32]

The canal belt extending from the northwestern to the southern side of the city was where most of the rich elite resided. It included the city's three principal canals: the Herengracht, Keizersgracht, and Prinsengracht. These exceptionally broad canals were each 26 to 28 meters in width, with a quay of roughly 11 meters on each side.

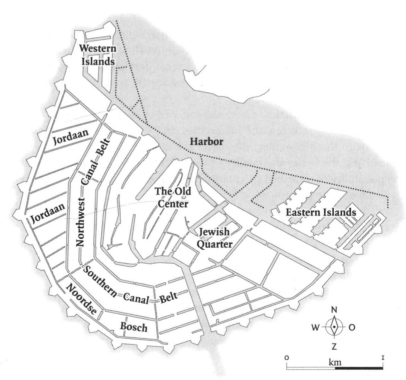

3.1 Amsterdam's Areas of Residence Around 1670. *Illustration by Derek Phillips and Kaartenkamer Universiteit van Amsterdam.*

The creation of the canal zone on the northwestern side of the city had been begun in 1612. The land bordering the canals was intended as the residential area for the regent elite and other wealthy people. The city fathers conceived and designed the system of canals for a small group of people like themselves: the rich and powerful.[33] The Herengracht was expressly intended for "persons of independent means and other well-to-do folk."[34] More of the political and financial elite lived there than anywhere else in the city.[35]

New regulations banned industry from this area intended for the rich. All trade or commerce by blacksmiths, masons, stone suppliers, timber merchants, or wine merchants, or any others using the anvil, was forbidden in the area between the north side of the Herengracht and the south side of the Keizersgracht.[36] As far as possible, unpleasant odors, dirty air, and excessive noise were excluded from this residential area.

In the 1650s and 1660s, the three canals were extended to the Amstel River on the eastern side of the city. In 1663, the list of prohibited industries also came to include sugar refineries, soap-works, breweries, and a number of other industrial activities offensive to the rich and powerful.[37] All had to be located outside the canal belt.

The wealthiest 10-12 percent of Amsterdammers thus came to be spatially separated from the rest of the city's inhabitants and from the most life-threatening aspects of the disease environment. Outdoor air pollution, chemical hazards, and sewage and waste problems were to be concentrated in the areas that the lower orders and the poor called home.

The Jordaan was the poorest and most densely populated of these areas, with roughly a quarter of the city's population living there in the last decades of the century.[38] At that time, it was made up of eleven canals and forty streets. Land in the area was also set aside for tanneries, textile dyeworks, and other industries banned from the newly-created canals.[39] The Jordaan became the center of the city's most environmentally harmful activities, and is described by one writer as a "great stinking garbage dump."[40] It was the intention of the city governors that the Jordaan be isolated from the area where the rich resided.[41]

The Western and Eastern Islands, the two areas where shipbuilding was concentrated, housed another 10-15 percent of the population. The VOC employed between 1,000 and 1,200 people in the industrial complex on Oosterburg, one of the Eastern Islands, and provided housing for the workers and their families.[42] Many were among Amsterdam's working poor.

The Noordse Bosch area and its surroundings in the southern part of the city was home to around 8 percent of the city's population, most of them also from the lower orders. The same was true for the 9 percent living in the Jewish quarter, an area containing many poor households.

About a quarter of the city's population lived in the city's old center, an area that had formed the core of the medieval city: the Singel, the Warmoess-traaat, and a few other streets and canals in the vicinity of the Nieuwezijds and Oudezijds Voorburgwal.[43]

People from the middling groups probably constituted the majority in the old center.[44] But it was also an area with some wealthy households and many people from the lower echelons of the civic and economic hier-archies. Most of the city's temporary inhabitants were found in this part of the city. It was near the harbor from which ships entered and left Amster-dam, and contained many inns and rooming houses.

Along with the temporary inhabitants living in the poorest streets in the old center, people living in the city's less desirable residential areas were especially vulnerable to the ill effects of the physical environment. With regard to inadequate sewage and waste disposal, the city's canals were the major problem. As well as being the main mode of transportation, they were essentially open sewers.

During the course of the century, the city governors issued different ordinances specifying what should not be thrown into the canals. They ap-parently had little effect, since new ordinances continued to be issued. An ordinance of August 2, 1695, outlawed the dumping of garbage, horse or cow droppings, human waste, animal intestines, hay, straw, and ash, among other things.[45]

Since the rich and the rest were considered different types of crea-tures, the city fathers considered it fitting and proper that people should inhabit areas commensurate with their positions in Amsterdam's civic and economic hierarchies.[46] All should be in their proper place.[47]

Moreover, the city fathers attempted to keep a check on people changing their residence from one neighborhood to another.[48] An ordi-nance dated January 1, 1652, decreed that anyone making such a move had to acquire a formal declaration from the neighborhood master (*buurt-meester*) which specified his (or her) trade or occupation, attested to his good conduct, and indicated the number of children in the family, years of employment, and years of residence in the old neighborhood.

The person wanting to move was required to hand over this declara-tion to the *buurtmeester* in the neighborhood to which he was moving.[49] But there is no evidence, according to Kuijpers, about the actual functioning of *buurtmeesters* and thus of the city fathers' ability to control where people lived.[50] Still, the very existence of such a decree underscores the regents' concern with maintaining social control and keeping people in their proper place.[51]

Housing Conditions

As a physical domicile, a home is meant to meet people's basic needs for shelter and security by protecting them from the extremes of outdoor temperature, against unwanted persons, and against unwanted intrusions by rodents, insects, dust, dirt, and other environmental nuisances. In regard to the outdoor temperature, something needs to be said about the climate at the time.

The weather in seventeenth-century Holland was much as it is today, with heavy rain, intermittent drizzle, and cloudy skies throughout much of the year.[52] Rain was a constant source of discomfort, leaking into poorly-insulated dwellings, creating mire and puddles in the streets, and soaking people's clothing.

Although there was more sun in the summer months, the climate was generally cool. Keeping warm was a problem for everyone. An open fire was the major source of heat, both for keeping warm and for cooking.[53] It was also the main source of inside light in most homes. On dark days, it was the *only* source of light in the majority of dwellings.

Although some families burned wood, peat was less expensive and was the normal fuel in most Amsterdam households.[54] It has been estimated that each inhabitant consumed between 1.0 and 1.6 tons of peat annually.[55] This amounts to about 10 pounds of fuel per person each day to provide warmth, heat water, and prepare meals. Though giving rise to thick smoke and unpleasant smells, peat was a basic necessity for virtually everyone.[56]

In addition to a fireplace, families who could afford it had small iron stoves that could be taken from one room to another.[57] And some used foot warmers in the cold months. These were small boxes made of metal or hard wood, about six inches square, containing a slow-burning cake of peat set in a small earthenware dish [58] But the most common way of keeping warm was to wear several layers of clothing inside as well as outside the house.

As we have seen, the majority of rich families lived along the city's three major canals. The houses in which they resided had several features in common, most especially those built at the time of the expansion in the 1650s and 1660s.[59] William Temple commented on their spaciousness and the fact that they were much more beautiful and costly than older houses in the city.[60]

Large and massive, the homes of the rich consisted of ten or more rooms and were often more than 10 meters wide and 15-20 meters deep, with large gardens behind. They were usually built against other houses on both sides, and thus had no side windows. Three to five large windows in the front and back of the house allowed outside light to penetrate into the deep interiors. Sometimes a sort of inner courtyard served as a light shaft for the inner rooms facing onto it.

The main entrance was usually above street level, in the middle of the fa-çade, with steps leading up to it. Within, most rooms were designated for specific functions, with separate rooms for cooking, sleeping, family activi-ties, conducting business, and receiving and entertaining visitors. Rooms designated specifically as bedrooms, when these existed, were usually on the upper floors.

The top two floors were generally used for storage, including doz-ens of baskets of peat, for hanging laundry, and for various other purposes.[61] The kitchen was usually located at the rear of the ground floor or in the basement so as to prevent as far as possible smoke and cooking odors from permeating the rest of the house.

It was not unusual for a household servant to sleep behind the kitch-en in the basement. Although often without windows, cold and dank in the winter, and airless and clammy in the summer, the basement was seen as perfectly suitable for a live-in servant. Moreover, it assured that she would not easily disturb her betters in the rooms above.

A *secreet* or privy was usually located somewhere at the back of the house, sometimes behind the kitchen.[62] In the early canal houses, these privies were located against the house's outside walls. Later the privy was placed inside the house. A sort of wooden cupboard, the *secreet* was a wood-en bench with a hole in it, usually located above a cesspool made of wood or brick. Through several outlets, the waste drained into the soil. In some instances, the sewage of several households flowed into a sort of communal cesspool. It was then emptied out through one of the houses, where it was collected and disposed of elsewhere.

Various sorts of sanitary conveniences were found in the Dutch sev-enteenth century: some with a wooden seat, some simply fitted to sit upon, and others nothing more than a pot in which to urinate. Judging by house-hold inventories from the time, an abundance of such conveniences were located throughout the homes of the wealthy elite.[63] Chamber pots seem to have been used with great frequency, especially when people had to get up in the night in a cold and dark house.

In wealthy homes one or more household servants saw that things were neat and clean, dusted and polished, scrubbed and shined, and emp-tied the chamber pots and bedpans regularly. In addition to the open fire in the kitchen for cooking, a half dozen or more fireplaces provided heat, and were a source of light as well.[64] Apart from the fireplaces, candles were the most common source of light at night and on dark days.

The rich elite were not the only people who inhabited a whole house. So, too, did households headed by doctors, lawyers, successful shopkeepers and merchants, bookstore owners, a small number of master artisans, and other well-to-do families. Smaller than the homes of the rich, they consisted of rooms of different sizes on several floors. Such houses were usually 5 or 6 meters wide, 10 meters or so deep, and had two or three fireplaces. These one-family houses were spread throughout the city.[65]

Relatively few Amsterdam families inhabited a house on their own. Instead, the majority rented as many rooms as they could afford. Some of these multi-family dwellings were located on side streets between the main canals, but many more were in alleys and passageways in the poorer areas of the city.

Although it is difficult to speak of a "typical" family home in seventeenth-century Amsterdam, most common was a small multi-family house shared by three households. Zantkuijl has uncovered building plans for small multi-family houses on the Kerkstraat built by a master carpenter in 1670. Like most houses in the city, they were adjacent to each other in a row, sharing common walls. And also like most smaller houses at the time, they had two front doors. These houses no longer exist.

Each house contained three separate living-units of about 4 x 6 meters.[66] The one entered at street level consisted of an inner room or *binnenhaert* and a small side room. The upstairs unit, reached by a narrow spiral staircase next to the dwelling downstairs, was just one room, covering the depth of the house. The third unit, in the basement, was reached through the second door at the front of the house. Each provided about 24 square meters of living space and contained a fireplace for cooking and keeping warm. Family members shared the use of the outdoor privy with the house's other residents.

These multi-family houses on the Kerkstraat seem to have been particularly small. Other multiple-family houses were somewhat larger. Another described by Zantkuijl was 4.7 meters wide and 9.4 meters deep.[67] One household occupied the basement, a second had two or three rooms on the ground floor and the floor just above, and a third lived in two or three rooms on the top two floors.

It was not uncommon for even more families to inhabit a multi-family house. Illustration 3.2 shows a house built around 1610. It is located at the corner of the Bloedstraat and the Gordijnensteeg in the city's old center. Jan van der Heyden (1637-1712), who had invented a more effective hosepipe for fighting fire, made the drawing after a fire on July 20, 1684. It was apparently intended to show how his invention had limited the damage done by this fire.

Still standing today, the house is 6 meters wide and just 5 meters deep. At the time of the fire in 1684, four different families were crammed into this tiny house. A tailor had his workshop and lived with his family on the ground floor, while the other three families occupied the rest of the building.[68]

The average multi-family house in Amsterdam contained nine people.[69] Individuals were born, grew up, fell sick, were nursed, and died in such buildings. Household members cooked and ate their meals, clothed themselves, slept, made love, raised their children, and entertained in a space of 40-50 square meters. Individuals had little privacy, and children learned about copulation, domestic conflict, and violence at an early age. The sounds and smells of neighbors were a constant presence.

So, too, was the odor of unemptied chamber pots. How often, I wonder, did people living in rooms on the upper floors walk downstairs to empty their chamber pots? And how often did they simply empty them from upper windows? And when people did leave the house to empty a chamber pot, the question is where. Perhaps some poured the household waste down the hole in the outdoor privy. But many more probably dumped their household excrement into the closest canal.

These small multi-family homes were heavily concentrated in the most undesirable parts of the city: the Jordaan, the Eastern and Western Islands, the Jewish quarter, and in the side streets and alleyways in the old city. Most people in Amsterdam lived without the amenities enjoyed by the rich and the middling groups.

Like other cities in early modern Europe, Amsterdam was characterized by constant noise: from carts and carriages, craftsmen working at home and in small shops, barking dogs, the ringing of church bells, drunken revelers, voices heard through the walls, and inconsiderate neighbors. The multi-family houses inhabited by the poor were especially subject to the intrusion of noise.

These dwellings were in areas characterized by intense noise and foul air from work activities, as well as the constant danger of fire for the many people squeezed into multi-family buildings made of wood. Many non-citizen residents and temporary inhabitants lived in such conditions. The city governors did not issue an ordinance forbidding wooden houses until 1669.[70]

The poorer the area of the city, the larger the number of families sharing a building. An especially high density was found in the Jordaan and the Eastern and Western Isles.[71] This remained unchanged until at least 1800. These were also the areas with the highest percentage of children.[72] In the Jordaan's most densely-populated houses, a whole family occupied a single room. It has been estimated that fewer than 6 square meters were available per person.[73]

Many buildings were barely fit for human habitation. With a single layer of bricks (or sometimes one and a half layers, while wealthy homes had two) separating a building's inhabitants from the outside elements, rooms were drafty, cold, and damp during much of the year. Dampness and mold are today linked to respiratory illnesses. People may or may not have realized this at the time.

The open fire produced soot and foul-smelling smoke. This indoor air pollution would also have had adverse effects on people's health. The dwellings were poorly ventilated and reeked of cooking odors. When the windows were open in the summer months, smells and noises were a constant presence.

While the homes of the rich elite contained a plethora of sanitary conveniences, the middling group had two or three chamber pots or bedpans in the house, the lower orders usually made do with sharing just one, and it was rare to find any at all in the rooms of the poor.[74]

Except in some wealthier homes, water had to be fetched from a distance. It was used for preparing food, cleaning, and washing, but never for drinking. When there was water in the house, it was usually in the kitchen. Few homes had either washbasins or bathtubs. Most homes, in fact, contained neither water nor soap with which to wash. People seldom washed and the unexposed parts of their bodies rarely saw soap and water.[75] Instead, those who could afford it doused their bodies liberally with perfumes and other smelly substances.[76]

It was the smells that mattered. The smell of scent was preferable to that of body odor. No thought was given to washing for hygienic reasons. It was not until the nineteenth century that people in early modern Europe were encouraged to wash their hands before eating or after urinating or defecating.[77] Hygienic awareness was generally lacking.

Household almanacs recommended a yearly bath in the spring so as to destroy the insects that laid their eggs in people's hair and clothes.[78] With a low level of personal hygiene and beds often being shared by two or more people, fleas and lice were commonplace. Head lice were picked out rather than washed away.[79]

The cramming of large numbers of unwashed men, women, and children into damp, poorly ventilated, and unsanitary rooms created the conditions in which the plague bacterium grew and spread. It was transmitted to people by fleas from infected rats carried by ships from port to port. Once infected with the plague bacillus, the rat flea was voraciously hungry. When a rat died of the plague, the flea looked elsewhere for food. If a human host was available, the flea moved there.[80]

In the absence of rats and fleas, there was no risk of plague. But this was not known at the time. With many people living in crowded conditions, it was easy for fleas to move from person to person. As a result, thousands died in epidemics of the plague. In 1664 alone, it took the life of one in every eight Amsterdammers.[81] Other diseases spread by parasites and proximity to an infected person also thrived in overcrowded conditions, and over the century would have been responsible for more deaths than the plague.

People who could not wait to use the building's communal privy used the ground next to it or anywhere else they could stand or squat to relieve themselves. Waste and sewage removal were infrequent, and the city's backyards and streets emitted putrid odors.[82] Privies for public use, located under the bridges, emptied into the canals. In terms of cleanliness, they would have left much to be desired.

Foul smells had their source in the excrement of horses, dogs, other animals, and, of course, the people themselves. Garbage, animal excrement, blood, and even dead animals were dumped into the canals. Noxious odors accompanied the (unhealthy) work activities of tanners, brewers, sugar-boilers, and glue-makers. The city's smells were often so bad in the summer months that they even irritated people's eyes, and scented water was sold on the streets.[83]

But, unknown to people at the time, it was not the noxious air that presented a direct danger to their physical well-being. Instead, the dangers came from the pathological consequences of overcrowded housing, the deplorable sanitary and hygienic conditions, the inadequate systems for sewage disposal, the air pollution, and even the eating implements people used and the clothing they wore.

People ordinarily used wooden bowls and dishes for eating. In the general absence of water in the house, the wooden tableware was cleaned with sand or grit. Wealthy families could afford pewter and, later, ceramic tableware. It could be cleaned much more effectively than wooden tableware, especially when there was water in the household, so bacteria and viruses were more likely to be destroyed.

I have already mentioned people's apparent aversion to washing their bodies. And their clothes were equally unhygienic. Ordinary people owned far less clothing than did the rich and changed what they wore much less often. Moreover, the rich sent their clothing out to be washed and then hung it to dry in the spacious upper regions of their homes.

Most people lacked water, could not afford to send their laundry out, and had no place to dry it in any case. So their clothes were washed much less often than those of the rich. Moreover, the clothing worn by the lower orders and the poor was usually of heavy, coarse wool and thus not conducive to washing. It was mainly the rich who could afford cotton clothing, which, notes Riley, simplified control of body lice and fleas.[84] The same was true for the washing of bed linen.

William Temple seems to have been correct, then, in his observations about the ill effects of Amsterdam's physical environment. Along with the extreme dampness, overcrowding and its side effects played a crucial role in people's life expectancy in the seventeenth century. Although he remarked on the early decay of men and women, it was mainly infants and young children who died prematurely.

Speaking about early modern Europe, Lindemann points out that "those who survived the perils of infancy and childhood were pretty hardy specimens whose immunological systems coped well with subsequent attacks of disease and infection."[85] But this was far more the case for native-born Amsterdammers than those coming to the city from elsewhere.

Newly-arrived immigrants lacked the proper immunities against diseases endemic to seventeenth-century Amsterdam and other large cities.[86] Though figures are lacking, they must have had higher rates of mortality than their "native" peers.[87] Smallpox especially would have taken a high toll among those persons never exposed to it in the countryside and lacking any immunity.

Not only was life expectancy shorter in Amsterdam than in the countryside, but it is likely that differences in expectancy between the wealthy elite, the middling groups, the lower orders, and the poor were greater in Amsterdam than outside.[88] Along with differences in immunological status, nutritional status also played a role as far as resistance was concerned. I discuss nutrition and infectious disease in a later chapter.

Death was a familiar occurrence and almost everyone had first-hand experience of the death of family members, friends, and neighbors. It was never far away. Short of an individual's own premature death, there was no more decisive a blow to well-being than the early death of a loved one.

Death's disruptions were, of course, considerable. And as with the likelihood of dying early, these disruptions differed in accordance with the survivors' positions in the city's hierarchies of civic status, economic position, and gender. Although I will be saying a great deal about other aspects of the wellness of being in seventeenth-century Amsterdam, death occupies an important position in all but one of the remaining chapters. The exception is the chapter that follows.

-III-

Along with inequalities among the city's households, inequalities *within* them had an enormous impact on people's well-being. Among these inequalities were those between household masters and mistresses and the domestic servants whom they employed. Their relationships were characterized by differences in power, the distribution of hard labor and dirty work, opportunities for independent initiative, and assaults on the self-esteem of those occupying subordinate positions.

My consideration of relationships between servants and other household members in the next chapter sets the stage, so to speak, for my subsequent discussions of the ways in which inequalities structured the lives and shaped the destinies of men, women, and children in families and households in Amsterdam's golden age.

Chapter 4

INTIMATE INFERIORS: SERVANTS IN AMSTERDAM

T he year is 1663. The place is Amsterdam. A young servant girl employed in the home of the wealthy silk merchant, Jacob Bierens, has been instructed to join members of the family for a family portrait. She may never have seen a portrait prior to going to work in a wealthy household, for only the well-to-do could afford to have their portraits painted.[1] She had certainly never seen a portrait in which a wealthy family is depicted in the kitchen of their home.

Portraits were normally painted in the artist's studio, and this one was probably no exception. However the scene portrayed in the painting may have been worked out, Hendrick Martensz Sorgh's *Portrait of the Bierens Family* (Illustration 4.1) shows family members and their young servant in a large and well-outfitted kitchen with a tiled floor, a fireplace, three landscape paintings on the wall, various kitchen utensils displayed in the foreground, and a spout for water (at a time when most households lacked water altogether).

In this portrayal of domestic tranquility, Jacob Bierens, the father, enters from the courtyard, displaying a large fish; ten-year-old Anthony accompanies him; Cornelia van Hoecke, the mother, is busy peeling vegetables; the fourteen-year-old daughter, Cornelia, next to her mother, is plucking the feathers from a bird; and Abraham, who is twelve, plays the viola da gamba. The servant girl, filling a jug, has been placed in the background, thus graphically expressing her separation from the family who employs her.

In "real life," of course, the three male members of the Bierens family would seldom have ventured into the kitchen. This was not true of the mother and daughter, who would have spent time there overseeing and helping prepare family meals. As well as being involved in preparing the food, the young servant girl was responsible for managing the fire, serving the meals, and cleaning up afterward.

Of family portraits surviving from the seventeenth century, that of the Bierens family is one of the few to include a servant. Nothing, however, is known about this young woman. Although scholars have established the identities and ages of her master and mistress, and each of their three children, the name and age of the servant remains unknown.[2] I am aware of no instance where a servant in a family portrait is identified by name.[3]

-I-

The young woman in the Bierens portrait was perhaps, like many other servants, born in Amsterdam. Or she may have been an immigrant to the city, perhaps from the east of the Netherlands, from the west of Germany, or from Scandinavia, all of which provided servant girls for wealthy Amsterdam households.[4]

Childhood officially ended at age twelve, and this was the age at which a girl could take up employment as a servant. But most girls who became servants left their parental homes in their teens, mainly through economic necessity. Either their parents sent them into domestic service to rid themselves of mouths they could not feed or the girls and young women themselves wished to better their situations.

While the city's guilds contained few women, more than 95 percent of servants were female. It was considered a job for young women between leaving the parental home and getting married, usually when they were around 24 or 25 years of age. A servant knew, of course, what it was to be treated as a member of the order-taking class. Yet at the same time she had relationships of considerable intimacy with the members of wealthy families.

A servant helped family members dress, prepared and served their food, cleaned up their dirt, made their beds, bathed their babies, picked up their dirty linen, ironed their clothes, emptied their chamber pots, touched every item in their house, and listened to them talk about intimate and private matters. A servant was privy to much of what went on between various members of the family: husband and wife, parents and children, siblings together.

These adolescents and young women from the society's lower ranks were employed almost exclusively by the city's wealthiest families, roughly 10-12 percent of Amsterdam households.[5] About three-quarters were one-servant households, in which an adolescent girl or woman was employed as a servant-of-all-work. Only the very richest families had two or more living-in servants. These families sometimes owned a country estate, horses, and a carriage. Some employed both male and female servants, four or more in a small number of instances.[6]

Servants at Work

Rich, poor, or in between, household relations were dominated by hierarchies defined on the basis of age, sex, and birth order. In households employing servants, there was a hierarchy of social positions as well. Having been subordinated to the authority of her mother and father, a servant came under the authority of the family that employed her. Still, initially at least, domestic service must have seemed like a welcome escape from the crowded conditions at home.[7]

Servants in England, France, and Italy were often regarded as children for whom the master of the house had a responsibility.[8] But such a patriarchal pattern was generally lacking in the Dutch Republic, where a servant was *not* generally treated as a member of the family.[9] Instead, wealthy families and their servants related to one another as employers and workers.

Servants were regarded as wage laborers. Haks's study of civil suits involving employers and their servants makes this clear. It was a businesslike relationship, with the woman of the house doing most of the hiring and firing.[10] She may herself have come from a relatively modest background. But in her relationships with servants, the mistress of the house knew how to give orders.

A servant's contacts were not, however, with her mistress alone. She also had face-to-face relationships with the master of the house, the couple's sons and daughters, perhaps other servants, and whoever else lived in the household. To a very large extent, the everyday world of a servant was determined by other people. In fact, interpersonal relationships in wealthy Amsterdam households go to the heart of gender and socio-economic hierarchies in the Dutch Golden Age.

When, as in the very wealthiest families, there was a male servant (*knecht*) in a household, he had two general types of responsibilities. The first was seeing to the needs of the master of the house, escorting him about the city (carrying a torch to light the way at night and perhaps a weapon for protection), collecting and receiving wood, peat, wine, and other household goods, delivering messages, and performing whatever other personal services the master required.

A male servant's second responsibility was caring for the garden and the stables, and seeing to the horse and carriage that provided transportation within and outside the city for the master and his family. Most of his work was outside the house, although he would have been expected to take on various duties inside when necessary. In the absence of a master, he performed his tasks for the mistress of the house.

A female servant's responsibilities were broad and unspecified. But they can be grouped into three general categories. The first was to maintain the home, a job encompassing an enormous number of different tasks. She saw to lighting the fires and keeping them going, lit and snuffed candles, cleaned, washed, sewed, ironed, swept, scrubbed, dusted, made beds, aired featherbeds and pillows, emptied bedpans, fetched and carried water, peat, and wood (often up several flights of stairs in Amsterdam's tall houses), prepared meals, scoured and washed the dirty dishes, cleaned windows, scrubbed steps, ran errands, went shopping for the mistress, and did whatever else was required to maintain the house inside and out. As Davidoff emphasizes, servants everywhere "dealt with the recurring by-products of daily life: excrement, ashes, grease, garbage, rubbish, blood, vomit."[11]

A servant's second general responsibility was to assist the mistress of the house in caring for infants and children, seeing that the older children got dressed, fed, and off to school on time, and tending to their everyday needs and wants. These sorts of tasks were especially burdensome when there were several children in the household.

It was not uncommon for a household to contain children of an age similar to that of the servant herself. She was expected to address them as Master or Miss. But they, like their parents, called her by her first or last name. This was a world in which adolescents were permitted to admonish a servant several years their senior. They were of the order-giving class, she of the order-taking.[12]

The domestic household was considered a microcosm of society, and relationships were thus regulated by formality and distance. Deference was a constant demand, not only with modes of address, but also with bowing, kneeling, and various other forms of servility. Failure to observe a rule of social intercourse was taken as an act of insubordination. Even an eyebrow cocked too high could result in a reprimand.

A servant's third realm of responsibility involved seeing to the personal needs of the mistress of the house, helping her dress, doing her hair, serving as a companion and sharing her secrets and perhaps her grievances as well, assisting her in entertaining, accompanying her on visits, and doing whatever else the mistress deemed necessary.

We should not, however, forget that in "ordinary" households – that vast majority who were unable to pay for outside help – most tasks were performed by a wife herself, sometimes with the help of older daughters. But the tasks in the homes of wealthy families were still more demanding. For one thing, there were many more rooms and considerably more furniture and decorations to attend to than in ordinary dwellings.

For another, the daily demands of cooking – over an open fire – far exceeded those of ordinary families. The complexity of lighting and tending the several fires in a large home, day in and day out through most of the year, was itself a daily challenge.[13] It is not surprising, then, that women who could afford it hired a servant to take over many of the household tasks.

Under the authority of the master and mistress of the house, a servant was available to meet the family's needs from early morning until late at night. Her hours were long, and she had little time off. A few hours on Wednesday afternoon and on the weekend seem to have been the norm.[14] Besides being at their beck and call and exhibiting the proper degree of deference, she was expected to show master, wife, and children obedience, respect, and loyalty. A servant's life was one of servility.[15]

In return for taking care of the personal and physical needs of family members, a servant was given a place to sleep, three meals a day, and a small wage. She sometimes had a room of her own, but she might also sleep in an alcove of her mistress's bedroom or above in an attic used for storage. Most often, as noted earlier, she slept in that part of the house commensurate with her status: the basement "underneath."

In accordance with her low status, the servant's room was plainly furnished: a bed, a table, a chair, and a clothes rack. The room (in some wealthy homes shared with one or two other servants) lacked a fireplace. "Being warm," notes Sarti, "was a prerogative which employers tended to keep for themselves."[16]

The hierarchical separation between a servant and members of the family was expressed in food as well. Although a servant ate higher quality food than she did at home with her parents, she ate less well than those she served. When she dined at the same table as her employees, it was probably so that she could look after the children.[17] In any case, she enjoyed a better diet than she ever would again.

There was some variation in what servants were paid, but wages seem to have been around 50-60 guilders a year in the last quarter of the seventeenth century. Half was received at the beginning of May and half at the beginning of November, the same times of the year when servants were permitted to terminate their employment.[18] Male servants were paid more than females. Added to a servant's wages, writes Marybeth Carlson, were "tips [from household guests], customary holiday bonuses, and hand-me-down clothing, not to mention amounts skimmed from the household's marketing budget or kickbacks received from tradesmen."[19]

-III-

Vulnerability and Conflicts
A servant observed the everyday interactions of her wealthy employers, their children, other household members, and the family's friends and visi-

tors from, so to speak, the bottom. Given her dependence and vulnerability, she could not afford to ignore differences in the sensibilities of the various people she encountered. As a subordinate, she noticed things to which the people themselves were often blind.

As is always the case with someone in a position of subordination, a servant recognized her dependency and vulnerability. This meant she had to be a keen student of human behavior. A servant learned to pay careful attention to what pleased and displeased her master, her mistress, and other people in the household, to the moods and personalities of different individuals, and to work out what stance to take in her relationships with various household members.

She had to be sensitive to nuances of behavior, anticipate anger, suppress any expression of emotion, and exercise caution in her relations within a precarious social environment. A servant's efforts were not always successful, though.

Conflicts about Earnings and Work

Servants' earnings were one source of conflict. Since the wage levels were low, the possibility of supplementing them was an important aspect of their employment. Bonuses were regularly paid at the end of the year and at the time of the annual city carnival, although it is difficult to determine the exact amounts. Servants with a long period of service with a family would sometimes receive legacies in wills. These were generally not particularly generous.[20]

Tips were the main way for servants to supplement their wages. It was customary for guests to tip servants for ushering them into the house, relieving them of their coats and cloaks, waiting on them at table, and serving them drinks. Family friends and relatives staying overnight were expected to distribute tips for the services received from servants. Employment in a house known to entertain frequently or in a grand manner was therefore particularly desirable.

"By providing a source of income that employers could not control," writes Carlson, "tips offered servants a certain latitude in their relationship with their employer."[21] Not surprisingly, many employers were strongly opposed to this custom. It was not only the cost to their guests (and to themselves when they visited other families) that they objected to. They also disliked their servants becoming less dependent on them. In some cases, employers forbade their servants from accepting tips. Perhaps more than their actual wages, tips were a continuing source of conflict in relations between servants and employers.

Conflicts about the work itself were frequent as well. Servants objected to the tremendous demands placed upon them in the large urban houses where they were employed. Cleaning, cooking, caring for children, and the other tasks performed by an often lonely adolescent girl were enormously tiring. Her duties also often involved what Davidoff calls "the potentially disruptive and polluting fundamentals of life: birth, infancy, illness, old age, and death."[22] Whether or not a servant had to deal with these fundamentals depended, of course, on the composition of the household where she was employed. Hard drudgery, however, was a constant in her work. A servant had much to complain about.

Given a servant's broad responsibilities, there were many opportunities for her mistress to find fault: the cleaning, the cooking, the ironing, the dusting, the bed-making, and on and on, through the myriad tasks that the servant was expected to perform. And there surely were many quarrels and frequent flare-ups in the relationship between the two. Warm relations were not unheard of, but a servant's work more often involved contemptuous treatment and assaults on her dignity.[23]

In light of their background and experience, young servants were unfamiliar with many of the rituals and practices they encountered in wealthy households when they first entered service. Those from outside the Dutch Republic or from other parts of the country spoke a different language or dialect from their employers.

Moreover, the elite often used Latin phrases and, towards the end of the century, spoke French at home. Being able to speak and read French was, in fact, one of the characteristics that distinguished the higher echelons from everyone else. No other country was considered to be as civilized as France, and the Amsterdam elite took many of their ideas about civility and proper behavior from the French elite.

What some employers considered impudence or a lack of respect on a servant's part was thus sometimes simply ignorance. It took time to learn the rituals of deference in a household's face-to-face system of hierarchy. Even so, servants were not always quiescent: they did at times purposely ignore or violate these rituals, answering back and threatening to leave. Much more often, they exhibited the expected deference while probably biting their tongues and seething in silent anger.

Conflicts about Dress

Dress was another source of conflict between domestic servants and their employers. Consistent with performing the hardest and dirtiest work in the household, a servant was expected to "know her place." Among other things, this meant dressing and conducting herself appropriately. All individuals were, in fact, expected to dress in accordance with their social positions.[24]

Clothes were expensive, even when purchased at one of Amsterdam's weekly markets for second-hand clothing. A second-hand outfit of breeches, coat, and waistcoat, for example, might cost a male worker a week's earnings.[25] In most families a couple's clothes, together with their beds and bedding, accounted for more than half of the value of their household goods.[26]

Dress was a material reminder of a person's place in society. Men and women at the top of the social scale dressed in colorful and carefully-tailored clothes made of silk, velvet, and other expensive fabrics thought suitable for their delicate skin. They were the only ones who wore colorful clothing. Ordinary people were clad in rough wool or perhaps dark cotton, and those at the bottom in worn and threadbare clothes.[27] Rough materials would have chafed and been uncomfortable, but they were viewed by the rich and privileged as perfectly suitable for the rough bodies of common folk.

Dress, like the food people ate and the size, furnishings, warmth and comfort of the rooms they slept in, distinguished between those occupying high and low positions in wealthy households. A servant was sometimes given hand-me-down clothing by her mistress. It was usually worn, out of style, or otherwise not something that the mistress herself wanted to wear any longer. In some instances, they were clothes she had inherited and then passed on to her servant. Some – a very few – employers provided their servants with clothing like their own.[28] This was perhaps a way of displaying their status and wealth. More often, the simple dress of a servant was in marked contrast to that of her employer.

Some servants, though, chose to wear clothes considered totally inappropriate to their lowly station, aping, it was said, their betters. Instead of the dark-colored and rough materials worn by most women from the lower orders, they spent their wages on stylish, colorful, and high quality materials. Some even wore bits of silk. Dress was, in fact, the major expenditure for servants in the Dutch Golden Age.[29]

Much of the clothing came from the markets selling second-hand clothes. The dealers did not belong to the tailors' guild and were supposed to sell only garments they had mended and altered themselves, but there were plenty who contravened the regulations and sold new items as well. Servants were among their customers.

Dress was anything but a matter of indifference to the wives of the high and mighty.[30] With only limited activities in the public sphere, their sumptuous clothing allowed them to demonstrate their wealth and assert a degree of individuality. It is also likely that husbands took pride in their wives' appearance. "The significance of female fashion in male-dominated societies," notes Stanley Chojnacki, "is a rich and fascinating subject."[31]

According to Carlson, the stylish and colorful clothes worn by some servants made a statement about the status to which they aspired.[32] The Amsterdam elite, involved in policing the conduct of everyday life, were outraged by the impudence of these young women. How dare a mere servant put on airs and resist the authority of her mistress? As a subordinate herself, the mistress was conscious of how important it was to conduct herself in a manner commensurate with her husband's position in the social hierarchy.

Well-placed women responded with ridicule, scorn, and contempt to the dress of their servants. When this failed to curtail the pretentious behavior of these adolescents and young women, some wealthy women appealed to the city fathers to forbid such inappropriate dress. The city fathers were apparently happy to oblige them, enacting an ordinance to assure that servants did not dress above their station.

This occurred at a time when regents and other members of the wealthy elite were increasingly preoccupied with putting the greatest possible social distance between themselves and the rest of the city's residents. Although not actually members of the nobility, some rich families had begun to use titles, invented coats of arms for themselves, often consumed extravagantly, adopted French modes of behavior and displayed genealogical charts in their homes.[33] An increase in punitive legislation and in the intensity of the repression of the lower orders reflected the patricians' wish to assert their dominance over the other strata of Amsterdam society.[34]

A servants' ordinance of January 23, 1682 included sumptuary provisions limiting the style and form of clothing that servants were permitted to wear.[35] Consider the wording of the law:

> And since such external haughtiness in the wearing of clothing, lace, curls, ringlets, bows, and so forth has been introduced among domestic servants for some time [so] that no or little distinction can be seen between their mistresses' clothing and theirs; and because the same conflicts with decency and good morals, over and above that domestic servants, who cannot acquire the same out of their wages, and yet wanting to seem equal to others, thus fall into unfaithfulness, theft, prostitution and other abominations.[36]

The ordinance, notes Carlson, "then went on to forbid servants from wearing any silk, velvet, lace, or embroidered trim – even on their underclothes – nor gold or gems." Male servants (*knechten*) were forbidden to wear lace on their scarfs, linen sleeves, or ruffles.[37]

It is striking that the city fathers not only found it inappropriate for female servants to dress like their mistresses or male servants like their masters, but also accused them of engaging in various sorts of unacceptable behavior so as to be able to afford what they wore: "unfaithfulness, theft, prostitution, and other abominations."

An article was consequently included in the 1682 ordinance stipulating that any thefts committed by male or female servants were to be punished with a severe whipping and an unspecified period of imprisonment in one of the city's jails.[38] A servant convicted of theft could also be branded, although this penalty was seldom imposed. The permanent scar, it was argued, would serve as a warning to future employers.

In fact, says Carlson, few servants were convicted of theft from the households where they worked. She suggests that it was their ambition to be respectable, "precisely the same ambition that their employers found so pretentious, that deterred servants from stealing".[39] Still, linking accusations of theft to the clothes that servants wore, and then imposing stiff penalties for theft, indicates how concerned the city authorities were with servants' dressing above their station. Threats to the existing hierarchy required action.

Conflicts about Sex and Intimacy

Another source of conflict, or at least of frequent tensions, arose out of the sexual vulnerability of young servant girls. Among married couples, a woman's sex life was supposed to be restricted to what occurred in the marital relationship. At the same time, a blind eye was usually turned to a man's sexual exploits outside marriage. This double standard of sexual morality was common practice as far as servants were concerned. As elsewhere in early modern Europe, sexual involvement with female servants was a widespread social phenomenon.[40] Although it usually had no adverse consequences for the reputations of a man, it was otherwise for the fair sex.

Rich and privileged men viewed servants as fair game, to be enjoyed sexually if at all possible.[41] These adolescent girls and young women were open to unwanted touching and sexual abuse by the men they encountered in the houses where they worked: fathers, sons, family friends, and male servants. The routines of servants and family members alike were known to everyone in the household. Since much of a female servant's time was spent working in rooms alone, a predatory male knew where he could find her at almost any time – day or night.[42]

Many adolescent boys had their first sexual experience with a servant, sometimes when they were away at school. One such was Jacob Cats (1577-1660), the widely-read Dutch moralist author, who warned his many thousands of seventeenth-century readers about the bad influence of female servants. As a youth, however, Cats enjoyed their bad influence.

In his autobiography, published forty years after his death, Cats recounts his own early sexual experiences with servant girls. He describes how, when he was twelve, his sexual education began under the tutelage of a female servant who visited him and other male students in the dormitory where they slept.[43] Then, as a sixteen-year-old studying law at the University of Leiden, he continued his sexual education with a servant named Louisa.

Cats describes Louisa as unusually attractive, and recounts spending time with her when she came to make up the beds in the boarding house where he lived with other students. Getting wind of this, the landlady fired Louisa and replaced her with a new servant. This young woman, writes Cats, was anything but attractive. He and his fellow students apparently treated her accordingly.

Angry about this, the landlady announced one day that Louisa was pregnant and that one of the students was responsible for her condition. In his autobiography, Cats reports having sleepless nights about this. The story proved, however, to be entirely an invention of the embittered new servant.[44] Jacob Cats, the great moralist, seems to have regarded sexual intercourse with a servant as part of a young male adolescent's education – it was one of the ways he sowed his wild oats.[45]

Female servants were seen as sexually voracious and out to seduce the unsuspecting male.[46] Two books that appeared late in the century made clear the sexual nature of the wanton servant. *The Seven Devils Rising* and *Enrapturing Maidservants*, notes Carlson, "helped popularize an image of maidservants that depicted them as man-hungry adventuresses. The books portray the uncontrolled sexuality of maidservants as a danger to the family estate, its men becoming the prey of the unattached woman who shared the intimacies of family life with them."[47]

This negative image of the servant was also found in plays, jokes, paintings, private diaries, and pornographic writings. It is no wonder, then, that female servants were treated by many men as sexual objects. And it is no wonder that men pursued them, since they were convinced that servant girls welcomed their attention. These young women consequently suffered the humiliation of being treated more as sexual objects than as fellow human beings.

The risk of seduction and sexual abuse by masters and their sons must have been well-known to female servants. But what, we might ask, was a servant to do if the master or one of his sons made sexual advances? With her master, she was well aware of the consequences of repulsing someone who had the power to dismiss her, who could refuse to provide a reference for another position, and who could spread stories about her sexual misconduct. Her future, both economic and marital, lay in her master's hands.[48] She was at the mercy of his sexual advances. The master's sons were also capable of ruining her life.

As Bridget Hill points out: "With an insistent master the life of a servant must have been made impossible. Little wonder then that in such circumstances some voluntarily succumbed."[49] Others gave in to the importunate demands of sons, some of whom promised marriage if only these vulnerable young women would satisfy their sexual appetites.

A servant who gave in or was raped and then became pregnant sometimes threatened to tell the mistress of the house what her husband or son had done. But she risked dismissal if she did.[50] Wives must have recognized and instantly understood the tonalities of sex in the household. Nonetheless, they were ready to protect their husbands and sons from accusations of wrong-doing and paternity.

Coupling the negative image of servants as sexually voracious with the stereotype of servants as thieving, gossiping, malicious, rebellious, and hypocritical, the likelihood of a servant being recognized as the victim of male domination was slim indeed.[51] She was unlikely to find a sympathetic ear in most households.

Nor could a servant expect to succeed if she took the master to court.[52] As with all sexual relations between an unmarried woman and a married man, the female servant had little chance of success before the law.[53] More often than not, she was alleged to have tempted the master to have sex with her. It was the servant, not the master, who was likely to be punished.

A servant pregnant by the master's son could, however, file a paternity suit against him. To avoid this, his family sometimes bought her silence. If the servant refused to be bought off and the son was found guilty, he might be obliged to marry the servant girl.[54] But this was not always the case.

An article in the 1682 Amsterdam ordinance referred to *hoererij* (whoredom) on the part of female servants. Although usually intended for a prostitute, the term also referred to a concubine or adultery. With the new ordinance, a female servant known to have had intercourse with any male member of her employer's household could be sentenced to six months in the prison for women (the *spinhuis*).[55]

Some servants may indeed have tried to ensnare a male member of the household, hoping for marriage and financial security. Others may have been lonely and simply sought affection and sexual pleasure when it seemed available. After all, many were adolescent girls and young women living in a strange household, away from their family and friends, and with somewhat limited opportunities to meet young men from outside the household. Even so, it seems unlikely that more than a few servants would have taken the initiative in sexual relationships with males in the households where they worked.

Understandably, however, some responded positively when sexual advances were made. Not only intercourse, but also kissing, hugging, touching, and fondling could surely be a welcome escape from the constricting discipline of their lives. But many more had to face and fight off unwanted advances by males in the families who employed them.[56] Whatever servants chose to do in such situations, unemployment in a largely unsympathetic world was a definite possibility.

-IV-

Changing Employers

Given the many sources of conflict between servants and others in the household, it is not surprising that these young women changed employers quite frequently. In an attempt to curb this, the Amsterdam authorities enacted laws limiting their right to seek employment. The servants' ordinances specified that only officially registered *besteedsters* (or go-betweens), women who had taken an oath to uphold the ordinance, were allowed to bring servants and prospective employers together. Moreover, servants were required to obtain written permission from their present employers before they were allowed to seek work elsewhere. A servant who failed to obtain such permission was fined, as was the employer who hired her.

The servants' ordinances eroded a servant's rights by weakening her legal position, thus making it more difficult for her to change positions and improve her economic situation. A servant who broke a verbal contract could be fined or even sent to jail. She could, in fact, be fired at any time. The female servant worked entirely at the pleasure of the household that employed her.

Although a servant lacked the freedom to simply leave an employer when it suited her, the turnover in domestic personnel in the seventeenth century was still considerable. There is, however, only limited empirical evidence about exactly how long servants stayed in one place. Haks reports that the servants employed by one wealthy family stayed an average of three years, with a spread from less than one year to more than five years.

Citing evidence from the eighteenth century, Haks says that ideas about a trusted servant spending her working life in service with one family are a "myth." But the turnover seems to have been somewhat lower than in seventeenth-century London, where Peter Earle found that nearly 40 percent of a sample of female servants stayed in a household an average of six months or less.[57]

Preparing for the Future

Servants everywhere must have looked for the same things in their work. Good working conditions and reasonable earnings were usually paramount, especially for a young woman seeking her first job. But every servant would also have hoped for decent treatment in the household that employed her. She did not want to have to endure insults, humiliations, unwanted sexual advances, or other attacks on her dignity. Employment was more than simply a matter of household tasks and earnings. Like anyone else, a servant preferred employers who treated her with respect and consideration.

Whatever the negative aspects of living in the homes of the rich and powerful, an important consequence of domestic service was to free thousands of young working-class women from parental control at an early age. It thrust an adolescent or young woman into contact with people with different ideas and sensibilities, and forced her to develop skills and strategies to cope with the complexities of her working environment. By the time she was an adult and left service, she was used to assuming responsibility and making numerous daily decisions on her own.

During their years of employment, servants cultivated "networks of sociability." These networks included other servants, as well as women working in the outdoor markets, in shops, and elsewhere. Tradesmen and men delivering goods to the house, friends and acquaintances from outside the households where the young women worked, and, for those from Amsterdam, family members and people from the neighborhoods where they had grown up were also part of these networks.[58] Servants from outside Amsterdam sometimes had contacts with brothers, sisters, or other relatives working in the city.

A servant's relationships outside the household were mainly with young men and women from the laboring classes, the kinds of people with whom she had grown up. Among them were men whom she would have regarded as potential marriage partners, for marriage was the aspiration of most young women. It was the sign of full adult status, offered a degree of economic security, and was the only legitimate sexual outlet open to a woman. A servant's preference would probably have been to marry a skilled artisan or another Amsterdam citizen rather than a soldier, sailor, or ordinary laborer.

As with most young women at the time, a domestic servant would have hoped to work for some years, accumulate savings to make herself more attractive as a potential marital partner, and eventually leave service to marry and start a family of her own.[59] Until that day arrived, home meant the household in which she was employed – but it was not usually the place where her heart was.

Young men and women alike usually spent several years in the single state before eventually marrying. But the experience of being single was vastly different for the two sexes. So, too, were the consequences of never marrying at all. In both instances, men and women differed in the wellness of their being. This is the subject of Chapter 5.

Chapter 5

A SINGULAR STATE: UNMARRIED MEN AND WOMEN

L ysbeth Sarragon and Johanna de Leeuw are domestic servants working in the household of the Amsterdam widow, Cornelia Bierens. We encountered Cornelia in the portrait of the Bierens family and their servant in the previous chapter (Illustration 4.1). Born in 1649, Cornelia was fourteen years of age when Hendrick Sorgh painted the family portrait. She grows up, marries the wealthy silk merchant, Adriaan van Hoek Janz, and has two daughters. The couple spend thirty-five years together, until Van Hoek's death.

Cornelia Bierens dies at age seventy. She is living in an expensive home on the Leidsegracht. She pays 700 guilders a year in rent, more than twice the annual earnings of the average household in the city.[1] Her everyday needs are met by Lysbeth Sarragon and Johanna de Leeuw.[2] Each is owed half a year's salary at the time their mistress dies: Lysbeth 33 guilders and Johanna 27. The former's higher earnings suggest that she had been in Cornelia's service longer. The two are left 40 guilders for the purchase of mourning clothes, as well as some of the widow's own clothing.

It is likely that Lysbeth Sarragon and Johanna de Leeuw have been working in Cornelia Bierens' household for quite some time, for each is willed an amount of 300 guilders.[3] This was a sizeable sum. Not only is the amount unusual, but so is the fact that the names of the two servants are stated in Cornelia Bierens' last will and testament. In most instances where anything is left to a servant, she is referred to simply as the servant, the servant girl, or perhaps as Maria, the servant.

As domestic servants living in the home of a wealthy widow, neither is married. If, as I suggest, they have been in her service for a long time, both are in their twenties or older. In that case, they would have had difficulty finding employment as domestic help in the future. Employers preferred younger women whose strength, energy, and good eyesight allowed them to carry out their duties with dispatch and efficiency. Competition for a position as a household servant must have been considerable.

Cornelia Bierens' generous provision is perhaps intended to help Lysbeth Sarragon and Johanna de Leeuw manage during their remaining years. Or perhaps she hopes to make the two women more appealing marital prospects than they would otherwise be. In either case, there is a good chance that Johanna and Lysbeth will never marry. Such was the destiny of many people in early modern Amsterdam.

-I-

The Years before Marriage
In the Dutch Golden Age, the nuclear family (husband, wife, and children) constituted the normative ideal of how companionship, affection, sexuality, child-rearing, and domestic finances *should* be organized. The family was viewed as society's most fundamental social unit. Domestic conduct treatises make this clear. So do the many paintings which depict the family as if it were the usual living unit. Father, mother, and children are represented as the embodiment of normality, harmonious relationships, and social order.

Such visual representations, like those of many other aspects of Dutch society, are highly misleading.[4] In fact, married couples with children made up only about half of all households. The other half consisted of individuals living outside a nuclear household: single men, single women, married couples without children, widows and widowers (with or without children), and orphans.[5]

The situation of single men and single women was to a large extent determined by the dominant marriage pattern in northwestern Europe. In contrast to eastern and southern Europe, India, China, and other societies at the time, marriage took place comparatively late, between similarly aged men and women, who chose their marital partners themselves, and then set up independent households, rather than being absorbed into households with other relatives.[6]

With this marriage pattern, most male adolescents left the parental home between the ages of twelve and fourteen to enter apprenticeships or go to work. Many female adolescents were employed as domestic servants or in other jobs when only slightly older. Some children left the parental home at an even younger age. For most, "home" was the place where they spent their childhood.

These young people then spent a decade or longer learning a trade or laboring at one type of work or another. It was also a period in which young men and women searched for a marriage partner and tried to accumulate savings for a married future.

The dominant marriage system was characterized by two unique features: women were relatively old when they married, and a high percentage of people never married at all. Although men in other parts of the world also married late, women did not. In northwestern Europe, including Amsterdam, women typically married ten years later than women elsewhere. This obviously meant a long period between sexual maturity and marriage.[7]

Many men and women in early modern Europe were single for a large part of their lives, living and working as single people for five, ten, fifteen years or longer, before eventually marrying. The figures were especially high for women. At any given time, writes Froide, "at least one-third of urban women were single in the early modern era."[8] Froide offers no estimate for the proportion of single men, but it was undoubtedly lower.

More than anything, late marriage resulted from the fact that it took young people several years to build up the savings needed to start a household of their own.[9] When they succeeded, that domicile was what they considered home. In the 1600-1700 period, the average Western European woman was about twenty-six when she married and the average man was twenty-nine.[10]

In Amsterdam the average ages at marriage were slightly lower: twenty-four for women in 1600, the same in 1650, and then rising to almost twenty-seven by 1700. The corresponding figures for men were twenty-six, twenty-six, and twenty-eight for the three periods.[11] This rise in the average age of marriage over the course of the century seems to reflect the deteriorating economic situation of wage laborers during the Golden Age.[12] It simply took longer for young people to save up enough to set up home.[13]

Throughout the century, Amsterdam-born brides and grooms were roughly two years younger than brides and grooms who had come to the city from elsewhere.[14] This was the result both of the latter's greater difficulty in accumulating savings and of their disadvantaged status in the marriage market as non-citizens. At the end of the seventeenth century, German-born women, for example, were about thirty when they married.[15]

The population of Amsterdam was quite youthful throughout the century. From 1680 to 1700, for example, roughly a quarter of the city's inhabitants were between fifteen and twenty-nine.[16] The 33,000 women heavily outnumbered the 22,000 men in this category. A large proportion of these young people remained unmarried for several years: from the age of sexual maturity until their mid or late twenties. Others never married.

Where and how single young men and women lived was related to their parents' civic status and economic position. In wealthier circles, unmarried sons and daughters could continue to live at home, enjoying a life of luxury. Unmarried sons were often away at university or traveling abroad, though, while daughters were likely to marry at an earlier age than those from ordinary families.

The daughters of doctors, lawyers, clergymen, and other professionals, successful merchants and tradesmen, and artisans in the more exclusive guilds also often remained at home until marriage. In such families, some boys lived away from home as apprentices. When a master artisan trained his son himself, the boy remained at home for the duration of his apprenticeship. Daughters could be kept at home to help their artisan fathers in their workshops.

In many Amsterdam families, sons and daughters left home at an early age to learn a trade or earn their own living. The majority of foreign-born adolescents and young people lived outside the parental household. The same was true of adolescents who came to the city from elsewhere in the Dutch Republic. Whatever the pattern for the native-born, many young immigrants were free of parental control from an early age. Most had to make their own living, males and females alike.

Being on their own, they could not generally count on help from their parents in case of need. Nor was there any expectation that adult children would help their parents should they become needy. In fact, the relationship between them was often almost businesslike. As soon as young men and women were able to make their own living, their relationships with their parents changed.

Young men or women living at home would often be expected to pay room and board. Similarly, a widow who lived with a married son or daughter was also expected to pay for her keep. Parents and children were seen as forming two separate households. In some instances, there was even a contract between a parent and a grown child.[17]

Young men and women differed dramatically in their opportunities to exercise independence. In law, most women were legally subordinate to a man. A married woman was under the guardianship of her husband, and was prohibited from carrying out legal transactions, entering into contracts, or appearing before a court of law. Her husband assumed those responsibilities for her. But in some instances, as when a seafarer was away for a long period, the city authorities could temporarily suspend the husband's guardianship over his wife.

Until she turned twenty-five, a single woman was under the legal jurisdiction of a guardian – her father, older brother, or another adult male. Once she was twenty-five, she was legally entitled to act independently: to own property, undertake legal transactions, and enter into contracts. In other words she was considered responsible in commercial activities. The law also allowed a single woman under the age of twenty-five to have herself declared of age by a letter of "venia aetatis" from the courts. This gave her the same legal rights as a single woman of age.[18]

Earning a Living: Single Men and Single Women

Throughout the seventeenth century, the Amsterdam work force contained large numbers of young men and women. Not all of the young men were always physically present in Amsterdam, many being away with the Dutch East and West India Companies or otherwise at sea.

Whatever their economic standing, single men were generally involved in the same sorts of work as their married counterparts. Being younger and with less experience, they earned less than married men. There was a noticeably high proportion of unmarried men among the male labor force working in guild-related occupations. The same was true for seamen and soldiers.

Females, of all ages, had far fewer ways of earning money than did men. The most common type of employment for a single young woman was as a domestic servant. Seamstresses probably made up the second largest category of employed women. Some single women made their living in the textile and clothing industry, although they did not do the same work as the men. The industrial sector was characterized by wage work, with a woman usually earning half or less than half of what a man earned.[19]

Single women worked as public vendors at Amsterdam's sixty or so specialist markets for bread, vegetables, meat, fish, birds, flowers, butter, eggs, cheese, tobacco, wood, peat, lace, needles, fabrics, and other products.[20] Others earned money as petty merchants and by selling wares on the streets.

The trade sector allowed women to work independently and earn a decent living, as there was little difference in what men and women could earn.[21] Trade did not require any special training or great financial investment. However, a single woman had to be over twenty-five or be declared of age by the courts before she could engage in trade.

Other single women earned wages in shops, cafes, and inns, by spinning, making lace, washing, filling and carrying peat containers, cleaning (in the town hall, the Admiralty, and the buildings of the East India Company) and toiling at other kinds of menial work.[22] Most of the city's many prostitutes were also single women.[23]

The majority of young unmarried women were engaged in low-paid, unskilled work.[24] They were, in fact, generally prevented from engaging in artisan activities or in other sorts of work with higher earnings. Working women threatened the hierarchical social order, and the city government kept a close eye on the restrictions on the work available to single women and the differentials in pay with men. As far as possible, a single woman was to be kept in a position of subordination.

The same was true elsewhere in the early modern period. In Germany, wages for single women were kept low to ensure that they were unable to support themselves and would be forced to move into a household headed by a man.[25] And in England special legislation meant that single women could not compete with married males and would have to work for a male master or artisan.[26] Married women, on the other hand, were sometimes sought for administrative positions in orphanages, hospitals, and other municipal institutions.

Little is known about the work young women did in Amsterdam and how they managed to survive. Some were married and no longer involved in the city's paid work force. Others were from families well-enough off that the young women did not have to worry about earning a living. Still others were kept at home to help their artisan fathers, to take care of a sick or widowed parent, a disabled brother or sister, or for other reasons. Even in middling households, a young woman's labor represented a family resource.

Along with the estimated 12,000 adolescents and young women employed as domestic servants, unknown numbers toiled at the various kinds of work I discussed above. Many others, an estimated 800, worked as full-time prostitutes. There may have been more.[27] These figures do not add up to anything approaching the estimated 33,000 young women between ages of fifteen and twenty-nine referred to above, but the estimate may be too high.[28]

Whatever the number, women from outside the city were always at a disadvantage when it came to paid work. Selling fish in the market and carrying peat were jobs available only to Amsterdam citizens, as was the trade of silk-twining; the guild for women sewing woolen garments was only open to Amsterdam women. Commenting on this, van de Pol and Kuijpers note that: "Much – perhaps most – of women's work was done in or for households, lodgings, inns, and workshops – as servants or as cleaners, taking in washing, nursing children or the sick, and repairing clothes."[29] There must have been many more ways of earning a living for a single woman, but evidence is lacking.

It was difficult for most single women to get by on what they earned from their low-paying jobs, and they would have had less access to credit than did single men. Single women had to find alternative ways of surviving. Their options were limited. Few had savings upon which they could draw. Nor were most able to count on long-term help from relatives, friends, or neighbors. Along with minimizing their consumption of life's necessities, many shared households with others in similar circumstances. Little is known, however, about how single women managed to survive.

Prostitution was certainly an option, especially for women coming to the city from elsewhere. The overabundance of women, a lack of suitable employment, and low wages played an important role in women's involvement in prostitution. For most women, however, selling their bodies must have been an act of desperation. They would have preferred to protect their bodily integrity and preserve their self-esteem.

Related to this was an exceptionally high level of female criminality in Amsterdam. The majority of women who were convicted thieves were immigrants. Crime, then, was one option for single women to support themselves.[30] Only rarely could a single woman count on the help of the city's charitable institutions as a survival option. Municipal poor relief was intended mainly for citizens and then for non-citizen residents of the city. Individuals had to be "deserving." This meant people who were destitute through no fault of their own and had a good reputation as well: usually the sick, aged, or disabled.

For the most part, single men and women were not considered deserving in this sense. On the contrary; they were seen as able-bodied and so perfectly able to support themselves. Some were viewed as having a dubious reputation. At the same time, city officials actually contributed to the poverty of single women by limiting their employment options and ensuring that their earnings were low.

Other women who might have qualified as deserving were denied relief because they were newcomers to the city and so not entitled to charitable help.[31] Then, as now, a distinction was made between people who deserved help and people who were entitled to it. Being deserving had to do with merit – a given individual *should* receive benefits. Entitlement had to do with institutional *arrangements*: what was set down in black and white (laws and rules) or at least embedded in social convention and practice (for instance, being a male rather than a female in seventeenth-century Amsterdam).[33] This meant that while a woman might have been considered deserving of help because of her good reputation, sterling character, Christian demeanor, dedication to helping others, or some other highly-valued quality, if she failed to meet the residence requirements, she would not be entitled to receive the benefits in question.

The city governors and church officials did not, however, let anyone starve or die on the street. Men and women who were not entitled to charitable assistance received enough for bare subsistence. Many of the strict rules were never adhered to. For one thing, religious conviction would have made a hard-nosed policy of total denial virtually impossible. For another, it was preferable that the poor be objects of charity rather than become thieves, prostitutes, or beggars. As recipients of charity they would be constantly reminded of their subordinate position.

The proportion of single women receiving poor relief was exceeded only by widows with young children. And it far exceeded the figure for single men.[34] Poor relief amounted to anywhere from a third to a half of what it cost to maintain a household. Recipients still had to find alternative ways to make ends meet.[34]

-II-

The Significance of Marital Status

Marital status was closely associated with adulthood in early modern Europe. For a man, marriage represented his establishment as head of a new household. For a woman, it entitled her to a privileged position in a new household. Marital status was an important marker of both male and female identity, although there were significant differences between the sexes.

In tax records, censuses, inventories of household possessions, and other formal documents, men were usually categorized according to their occupation. Women, on the other hand, were categorized in terms of their marital status: single, married, or widowed. An unmarried woman was generally referred to as a *jongedochter* (girl, young woman), even if she was legally an adult.

Recent work in women's history shows how gender and marital status interacted to influence attitudes toward men and women.[35] Unmarried men and women were distinct not only from husbands and wives, but also from widowers and widows. The latter had already been married, and had often been parents as well. The distinction was especially significant for women.

Ever-married women, in other words both wives and widows, were entitled to assist in running a household or to do so on their own. But for the *never*-married woman, in Froide's words, the only acceptable role was "as a household dependent, not as an independent female head of household, outside the control of a father or master."[36]

Though true for early modern England, this was not always the case in the Dutch Republic. Unmarried women over twenty-five were sometimes authorized to act independently, as were some women under that age. These women may or may not have headed their own households. But it was one thing for a young single woman to be legally independent and another for her to remain single for too long.

To be a son or daughter, a husband or wife, a father or mother, and then perhaps someday a widower or widow, were viewed as normal steps in the life-cycle of everyone.[37] Everyone began adulthood as single and usually remained so for several years before eventually marrying. But for someone to spend too many years in the single state or, worse yet, to be a lifelong single man or woman, was to incur the disapproval of the wider society. Such individuals, especially women, were viewed with suspicion.

2.1 *Jacob van Loo*, Allegory on the Distribution of Bread to the Poor (1657). *Oil on Canvas, 260 x 154 cm. Amsterdam: Amsterdams Historisch Museum.*

3.2 Jan van der Heyden. A house in the Bloedstraat damaged by fire on 20 July 1684. *Crayon drawing, 32.2 x 20.2 cm. Amsterdam: Amsterdams Historisch Museum.*

4.1 *Hendrick Martensz Sorgh. Portrait of the Bierens Family (1663). Oil on panel,
52.5 x 71 cm. Amsterdam: The Netherlands Institute of Cultural Heritage.*

6.1 Gabriel Metsu, The Sick Child *(c.1660).* Oil on Canvas, 32.2 x 27.2 cm. *Amsterdam: Rijksmuseum.*

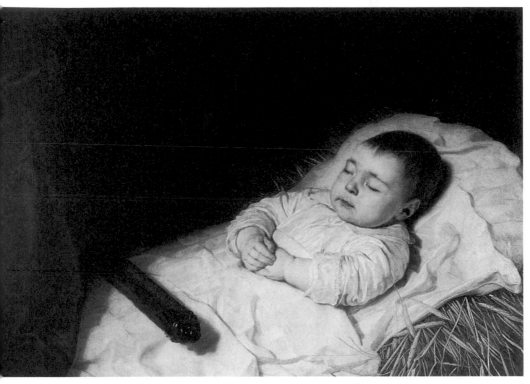

7.1 Bartholomeus van der Helst. Portrait of a Dead Child (1645). *Oil on Canvas, 63 x 90 cm. Gouda: Stedelijk Museum.*

8.1 Gerard ter Borch. A Widow Peeling Apples (c. 1660). *Oil on Canvas, transferred to panel, 36.3 x 30.7 cm. Vienna: Kunsthistorisch Museum.*

8.2 *Wallerand Vaillant.* Portrait of Gaspar Pellicorne (no date). *Oil on Canvas, 66 x 55 cm. Private Collection.*

,3 *Wallerand Vaillant.* Portrait of Clara ʾalkenier (no Date). *Oil on Canvas, 67 x 6 cm. Private Collection.*

9.1 Adriaen Backer. Four Regentesses of the Amsterdam Orphanage (1683).
Oil on Canvas, 193 x 282 cm. Amsterdam: Amsterdams Historisch Museum.

By not occupying their proper place, they threatened the existing moral and social order.

In the Dutch Republic, as elsewhere, the years between sexual maturity and marriage were considered a particularly dangerous time of life. The need for supervision, strict discipline, and control was emphasized by religious and medical authorities, as well as by the writers of domestic treatises.[38] Once again, women and men were treated differently.

Young single men were criticized for the way they dressed, for wearing their hair long, for drinking, rowdy behavior, and sexual misconduct.[39] This held for young men at all levels: from unschooled soldiers and seamen, to apprentices and journeymen, to students from wealthy families at Leiden University.[40] But the behavior of these young men was generally tolerated. For one thing, it was held that boys will be boys and that every young man needed a period in which he could enjoy himself and sow his wild oats before settling down as a husband and father.

For another, there was widespread recognition that the city needed large numbers of young men to labor in jobs associated with the craft guilds, to take on work as seamen, as soldiers, and as ordinary day laborers.[41] Better to put up with their sometimes irritating conduct than have them migrate elsewhere.

As to young men from wealthy families, they were protected both by their families and by university authorities. They were to some extent outside the law. At the University of Leiden, for example, the rowdy behavior of students included sexually molesting servants, prostitutes, and other young women from the so-called lower orders. Groups of students grabbed women under their skirts, fondled their breasts, and sometimes sexually assaulted them.[42]

Most, if not all, women, must have found such unwanted fondling, the efforts of men to initiate sexual relations, and other types of sexual aggression humiliating.[43] Some were able to resist, while others were coerced into sexual relations. Rape and the threat of rape were a major force in the subjugation of women in the Dutch Republic.

If a victim of rape became pregnant, her assailant was often acquitted, for the pregnancy was seen as an indication that the woman had enjoyed the act and experienced the orgasm thought necessary for conception. Since male ejaculation was known to be necessary for conception, the logic of physiological analogy indicated that female orgasm was also necessary. Medical and legal authorities consequently assumed that a pregnant woman had achieved an orgasm and experienced pleasure. She must, then, have consented to sexual relations.

When a woman accused a man of rape, the court took into account her age and sexual experience as well as the behavior of the offender. The rape of a young woman with no previous sexual experience was taken much more seriously than that of one who had already lost her virginity. The court was particularly unsympathetic towards a married woman who claimed to have been raped, believing that her sexual nature and sexual experience made her the perpetrator rather than the victim. But married or unmarried, a man was unlikely to be convicted of rape in the absence of witnesses.[44]

Needless to say, a single young woman was not given some time to do what she herself wished before embarking on marriage and motherhood. If she was the victim of sexual assault, she was likely to be accused of having invited attention because of her dress or comportment. It was, after all, a woman's responsibility to avoid arousing sexual desire in men.

Any young woman living otherwise than under the benevolent control of a male-headed household or a male master was perceived as a potential source of sexual immorality. A poor woman was especially suspect. As Froide notes about seventeenth-century England, a woman who was poor and single seemed "to threaten a social order run by adult, married males of middling elite status."[45]

Many young migrant women in Amsterdam were living at a distance from their families of birth. Their anonymity almost certainly raised fears among older men and women about immoral conduct. It is no wonder that employment as a domestic servant was viewed as the most appropriate position for a young woman to spend her single years. Never mind that she was vulnerable to the unwelcome advances of the master of the household and his sons.

-III-

Courtship and Marriage

When it came to courtship and marriage, domestic conduct books in the Dutch Republic formulated ideals about the roles of the two sexes, the conduct of young men and women, and the sanctity of marriage and the family. Written exclusively by men (Jacob Cats, who as we saw in the previous chapter had his pleasure with servant girls, was one of them), they set forth ideas widely embraced in the theoretical and popular writings of Catholics and Protestants, humanists and scholastics, Europeans, and Englishmen.

These writings are often taken as evidence of the actual behavior of men and women. It is better to regard them as exhortations about how people *ought* to act, as prescriptive rather than descriptive. Because many young men and women acted otherwise, these male writers were insistent on setting forth ideals of conduct that they should aspire to.

The authors of the conduct books were united in their views on sexual conduct, cautioning young women to avoid temptation and to remain chaste until marriage. They must have foreseen that this was unlikely. Even they recognized that sexual pleasure was natural and desirable, although procreation was its legitimate object. Sexual relations were thus permissible only between husband and wife. Despite the strong social, religious, and legal prohibitions against intercourse prior to marriage, love between young people, and the sexual yearnings connected with it, were acknowledged.

Under the circumstances, it could not have been otherwise. A minority of unmarried young people lived at home with one or both parents or other relatives. Far more were women than men. Many young men lived as apprentices in the homes of their masters and some with employers, while many young women lived in the homes where they performed domestic service. Some young people shared lodgings or households with unmarried people of the same sex. And some, more often men than women, lived on their own in rented rooms.

Foreign visitors remarked on the unusual freedom enjoyed by young people in Amsterdam, and several seventeenth-century books provided lists of the most popular locales for meeting members of the opposite sex. As is always the case in relations between the sexes, romantic longings, infatuations, fantasies, and frustrations would have been familiar to virtually every young person. When love entered their lives, it was surely welcomed and eagerly embraced.

Since the majority did not marry until well into their twenties, sexual relationships prior to marriage were almost inevitable. Despite the ideals set forth by the authors of domestic treatises, a woman's respectability rested more on avoiding the shame of bastard-bearing than it did on her chastity.[46] It was understood that if a woman became pregnant, the man responsible should marry her. Most did. Roughly one in five brides was pregnant when she married, but illegitimate children were extremely rare.

Love, or at least mutual attraction, was probably the primary reason for marriage. But economic considerations also played an important role. Setting up a new household often depended on a financial investment by both partners. This amounted to whatever each had been able to save during ten to fifteen years of wage-earning activity. Since women generally earned so little, their savings were often minimal.

Future inheritances probably also played a role in decisions to marry or propose marriage. Males and females were equally entitled to a share of inheritance upon the death of their parents, so single men and single women alike were assured of money coming to them sometime in the future, although these inheritances were unlikely to amount to much.

For many single men, a self-employed tradeswoman or any other young woman earning a reasonable income was a favored candidate for marriage. Literacy also increased a woman's value as a potential wife, since it meant that she could attend to an artisan's or merchant's accounts. A woman with no money of her own was less favored as a marital prospect. The same was true for a woman who was infirm, in ill health, suffered the ill effects of rickets, was grossly overweight, had facial blemishes, or unusually bad teeth.

Although few people enjoyed unblemished skin, good teeth, or completely healthy bodies, these physical characteristics were highly valued. This is evidenced in surviving portraits from the time, most of which are idealized depictions. Such portraits only rarely show freckles, moles, warts, large pores, bad complexions, or even wrinkles. No one has discolored or yellow teeth. In fact, teeth are seldom shown at all. Since the condition of many people's teeth would have been deplorable, it is understandable that they kept their mouths shut.[47]

Advertisements in the *Amsterdamse Courant* promised to remedy at least some shortcomings in people's appearance. Consider teeth. Cavities and diseased gums were common, and teeth were often decayed, stained, or missing. In this regard, an advertisement on July 8, 1692, refers to "the woman from Rotterdam who is able to set [artificial] teeth in the mouth in a way that allows people to eat, speak, and sing. She can also make teeth clean, however black and ugly they might be. This woman from Rotterdam is presently living in the Sail-straet, above the Zuyderkerk in Amsterdam." She was still in business three years later when a similar advertisement appeared.[48]

Facial blemishes, according to another advertisement in the *Courant*, could also be dealt with. "Senor Allonel [presumably someone from Spain or Portugal], who lives on the Herengracht near the Hysteeg, makes known that he possesses a certain water which is able to remove all freckles, red marks, and spots from the face and make it completely white."[49]

No such claims were made about removing smallpox scars. Visual facial scarring was common at the time and was remarked upon with surprising regularity in the *Courant*. A pockmarked face was mentioned as an identifying feature in notices about theft and missing persons. In one instance, the accused thief is described as "a Jew, with a pockmarked nose, and somewhat black and uneven teeth."[50]

Many people's physical appearance had been marred by smallpox. As I remarked earlier, immigrants who had never been exposed to it in the countryside had no immunity to the disease and would have had a higher rate of smallpox than native-born Amsterdammers. For individuals who survived smallpox, the scarring left them disfigured for life. It could put an end to a woman's prospect of marriage, particularly in a city with a surplus of single young women.

Then, as now, looks played a role in a woman's marriage prospects. Much more than with men, there was a hierarchical grading of female figures and faces.[51] A man's appearance was of less importance: he was the one with the earning power and therefore had the advantage in choosing a marital partner.

An older woman was also disadvantaged.[52] If she was past childbearing age, she was certainly unlikely to be sought as a marriage partner. A woman who had remained at home or returned home to care for a sick parent or sibling might never marry. Of course, some women chose to remain single. Some had seen no happy marriages while growing up, and others did not want to yoke themselves for life to a husband and children.

But the most important reason for a woman not to marry was the unbalanced sex ratio, at least during the second half of the century.[53] There were simply too many others in the same boat for every woman to find a marital partner. Most European cities had a disproportionate number of women. Amsterdam had an exceptionally high proportion. At a time when marriage was an economic necessity for most women, this made their prospects rather grim.

The ratio of adult women to adult men in late seventeenth-century Amsterdam was especially high in poor neighborhoods. Van de Pol calculates it as three-to-two. That is to say, 60 percent of the residents were women.[54] This was the result of many thousands of newly-arrived immigrants and other poor men leaving Amsterdam with the East and West India Companies.[55] The universe of possible marriage partners was therefore much smaller for women than for their male counterparts.[56]

As we have seen, men generally enjoyed a higher level of material well-being while they were single, whether for only a few years or for the rest of their lives. Single women, it has been written, had a dreadful propensity for being poor.[57] There was thus an enormous pressure for women to marry. Fear of poverty may well have turned many women into husband-hunters. For some, at least, any marriage was better than none. Not all did, in fact, marry.

-IV-

Never-Married Men and Women
Estimates of the proportion of people in early modern Europe who remained single throughout their lives vary according to gender, time, and place. Because of the efforts of female historians studying other women, more is known about the situation of women than men, although comparatively little attention was given to either single men or women until re-

cent years.[58] While there are differing estimates for the proportion of adult women who remained single throughout their lives, it is safe to assume that the figure was at least 20-30 percent.[59] It was lower for men.[60]

No reliable figures for the percentage of never-marrying men and women exist for seventeenth-century Amsterdam. But the percentage of women was almost certainly higher than elsewhere in Europe at the time, especially towards the end of the century. It seems likely that a third or more of the city's adult women never married.[61]

Only a minority of foreign-born women ever found a marital partner in Amsterdam. Whatever their hopes and desires, many ended up as temporary inhabitants, eventually leaving to return whence they came.[62] Other immigrant women settled permanently in the city, remaining unmarried. The numbers in the two categories are unknown.

Except for the wealthy, differences between the situations of a never-marrying woman and a never-marrying man were enormous. Although marriage might have been the eventual goal of both, it was much more a matter of necessity for a single woman than a single man.

Women working as domestic servants managed to get by economically, though often unable to accumulate much in the way of savings. Some remained single and self-supporting throughout their lives, spending their entire working life as a servant. Some found other types of employment after a few years, and others still returned to their birthplaces with such savings as they had managed to scrape together.

Most permanently single women had difficulties making ends meet, and the threat of poverty was ever-present. Little is known, however, about alternatives to marriage for women or how many found security, care, and intimacy outside the married state.[63]

A single man, especially one with decent earnings, was not only better off economically than a single woman, he was also usually better off than a married man, especially one with children. A single man could spend his earnings on himself, rather than having responsibility for other family members.[64] He was relatively free to live as he chose, perhaps hiring a young servant girl to see to his domestic needs.[65]

-V-

Although there were differences in the proportions of adult men and women who remained permanently single, the majority of both sexes *did* eventually marry and start a household of their own. Just as getting married was more of a necessity for a young woman than a young man, being married was more of a radical break from single life for her than it was for him.

Whatever the greater security, status, and respect provided by marriage, a woman was now expected to subordinate herself to her husband and to take on the reproductive responsibilities (and dangers) associated with being a wife.

Chapter 6

THE FAMILY HOUSEHOLD: HUSBAND, WIFE, AND CHILDREN

I t is January 23, 1665. Arent van Deurs and Christina Pelt are registering to marry in Amsterdam. He is twenty-six years old and she is twenty-four, rather younger than most people marrying at the time. Since they are from the upper echelons of society, there is no need to worry about saving money in order to marry. Arent, a merchant living on the Herengracht, is originally from Haarlem. Christina, the daughter of a broker, lives with her parents on the Singel. She is a native-born Amsterdammer.

-I-

Family Orientation

Young men and women from wealthy families, like Arent van Deurs and Christina Pelt, differed from most people in their family orientation. Among the regent elite, in particular, primary kinship loyalty was to the family of birth rather than to the family of marriage.[1] Blood relations, in other words, took precedence.[2]

The rich located themselves in relationships with members of their birth family both socially and psychologically. It was from these relationships that they acquired their sense of status and identity. In such families, young people sometimes married first cousins and other people related by blood.[3] Most, however, married the sons and daughters of other rich families.[4]

The vast majority of young men and women in Amsterdam had a different kinship orientation. Rather than biological ties, individual preference was paramount in choosing a marital partner and in family life more generally. By the time they came to marry, most young people had enjoyed several years of independence and freedom from parental control. The wishes and desires of their parents counted for little.

Migrants from other lands or from elsewhere in the Republic were often isolated from their biological families, having left them for a new life. Whatever their earlier family loyalties, it was difficult to maintain affective ties at a distance. Even young men and women with relatives in Amsterdam, usually brothers or sisters, were not embedded in webs of family relationships.

Evidence about adherence to the rules and regulations regarding marriage is informative in this regard. The Politieke Ordonnantie of 1580 stipulated that prospective bridegrooms under the age of twenty-five and brides under twenty required the permission of their parents to marry, or, if they were no longer living, that of other relatives or a guardian.[5] Normally this was only a formality; there had to be an extremely good reason for refusal. In fact, most prospective brides and bridegrooms had attained their majority so they did not actually require permission.

Among brides and grooms registering to marry in 1650, around 60 percent of Amsterdam-born brides and grooms received permission from their parents. For the rest, permission came from older brothers and sisters, aunts and uncles, now and again grandparents, or guardians if there were no living relatives. Although some immigrants came with letters purportedly giving their parents' permission, the vast majority married without parental permission: most claiming that both parents were dead.[6] Again, permission came from others.[7]

Another law obligated parents, other relatives, or guardians to be present as witnesses when children registered to marry. Generally, however, parents were not present, nor were other relatives. In 1650, more than two-thirds of men and half of women had no witnesses at all. For migrants, the figures were even higher: 83 percent for the men and 71 percent for the women.[8] It was difficult to enforce such marriage regulations in a migrant city like seventeenth-century Amsterdam.[9]

-II-

Starting Married Life: Husband and Wife

Upon marriage, a couple formed their own family household. This usually meant renting several rooms in a multi-family dwelling and setting up housekeeping. From then on, the primary orientation of most married couples was towards the family they created themselves: spouse and children.[10]

Husband and wife were expected to occupy their proper place in the marital relationship. According to religious doctrine and domestic conduct books at the time, males and females possessed distinct characteristics. Men – the superior sex – not only had greater intelligence and physical strength, but also such distinctive virtues as boldness, honesty, ambition, determination, vigilance, responsibility, and, most importantly, reason.

Women were more pious, devout, meek, modest, humble, and dutiful than their male counterparts. These were largely qualities associated with the emotions. Both men and women were, however, prone to lust. But a man's lust was controlled by reason, whereas a woman's was governed by passion. Since passion must be disciplined by reason, a wife must be submissive to her husband. A woman's perceived inferiority was a result of her physiology.

In line with the distinctive characteristics of men and women, husband and wife were to perform the tasks fitting to their respective natures. A husband had to go out into the world to earn a living, provide for the material and physical well-being of his wife and children, ensure their protection, provide guidance, and govern the household.

A wife had to see to the needs of her husband, bear and raise their children, manage the household, maintain contact with other relatives, and do whatever else was necessary to create a comfortable domestic environment. The marital relationship was hierarchical and asymmetrical, with the wife occupying a subordinate position. In this sexual division of labor, ultimate decision-making power rested with the husband as head of the household.

In theory, then, husband and wife occupied different spheres of activity. In reality, however, the sexual division of labor was seldom so sharp. Women did not live entirely in the domestic domain, nor did men function entirely outside that domain. Some women augmented their husbands' income by working outside the home as well as performing myriad domestic tasks within, and most men spent a great deal of time at home in the family household.

Also in theory, the husband exercised authority over his wife. But in reality, his authority was not always in line with the prescriptive literature. It is true that whatever the financial resources a woman brought to her marriage, she was economically dependent on her husband for her material and physical well-being. And, as always, economic dependence bred other types of dependence: on the good will, approval, praise, admiration, benevolence, or indulgence of the family head. Excessive concern for the reactions of the more powerful person always undercuts or threatens self-respect and integrity.

It is also true that a wife's legal status was inferior to her husband's. She was not allowed to administer her own property, carry out legal transactions, enter into contracts, or appear before a court of law. It was only in the realm of household expenditure that a wife had the legal freedom to make decisions independently of her husband.

There were, though, exceptions to what a woman's legal status entailed. The wives of men of higher economic standing were entitled to take over various administrative responsibilities when their husbands were out of the country in connection with trade or other business activities.

Similarly, women married to sea-going men managed things when their husbands were away, and the wives of shopkeepers often had legal authority to handle business and money affairs.

Still, overall being a married woman was associated with a pattern of cumulative disadvantage. Her relationship with her husband was certainly not one of raw exploitation. More often than not, in fact, a husband probably had a benevolent concern for his wife's well-being. Love and affection between husband and wife seem to have been characteristic of marriages at the time.[11] Nevertheless, a wife had to adapt to the reality of her lack of control over critical resources and her consequent dependence and vulnerability. But she was certainly not a passive and helpless victim of the existing marital arrangements.

We should not forget that most newly-married women had spent a decade or more earning their own living, finding ways to keep their heads above water, and exercising independence from parental control. Moreover, they had dealt with sexual desire and temptation, negotiated their way in relationships with men, and exercised choice with regard to a prospective husband.

Nor should we forget that a wife brought her accumulated savings to the household she established with the man she chose to marry. In many instances, her savings were instrumental to the creation of the household. This fact must have sharply reduced the domestic authority of a husband as the head of the household.[12]

Furthermore, many wives worked alongside guild-master husbands in their workshops, and took over their activities when they died. Most female public vendors were married women. Other women were engaged in wage labor outside the home. Although exact figures are lacking, a large number of married women contributed to the household income.[13] Their earnings were crucial to the survival of the two-fifths of Amsterdam households that lived either below or just above the poverty line.

A husband acknowledging his wife's contributions could not easily exclude her from involvement in important decisions affecting the well-being of the family. A husband who did not do so could be reminded of this fact by his wife. His authority as head of the household was, then, less absolute than is suggested by the prescriptive literature.

In that regard, Schmidt argues that women in the Dutch Republic had more room for asserting themselves as marital partners than did women elsewhere in Europe.[14] They seized whatever opportunities were available for exercising autonomy in their lives. Sometimes at least, husband and wife were what Hartman terms "relative equals" within their own households.[15]

At the same time, many a husband would have been deeply ambivalent about his wife's relative equality. On the one hand, he welcomed her contribution to the creation and maintenance of the household, and perhaps valued her character and personality as well (he had asked for her hand in marriage). On the other, he would have been threatened by her acting in ways inappropriate to what was expected of a married woman. Theologians, after all, stressed the divinely ordained obligation of a wife to subordinate herself to her husband. Domestic conduct books were dominated by misogynist rhetoric, insisting that a wife defer to the authority of her husband. Literary texts, drama, and popular writings mocked the bossy controlling wife and her subordinate husband. Painters depicted the domestic upheaval resulting from a housewife acting like a man.

Contemporary male commentators often showed contempt for and distrust of women. They warned against women gaining the upper hand and reiterated the need for a husband to fill his God-given position as head of the household.[16] These men were disturbed by independence in women, by competition from women, by women thinking and acting for themselves. Too many women, they seemed to believe, were dangerously uncontrollable. For some men at least, *any* manifestation of ambition or self-assertion by a woman was a source of alarm.

The position of a married woman was, then, one thing in ideology, another in the law, and yet another in everyday relationships with her husband. As in any society, there were women with stronger personalities than their husbands, a greater need to take charge, or a simple unwillingness to accede to the authority of the head of the family. But more than anything else, it was a wife's contribution to the establishment of the family household that allowed her to enjoy a degree of autonomy and maintain a sense of her own worth.

This is not to deny the existence of a hierarchy between members of the two sexes or the privileged positions of husbands vis-à-vis their wives. But more often than not, everyday relations between husband and wife necessarily involved cooperation, conflict, compromise, and negotiation.[17] The proportions and circumstances for each differed, of course, from one couple to another.

Virtually nothing is known, however, about the internal dynamics of husband-wife relationships, about the everyday goings-on between them, or about how decisions were reached about household matters, even with regard to such matters as family spending.[18] Nor is anything known about a woman's participation in decisions about having children.

Having Children

It was considered the duty of every Christian couple to beget children, and most men and women seem to have actively sought parenthood. An estimated 16 percent of married couples were without children.[19] This was seldom by choice, since the absence of children represented failure and inadequacy. To be barren was a judgment from God, always regarded as the woman's fault.[20] In an unknown percentage of childless marriages, there had been miscarriages or still births.

As a consequence of the dominant marriage pattern in northwestern Europe, described in the previous chapter, households in Amsterdam were small. Newly-wed couples set up their own households rather than sharing households with other relatives. For that reason, extended families, with parents, aunts and uncles or other relatives living under the same roof were rare. They were particularly rare among foreign-born families.

Late marriage also had an influence on the number of children that women bore, since every woman will at some point in her life become incapable of conceiving a child.[21] Women who married when they were about twenty-six would have had an average of five children before the end of the childbearing period as compared to an average of seven children among women in eastern and southern Europe at the time.[22]

Typically, the family consisted of a husband and wife, and two or three surviving children. The vast majority of wives spent their married life alternating pregnancies and births with periods of mourning. Death was a familiar occurrence, and almost every family experienced the loss of at least one child.

Just as the physical structure of the family dwelling had an impact on eating and sleeping arrangements, the level of hygiene, sexuality, intimacy, and other aspects of everyday life, so it shaped and limited the patterns and quality of relationships between parents and their offspring and influenced the well-being of both.

Children were born at home. Wealthy families were able to set aside a room for childbirth. Ordinary families, often living in crowded conditions in small dwellings, could not do so. Some may have screened off part of a room to create a sort of birth room. The pregnant mother was, in either case, delivered in the presence of other women whom she specifically invited to the birth: a midwife, female relatives, friends, and neighbors.[23]

When no female relatives were available, as with most families who came to Amsterdam from elsewhere, the woman's husband attended the birth. For families living in just two or three rooms, his presence was at times unavoidable. Husbands are known to have been in attendance in wealthy families as well.[24] This probably occurred among families at every economic level.

Childbirth in the early modern period was dangerous and painful. It was often perilous and sometimes traumatic for a mother. Little is known, however, about this aspect of a married woman's life. For, as Bonnie Smith notes, "there has been virtually no historical consideration of women's trauma from sexual, gynecological, and reproductive pain and powerful bodily dysfunction as a result of childbirth,"[25] Women's sexual uncertainties, fears, and sufferings remain unexplored.

The presence of a midwife was required by law, both to assist the mother in the birth of her child and to assure that no secret births or concealed infanticides occurred. The midwife instructed the mother how to prepare for the birth. At the actual birth, she told her when to bear down and when to rest, and which positions to adopt, and then delivered the baby.[26]

The midwife was also required to find out and report the name of the man who fathered the child. In the case of an unmarried woman, it was particularly important for the midwife to ascertain the father's name. He could then be held legally responsible for providing economic support for mother and child. Otherwise, the community would be saddled with this burden, something that municipal and religious authorities alike tried to avoid. The law demanded that the midwife perform her task in the presence of witnesses who could testify, if necessary, that she had done her job correctly.[27]

Midwifery was a profession with a specialized and extended period of training. During the first two years, an aspiring midwife was required to witness a minimum of sixteen births. She needed (from 1668) to be examined by the *Collegium Medicum* of Amsterdam and obtain a certificate of expertise, and (from 1675) to have worked as an assistant to a qualified midwife for at least four years before being allowed to take the examination that would qualify her as an official midwife.[28] This examination was only open to women who were citizens of Amsterdam, could read and write, were more than twenty-five years old, either married or widowed, and had children of their own.

Women who qualified for and passed this examination were then entitled to hang out a sign indicating their professional status. In addition to those midwives paid by individual families for assisting at a birth, others were employed by the city of Amsterdam to help poor women who were unable to pay for their services.[29]

Midwifery demanded special training, was the most respected profession open to women, and was probably better paid than any other sort of work done by women at the time. It has been estimated that a typical midwife was involved in roughly 120 births a year and was paid an average of two guilders a birth, so that she would earn around 240 guilders a year. Her earnings were, however, below those of men with a similar period of specialized training for their occupations.[30] In Amsterdam, as elsewhere in the Dutch Republic, the city fathers and the guilds assured that the female-male wage ratio was always to the detriment of women.[31]

Despite a midwife's special training and experience, mothers died giving birth.[32] Negligence on the part of midwifes, unsanitary conditions, and a mother's nutritional deficiencies were among the factors responsible for high-risk deliveries.[33] Poorer women were especially vulnerable.

Maternal mortality was not solely the result of childbirth. It was also a result of the mother's immune system having to adjust to the presence of the fetus, an adjustment making mothers more susceptible to fatal infections. Maternal mortality was consequently much higher than normal during the first six months following a birth, and it continued to be high during the infant's first year.[34]

A baby that survived its mother's death had, of course, to be fed. So, too, did a baby whose mother was unable to feed it. Two possibilities existed: either milk from the breasts of a wet-nurse or a sort of porridge (pap). The latter was less expensive, but provided little nourishment and so dramatically lessened the chances that the baby would survive. Infants suckled by wet-nurses, on the other hand, acquired the right antibodies to provide at least some protection against gastrointestinal and respiratory infections.[35]

Such protection was unavailable to infants fed porridge. For most families, however, porridge was the only option.[36] A wet-nurse cost 7 guilders a month, more than a week's wages for a skilled artisan.[37] A live-in wet-nurse cost even more. Since infants were kept on the breast for a year or longer, only well-to-do families could afford to engage a wet-nurse if the mother died in childbirth, was physically unable to breastfeed the baby herself, or chose not to do so.

Wet-nurses were women who were either suckling their own babies or had just weaned or lost them. No more intimate or personal labor is imaginable. Sometimes the infant was lodged in the home of the wet-nurse, frequently in the country. As with the earnings of married women more generally, nothing is known about the extent to which wet-nurses controlled the income they earned from nursing other people's infants.[38] It was labor undertaken for reasons of financial necessity rather than intrinsic pleasure.

Most families had insufficient savings on which they could draw to engage the services of a wet-nurse, could not count on long-term help from friends or neighbors, and did not qualify for financial help from the church or the city in such circumstances. As with other situations involving limited financial means, husband and wife had to decide on the allocation of available resources. In this instance, it was a decision that affected their child's chances of survival.

Only rarely did a family of modest means take on the economic burden of hiring a wet-nurse. Hermanus Verbeeck and his wife, Clara Molenaers, were a couple who did. They had married in 1649, and she was pregnant soon after. A daughter was born in 1650, following a painful delivery. In 1652, Clara gave birth to a son. An infection meant that she had difficulty breast-feeding the infant, and he died within four months.

A second son was born in 1655. Again, an infection prevented Clara from breast-feeding the child. This time, the couple decided to engage a wet-nurse. They were not poor. The family's income, about 400 guilders a year, was above average. Even so, the services of the wet-nurse consumed a quarter of that amount. According to Verbeeck's autobiography, friends and relatives regarded this as exceeding all normal expectations for what should be done to keep a newborn infant alive.[39]

This was not because of any emotional indifference on people's part towards infants and children, but because of the hard struggle faced by most families in simply surviving and getting by. Families faced difficult decisions about how to divide available resources. As far as I can tell, parents usually did as much as conditions would allow to promote the survival and well-being of their loved ones.[40]

Clara Molenaar had long been involved in providing a share of the family income. For this reason, she probably had a greater say about hiring a wet-nurse than did many other wives at the time. Her husband, Hermanus, had worked at a variety of jobs during the couple's marriage: as a furrier, bookkeeper, broker, and clerk. But severe health problems, bad luck, and a degree of ineptitude made it impossible for him to make an adequate living.

Clara became the main breadwinner, taking over the management of a grocery store previously owned by her father. At other times, she worked as a seamstress. Clara was in a position, then, to be quite insistent about spending a large portion of the household income to try to assure the survival of her infant son. Despite the couple's serious concern and financial sacrifice, the baby died after a year.[41]

Although the highest frequency of deaths among infants was for those fed porridge, Clara Molenaer and Hermanus Verbeeck must have been aware that infants suckled by wet-nurses died more frequently than those breast-fed by their mothers. This was a consequence not only of differences in the quality of the milk, but also of less touching and physical contact from a hired wet-nurse than from a mother.

Maternal breastfeeding had significance beyond its role in infant mortality, and was advocated in virtually all medical treatises and advice manuals. Blankaart, a Dutch physician, and Cats, the famous moralist, gave both medical and moral reasons as to why mothers should breastfeed their children.[42] Cats argued that nursing strengthened a mother's affective bond with the child.

Controlling Fertility

Breastfeeding was a form of birth control as well. The principal means of voluntary birth control at the time was undoubtedly *coitus interruptus* – withdrawal before ejaculation – "assisted no doubt," writes Lawrence Stone, "by oral, manual and anal sex."[43] Although a crude type of condom existed, it was used mainly for protection against venereal disease. Stone apparently does not consider breastfeeding a form of voluntary birth control.

For the vast majority of women who breastfed their children, the process of suckling acted as a natural contraceptive.[44] Ovulation took much longer to return and the chance of conceiving was reduced. At least some women knew that lactation was a natural suppressant of fertility.[45] It was a way of preventing unwanted pregnancies, a concern of women throughout history.[46]

If a woman feared becoming pregnant again too soon after her confinement and was anxious to ensure her children's health by spacing them, extending her lactation up to two years provided a margin of safety against a subsequent conception. Reproductive decisions were of enormous significance for most women. They recognized the dangers of pregnancy to their health and that of their children.

Surveying the relevant literature, Roberts concludes that "the employment of a wet-nurse was unusual and only in cases when a mother was incapable of breastfeeding her child or if the mother died."[47] But employing a wet-nurse was much more common than Roberts suggests, and it was not always because the mother died or was unable to breastfeed her child. It seems, in fact, to have been quite common among the wealthy elite in Amsterdam and elsewhere.[48]

Researchers classify birth intervals of less than 16 months as evidence that mothers were not themselves breastfeeding.[49] Applying this standard, my examination of the birth intervals for children in thirty wealthy Amsterdam families reveals that three-quarters employed a wet-nurse with one or more of their children.[50]

Wealthy women had a variety of reasons for engaging a wet-nurse: the mother's inability to nurse the baby, considerations of her health, the wish to avoid being tied down to a nursing schedule, vanity about her figure, a husband's jealousy at having to share his wife's body with an infant, and the desire to escape the cultural proscription against sexual intercourse as long as lactation continued (sexual relations were thought to spoil the mother's milk).[51]

Another reason for hiring a wet-nurse was the desire of some women to become pregnant again as *quickly* as possible. Consider the merchant Willem Noltenius and his wife, Catharina de Wit. They almost certainly employed a wet-nurse. The couple lived in a large house on the Keizersgracht, one of the city's most desirable locations.[52] Catharina was from a well-to-do Amsterdam family.[53] Willem, originally from Dordrecht, was involved in international trade.[54] They married in February 1697.

No children were born during the first five years of their marriage, or at least none lived long enough to be entered into the baptismal records. Except for the stillborn, all children in seventeenth-century Holland were baptized and named. It was vital to do so as soon as possible so as to assure the child's admittance into the Kingdom of Heaven.

The first recorded birth in the Noltenius household was for a son, Govert Rookus, who entered the world in August 1702. Then, like clockwork, a second son and two daughters followed in August of the following three years. The only way that the children could have been born just one year apart is if a wet-nurse had been hired to suckle each of them.[55]

Govert Rookus was born, a wet-nurse was hired, and ovulation returned for Catharina.[56] And so it went with the following children. The couple's motivation, it can be assumed, was to make up for the absence of any (live) births during the first five years of their marriage.[57] They wanted to control Catharina's fertility, and seem to have continued to do so in the following years.

Catharina must have returned to breastfeeding after the birth of the couple's fourth child, judging by the birth interval of thirty-one months before the next one. With two further children, the birth intervals were each twenty-six months. These longer birth intervals may represent a deliberate effort at spacing subsequent births. As we have seen, extended breastfeeding was a form of family planning. It was basic to the survival of young infants as well.

-IV-

Vulnerabilities and Early Deaths
Infant mortality was high. The greatest risk of dying was in the first days after birth, but it continued to be high for several months. A quarter of all infants died within the first year. Although the level of risk is much lower today, first-year mortality has remained remarkably constant over the cen-

turies. This pattern points to the biological roots of early infant deaths.[58] Biological factors are a primary determinant of infant mortality until the time that an infant is weaned, the real transition between infancy and childhood.[59] Breastfeeding plays a major role in this regard, as does economic status. An inverse association exists between economic status and infant mortality, in contemporary societies and in the past. Although evidence for early modern Europe is limited, a recent study shows a clear relationship between economic status and the survival of infants and young children in pre-industrial England.[60]

In the case of seventeenth-century Amsterdam, the ability of families to employ a wet-nurse was a major factor in this association. But once an infant was weaned, the disease environment played the dominant role in mortality.[61] I considered this in Chapter 3, where I described differences in the residential and housing environment in Amsterdam.

Just as families differed greatly in their housing and hygienic conditions, so they differed in the nutritional value of their diets. The quantity and quality of what men, women, and children in Amsterdam ate and drank depended on their economic position, as did the demands made on that nutritional value by cold, disease, and physical activity.[62]

Most people ate three meals a day, but those engaged in demanding physical labor would also eat once or twice in between. Breakfast consisted mainly of bread, butter, and cheese, although some wealthy families also ate meat at breakfast. For most families, bread was the main staple in the morning. Its quality varied according to the social level of those consuming it. Milk was mainly consumed as the liquid ingredient in different types of porridge. Beer was the usual drink, since water was not available in most houses.

The principal repast of the day was a hot midday meal, eaten around noon by wealthy families and somewhat earlier by other families where the husband was able to be at home for a midday meal. For individuals working away from home, the time of lunch depended on how early they had begun work in the morning. In some families, the times of breakfast and the midday meal were also governed by school hours.

Wealthy families ate generous portions of meat and fish (both of which were expensive), accompanied by such vegetables as carrots, onions, cabbage, peas, and beans; often followed by eggs, bread, butter, cheese, or a salad. Fruit, sometimes from their own country garden, cakes, biscuits, waffles, and pancakes were also consumed at the midday meal. These families often ate a similar, though smaller, meal in the evening. They drank beer or wine with their meals.

The rich were anything but moderate in what they consumed. The amount and quality reflected both what they could afford and their beliefs about what was appropriate for people like themselves. Physiological necessity was relatively unimportant.

The nutritional value of rich people's diets was more than adequate. They were, in fact, overfed. Though not living completely sedentary lives, they expended insufficient energy to avoid becoming overweight. In wealthy families, many men, women, and children would have been grossly overweight.

Most other families ate vegetables, with perhaps a small amount of meat at midday, along with a large amount of bread, butter, and cheese. At dinner, they ate leftovers, and the ubiquitous bread, butter, and cheese. Poorer families rarely ate meat or fish. They consumed large quantities of vegetables at midday, followed by bread, but seldom butter or cheese. Their evening meal consisted of a large amount of bread. Both adults and children drank beer, since it was cheaper than wine.

The work performed by guild masters, journeymen, and apprentices was physically much more demanding than that done by the regents and other highly-placed citizens. The same was true of the labor performed by their wives at home. Other people located midway in the economic hierarchy faced similar physical demands. Their nutritional intake and their expenditure of energy were usually much more in line than in the case of the rich.

This was not true of the majority of workers, and certainly not of the city's immigrants. The labor done by working men often demanded an enormous expenditure of energy, carrying out heavy work involving movement of the whole body from eleven to thirteen or more hours a day in the summer months and a few hours less in winter.[63] The labor of women at home was also heavy, as was that done by many children. Their nutritional intake was not always enough to satisfy their energy requirements.

People living a hand-to-mouth existence were certainly undernourished. For the poorest 15-20 percent of the population, the nutritional value of the proteins, fats, and carbohydrates eaten by men, women, and children provided insufficient calories to meet the demands of cold, disease, and heavy labor. The energy they expended in keeping warm, fighting disease, and performing physical labor inside and outside the rooms they called home stunted their growth and made it difficult to maintain an adequate bodyweight. In poor families, parents and children were often frail, pale, and in a constant state of ill health.

The lower a family's position in the economic hierarchy, the higher the percentage of income spent on food.[64] In the course of the seventeenth-century, as the price of necessities rose while wages remained stable, most families experienced a decline in nutritional intake. This led not only to an increased susceptibility to illness at the time, but later in life as well. Poor nutrition in the early years has a lasting effect on people's health.[65]

Nutritional intake had a direct impact on infant, child, and adult mortality. The interaction of infections and nutrition was especially significant in this regard. It always is.[66] On the one hand, infections reduce appetite and decrease the absorption of nutrients. On the other, nutritional deficiencies reduce resistance to infections by weakening the human defense system. Although infections always influence nutritional status, the reverse is sometimes not the case.

Some infections are so virulent that they spread and become fatal no matter how well-nourished someone may be. Plague, smallpox, and typhoid belong to this category. With others, the outcome is to varying degrees dependent on the resistance provided by nutritional status. Tuberculosis (consumption as it was known in the early modern period), measles, diarrhea, respiratory infections, and most intestinal parasites are examples of infections that caused more disease in the malnourished than in the rest of the population.

The foremost killers among infectious diseases in Amsterdam would have been plague, consumption, fever, smallpox, and diseases afflicting infants and young children.[67] Plague, fever, and smallpox were fatal to virtually everyone, regardless of how well-nourished they may have been. Consumption, on the other hand, was significantly influenced by the standard of nutrition. And, as we have already seen, infants who were breastfeeding acquired a degree of protection against infections. Once weaned, however, children became particularly vulnerable to gastric disease spread by contaminated food and water.

Childhood mortality seems to have been highest among the poor and lowest among the wealthy elite. The same was true with morbidity (sickness).[68] Little is known, however, about morbidity rates. In any case, many children fell sick but did not die. Even so, a sick child would have been a terrible worry in a period with few resources or remedies for childhood illnesses.

Depictions of sick children are rare in the art of the Dutch golden age. Illustration 6.1, Gabriël Metsu's *The Sick Child*, is a rare exception.[69] It shows a pale, languid child lying in the lap of a large, worried-looking woman. A spoon in the small stoneware bowl at the left suggests that she is trying to get the child to take some soup. This poignant image has surely awakened many viewers' memories of the agonies of childhood illness.

The poorer areas of seventeenth-century Amsterdam acted as a reservoir of disease, and individuals living in proximity to one another were exposed to similar dangers. But better-off areas were not immune to infections and many people suffered the consequences of plague, fever, smallpox, and other virulent infections that produced diseases that were deadly for almost everyone.[70]

Some rich families had the means to escape to a second house in the country, where there was pure air, clean drinking water, and the danger of contagion was far less. They left the city on weekends and holidays, and during the summer months. They were also able to retire to their country estates during epidemics of the plague. Often four or five hours away by horse and carriage, far removed from the bad air and possibilities of contagion in the city, these second homes afforded protection against the ravages of infectious diseases. No such possibility of escape was available to the vast bulk of the population.

-V-

This chapter has examined various aspects of life in family households in seventeenth-century Amsterdam. But I have had little to say so far about face-to-face relations within the family setting and their influence on the wellness of people's being. For the many people living in cramped quarters, their emotional life was inevitably anchored in relationships with other family members.

Feelings of solidarity, happiness, joy, satisfaction, pride, and accomplishment arise from being embedded in families. So, too, do such feelings as sorrow, grief, jealousy, and humiliation. Intimate relations within the family are a source of both intense pleasures and intensely felt hurts. As everyone knows, families are potent and affect the well-being of virtually everyone.

Just as it does today, family life in early modern Amsterdam involved patterns of relationship between husbands and wives, parents and children, and between siblings as well. More often than not, these familial relationships were characterized by hierarchy, dependence, and subordination. I have given some attention to husband-wife relationships. Parents and children, and brothers and sisters are my focus in the chapter that follows.

Chapter 7

PARENTS AND CHILDREN, BROTHERS AND SISTERS

I t is December 26, 1679. In Amsterdam's Waalse kerk two infants are
baptized. Susanna de Bane has recently given birth to twins: a boy and
a girl. Originally from Leiden, she and Abraham Muyssart, a successful Amsterdam merchant, were married in 1675. The birth of twins is an
unusual occurrence, much rarer than today when delayed childbearing and
fertility treatments have increased its likelihood.

The parents are ready with names for the newborns: Susanna Catarina and Abraham. Susanna is the mother's name and was also the name of
the couple's first-born daughter who died a year earlier. Abraham is named
after his father. Though the two children are twins and will grow up in the
same household, they will experience radically different upbringings: for
one is female and the other male.

-I-

Mother-Child Relations

A seventeenth-century mother had primary responsibility for introducing a
couple's children to the ways of the world. This included teaching a boy or
girl the behavior appropriate to its birth order, gender, and social standing.
Susanna de Bane had to take care of the well-being of a son and a daughter
at the same time.

With twelve or so rooms, the Muyssart home was large enough to
set aside a lying-in room for the mother and her two babies. The family had the wherewithal to employ maids to take on the extra burdens of
housework while Susanna recovered from childbirth. The Muyssarts may
even have hired a nurse to wash the two infants and change their napkins
regularly.

"Children must never be left wet or soiled for long," wrote the Amsterdam physician Stephanus Blankaart, "as this causes them discomfort
and makes them cry. The wet fabric will, moreover, rapidly become cold
against the body, which is harmful to the infant."[1] Each time it was changed,
an infant was placed in a clean napkin.

The infant was then wrapped in swaddling clothes: narrow strips of cloth that restricted its movement and kept it warm. Swaddling was also intended to assure that the child would not grow up physically deformed. For, according to another seventeenth-century physician, "the soft and tender limbs can give and bend like wax, with the result that incorrect swaddling frequently leads to a deformed body, crooked legs and other shortcomings".[2] Swaddling continued for the first few months.

Every infant had to have its napkin changed regularly and be re-wrapped in swaddling clothes. But only the well-to-do could hire a servant or nurse to help. Only they could afford to send the napkins and swaddling clothes out to be washed. In the majority of families, the mother performed these chores herself. Since she had to fetch water to do them, the napkins and swaddling clothes were probably changed less often than in wealthy households.

Ordinary families did not have a special lying-in room, and few mothers had time to stay in bed in the days and weeks following a birth. Some had to be on call to assist their artisan husbands. Others were kept busy with the numerous household tasks taken on by domestic servants in the homes of the rich. When there were other children in the family, the mother had to be available to them as well. The recovery period for most women in Amsterdam had to be kept short.

During the early months, an infant's most intense emotional tie was with its mother. She was the person who suckled and otherwise took care of it, although this was not necessarily the case in wealthy families. If a mother died, another woman became the primary caretaker. It was always a woman who inculcated the knowledge on which all subsequent learning was based, whether a family lived in a large house or in just one or two rooms.

It was from its mother that a child learned to walk, to talk, to eat, to control bodily functions, to recognize what was dangerous or threatening, and to relate to other people. It was within that relationship that a child came to have a sense of itself as masculine or feminine, and learned the emotions appropriate for males and females and how to display them. Boys and girls were encouraged to develop the traits considered appropriate to the two sexes.[3] From birth onward, an infant was treated in accordance with its sex.

So it was with the twins Abraham and Susanna Catarina in the Muyssart family. Gender identity is firmly established by the age of eighteen months.[4] By that time, Abraham would have been aware that he was a boy and Susanna would have known she was a girl. But the acquisition of gender identity was different for the two sexes.

Mother-child relationships and the mechanisms involved in the acquisition of gender identity are basically the same in all societies.[5] A mother identifies more closely with a daughter than with a son. She has, after all, been a girl herself. Her sense of oneness and continuity with a little girl is stronger and of longer duration than with a little boy. A mother prolongs the period of close connectedness with a daughter beyond what occurs with a son. A daughter is encouraged to identify with her mother and take her as the model for what it is to be female.

A little boy, on the other hand, has to learn to stop identifying with his mother and to separate himself imaginatively from her.[6] To acquire a sense of maleness, he needs to identify with his father. In the absence of a father, he still faces the task of shifting his primary identification from a woman to a man. This, too, is first learned in a relationship with his mother. She is the one who encourages him and insists that he act and define himself as being different from her and like his father (or another male). Masculinity is identified by a rejection of what is "female."

In seventeenth-century Amsterdam, a mother had to ensure that her child honored and obeyed its father and mother. She was expected to inculcate the importance of submission to those in authority more generally, including the proper ways of showing deference and respect to one's betters. As a child grew older, this was reinforced by religious teachings.

Although it spent far less time in the presence of its father, a child quickly became acquainted with male precedence and advantage. A child's father stood for freedom and independence. He was the one who left the house, "went to work," had contact with the outside world, and was the main breadwinner.

A child saw that its mother and other women raised the young and oriented themselves to the needs and interests of other persons. Even in those instances where a mother labored outside the house, she had primary responsibility for food preparation, housework, and childcare. Whatever the extent of their recognition, boys and girls alike were aware that their mother had less control over her life than their father did over his. In ways unavailable to her, he was able to exercise at least a degree of autonomy and control over his life.

We now know that parental time and presence in a child's world affect its general health, and play a critical role in cognitive, educational, and social development. Conversely, parental absence and lack of contact are detrimental to a child's general well-being.[7]

In seventeenth-century Amsterdam, a mother's presence differed from one household to the next, depending on the time and attention she devoted to her husband, the number of other children in the family, and on whether she had household help from a servant or perhaps from an unmarried sister or another relative.

Her presence was also influenced by the size and layout of the family's home. In the large homes of the rich, rooms often had a specialized use and household members were spatially separated much of the time. Husbands and wives, sons and daughters, and sometimes household personnel as well, were likely to have rooms of their own. An infant or young child might not sleep in the same room as its mother. When a wet-nurse was hired to suckle an infant, it may have spent more time with her than with its mother.

A wealthy woman was also apt to have a busy social life: entertaining and visiting friends and relatives. In wealthy households, then, an infant or young child spent considerable time outside the physical presence of its mother.

In smaller single-family houses, the use of rooms was much less specialized. A young child often slept in a room with its parents, and rarely was a wet-nurse employed. Mother and child spent considerably more time together than in a wealthy household, much of it while the child's father was absent.

The situation was different for the vast majority of families, few of whom inhabited a house on their own. The limited amount of interior space in dwellings of two or three rooms made it virtually impossible for family members to be out of sight and sound of one another. Intimate space was virtually nonexistent. Husband and wife had to wait for some privacy for love-making. Not all did so.

A mother prepared a thousand or more meals a year in the room where the family ate, gathered for warmth, spent time together, and where at least some members of the family slept. She breastfed her young infant and changed its napkin and swaddling clothes there as well. In such circumstances, the mother's physical presence was almost a constant in the experience of the young child.

-II-

Father-Child Relations
As in most other times and places, a young child had a weaker and less intense relationship with its father than with its mother.[8] A child whose father was regularly at sea had only intermittent contact with him, and some children never knew their father at all. But most children spent some time with their father, since he was usually present for at least part of the day. Here, too, the size of the house made a difference. So, too, did a father's work.

In wealthy families, fathers were able to be at home for large stretches of the day. The activities of Amsterdam regents seldom required a full day's work, and they spent a considerable amount of time at home.[9]

Although they had other responsibilities and other meetings, and devoted some time during the afternoon to their investments and business interests, the city fathers had plenty of free time.

High-placed members of the city government usually had an office in the house. So did merchants, traders, and other men active in business. Visitors were common. City officials and officers of the Dutch East India Company entertained their colleagues, merchants discussed business, and women received friends and relatives for afternoon tea. Eating and drinking were central to the everyday activities of the wealthy elite. Home was the center of their lives.

But while physically present, wealthy fathers had little involvement in the everyday lives of their young sons and daughters. Not only was there a separation of gender domains in the houses of the rich, but the physical and social differentiation of space assured that fathers seldom encountered their children during normal daily life.

Higher-placed personnel worked longer hours than wealthy men, but far fewer than those who did physical labor. Bookkeepers and clerks employed by the East India Company, for example, worked from six or seven in the morning until eleven o'clock. Returning to work at two, they would work until six in the evening: an eight- or nine-hour day, compared to the twelve-hour days of ships' carpenters and the thirteen-hour day of laborers working for the East India Company.[10] In theory, at least, this gave them more time to spend with their children than most manual laborers would have had.

Master artisans, who often worked at home, probably spent more time in the presence of an infant son or daughter than any other category of men. An artisan was never far from where his young son or daughter slept, was suckled, and otherwise cared for by its mother. Since his wife often helped him with his work, mother and child spent part of the day together in the same room as the father. This continued until the child went to school.

The separation of gender domains did not exist for most artisan families. Their dwellings had too few rooms and too little space to allow such a separation. Of necessity, a father took over some of his wife's chores (just as she took over some of his), including looking after, handling, and playing with their children.[11]

Fathers doing unskilled and menial sorts of work – the most common type of employment in Amsterdam – would have had the least intense relationships with their children. This was simply a consequence of their long hours of heavy and physically demanding work away from the family dwelling.

It is easy to imagine a father returning home exhausted from a twelve- or thirteen-hour work day, eating some bread and cheese, and then immediately falling into bed – a bed often shared with his wife and children. Although sleeping in close physical proximity, he was not in a position to be active in their care and upbringing.

-III-

Growing Up

Having been wrapped in swaddling clothes for several months as infants, both boys and girls were dressed in skirts for the next few years. There were apparently some differences in the details of the skirts worn by the two sexes.[12] From around the age of seven, if not before, boys exchanged their skirts for breeches. At least this was the custom among those wealthy families whose portraits of children survive today.[13]

As boys and girls matured, relationships with their mother and father changed, differing in duration, content, intensity, and strength. The amount of time they spent with their father usually increased, but they still spent more time with their mother. A daughter continued to have her strongest relationship with her mother. A son gradually came to have his strongest relationship with his father. Gender differences were more and more accentuated.

Schooling reinforced these differences. It also helped preserve the hierarchical distinctions in Dutch society. Formal education was considered less necessary for children from the lower than the higher orders and for girls than for boys. Although children were not required to attend school, most did have some schooling.[14]

Elementary schools, for children between the ages of five and ten, taught reading, writing, and some arithmetic, and provided a religious education. Girls also learned to sew and perform other "feminine" tasks, tasks they often already performed at home. The expectation for both boys and girls was that they would eventually do the same kind of work as their parents did.

Children from poorer families – many of them immigrants – had the least schooling, often having to help out at home or go out to work when they were no more than six or seven.[15] Some children never attended school at all. Others left school after learning to read, but without learning to write or acquiring any skills in arithmetic.

Being able to read was itself an important skill and enhanced an individual's well-being. It allowed someone to understand contracts, leases, and other legal documents, and provided access to newspapers, pamphlets, and the like. More generally, it provided access to the world of knowledge, ideas, and information. An individual who could read would be able to enjoy the written word and his skill would have given him a sense of accomplishment and self-esteem.

Boys from the lower orders went on to labor at menial and unskilled occupations, spending their working lives taking orders. Girls often became domestic servants in the homes of the rich. These children were not only worse off materially than the better-situated, they had less autonomy. Girls had less autonomy than boys.

Artisans generally saw to it that their sons received training for a career with at least some autonomy and independence. A master artisan often prepared his son in his own trade, actively supervising several years of preparation in the craft. When a family had to pay for a boy's training, he almost always left home. Girls, however, usually remained at home a few more years. Females spent a much greater proportion of their time in the family context than did males.

Wealthy fathers were deeply involved in the education of their children, especially their male offspring. Both sons and daughters received an education entirely different from that of children in ordinary families. Some sons, but probably more daughters, were educated at home with the help of private tutors.[16] A small number of sons were sent abroad for their schooling when they were about thirteen.

Most boys and girls from wealthy families attended the expensive and elite "French" secondary schools between the ages of six and ten. They were taught history and geography, to speak and write fluent French, and to conduct themselves as young ladies and gentlemen. Boys were also taught mathematics and bookkeeping, while girls had lessons in music, dancing, and needlework.

Boys were then usually enrolled in the Latin school, preparing them both for university study and for their responsibilities as part of Europe's social and cultural elite. At the core of the curriculum was instruction in Latin grammar, literature, and rhetoric. Ancient history, logic, ethics, geography, physics, and the history of religion were also taught. The emphasis was on the classical tradition, especially Roman authors such as Cicero, Virgil, Horace, and Ovid. The boys read Aristotle and Plato as well, although Greek writings were secondary.[17]

These Roman and Greek authors would have reinforced the boys' views about natural hierarchies, about the inferiority of women, non-citizens, and anyone involved in manual labor, and thus about the importance of people being in their proper place.[18] As sons of the future political and economic elite, they learned that the good of society required that authority be in the hands of rich and powerful members of the male sex.

Neither the Latin school nor the universities were open to girls.

More women than men consequently lacked knowledge of classical languages, history, and culture. Girls educated at home by private tutors were an exception. While wealthy young men were attending the university, their sisters often spent time in Paris, learning about much-admired French culture first hand.

At every social level, mothers and daughters spent more time together than mothers and sons, fathers and sons, or, of course, fathers and daughters. Father-son relationships, though often not close and frequently marked by conflict, had an emotional intensity lacking in other family relationships.[19] Father-son solidarity was particularly strong among adolescents and young men.

-IV-

Siblings
Most literature on family relationships – whether sociological, psychological, psychoanalytic, or historical – focuses on relationships between husbands and wives, and parents and children, ignoring almost entirely those among siblings. Although many of us are aware of the importance of siblings in our lives, sibling relationships receive little scholarly attention.[20]

Central to many family relationships in seventeenth-century Amsterdam were those among siblings. The saliency of ties with siblings arose from what was shared in childhood: parentage, name, traditions, practices, and experiences – all in the same household.[21] So, too, did rivalry among siblings for parental time, love, attention, privileges, and resources.

Although growing up in the same household, siblings have different experiences and memories. The number of children in a family, birth order, and gender all have an influence. The more children in a family, the larger the number of sibling connections: just one with two children, three with three children, and then six with four children. Possibilities for coalition-forming in situations of conflict increase as well. And the more children in a family, the less parental time, attention, and so on, there is for each.

As to birth order, the first-born is an only child until another comes along. During that period, a child receives more undivided time, concentrated attention, and focused care than will ever again be the case. The birth of the first sibling has a special impact, and the oldest child often reacts badly to the withdrawal of its mother's time and attention.[22]

Parents in seventeenth-century Amsterdam had to consider the well-being of each child in distributing resources such as time, attention, space in their house, money, and what money could buy. For many, the distribution of available resources was a constant source of apprehension and worry. In some poor families, an older boy had to go out to work to help his parents support younger siblings. When food was scarce, he received more than his siblings. Material resources were not distributed equally. Most families, and especially poor immigrants, faced hard choices about which child got what.

Even in wealthy families, with no worries about material resources, equality was seldom the norm. Parental energy, time, love, and affection are always in short supply. There is never enough to go around. With siblings, who gets how much of what is always an issue. Then, as now, every parent was likely to have heard the question "Who do you love most?"

Sibling relationships were an important aspect of the everyday lives of boys and girls in seventeenth-century Amsterdam. But with the city's high mortality rate, a sibling was often not there for very long. Death brought many sibling relationships to an abrupt end. The family of Lucas Wateringe and Johanna Timmers provides a dramatic example.[23]

The couple married in December 1661 when he was twenty-three and she was nineteen. Both were from wealthy Amsterdam families. Lucas's parents were no longer living and permission to marry came from an uncle who was his legal guardian, while Johanna's mother and father gave their approval.

The couple's first child was born in June 1663. During the following twenty-two years, Johanna gave birth to another thirteen children. At least, this is the number baptized. Her last child was born in 1687, when Johanna Timmers was forty-four. Eight of the fourteen children died before reaching the age of two. This was an unusually high rate of mortality, especially for a family from the upper echelons of society.

Birth Intervals: A Matter of Life and Death
It is informative to examine the pattern of births for some of Johanna Timmers's fourteen children, particularly the length of the birth intervals between one child and the next. A close association exists between the length of a birth interval and infant mortality: the shorter the interval, the greater the chance of a child's dying within the first year of life. A child born to a mother who has given birth to another child within the previous two years has a significantly higher risk of dying early.[24]

In early modern Europe, a higher death rate was due partly to infants not being breastfed by their mothers. Beyond that, the relationship between birth-interval length and level of infant mortality has been accounted for in three different ways: (1) short birth intervals do not allow adequate maternal recovery time; (2) the newborn child must compete with its older sibling for food and care; and (3) closely-spaced children are more likely to spread infectious diseases.[25] Given the economic standing and circumstances of Johanna Timmers and her husband, the first explanation is the most relevant.

The birth intervals for Johanna Timmers' first four children (1663-1667) averaged 15 months. Only one child lived beyond two months. With the last four births (1680-1687), the intervals averaged 30 months. All four children survived. It seems likely that the short birth intervals did indeed provide inadequate recovery time for Johanna Timmers. By her later childbearing years she had apparently learned the importance of extending the intervals between pregnancies.[26]

As I noted earlier, longer birth intervals suggest a conscious attempt to regulate the spacing of births.[27] No reliable data in this regard exist for the seventeenth century, and there is no way of knowing the extent to which married couples consciously practiced birth control.[28] Whether Lucas Wateringe and Johanna Timmers did so must remain unknown.

In any case, the pattern for the births of the couple's fourteen children is informative in another way as well: it highlights the phenomenon of "replacement" that was so common at the time. They named their firstborn child Johannes after Johanna's father. Born in June 1663, the baby died two months later. A son born in 1666 was also given the name Johannes. He died after ten months. Then came another Johannes, and three more until a son born in 1683 carried the name until adulthood. Johanna outlived the sixth Johannes as well. In fact, she outlived all but two of her fourteen children.

What was it like for a mother, a father, and siblings, when a child with a particular name died and was then "replaced" by one or more other children with exactly the same name? This is particularly intriguing in light of the practice at the time of parents including dead children when responding to a question about the number of children they had.[29] Dead children remained part of the family.[30]

Grieving for Lost Children

Although few mothers lost as many children as Johanna Timmers, the death of a child was a common occurrence. Nevertheless, it was a tragedy for the whole family.[31] A variety of factors influenced the emotional reactions of family members: the child's age, whether its death was expected or not (as with a child who had been sick for some time), and the relationship between the child who died and different members of the family.[32]

A mother surely grieved more deeply than a father when a child died, a consequence of her physical attachment to it during pregnancy, her bonding with it during infancy, and her absorption with it during its childhood years.[33] When a baby was stillborn or survived only a short time, a mother experienced not only a feeling of loss but also of emptiness for the infant who had so recently shared her body. This would have been the case with the early deaths of three of Johanna Timmers's children. What was it like to have this experience?

Married in December 1661, this nineteen-year-old woman became pregnant within nine months. Over the following nine months, she would have followed the advice of medical and moral treatises to safeguard her unborn baby's health by eating and drinking judiciously, and by avoiding physical and emotional strain.[34] During that time, her body underwent a slow and continuous adjustment to pregnancy. She experienced various physiological changes: in hormones, in weight, and in body shape. Along with immobility, nausea was an attendant discomfort.

In June 1663, Johanna Timmers gave birth to an infant boy whom they named Johannes. He died in August. The stress on her body, the limited sleep cycle permitted by the newborn infant, and then his death, resulted in her being weakened, fatigued, and depressed. Such an ordeal left her very little in the way of physical and emotional energy.

Two months later, Johanna was pregnant again. Once more her body went through the adjustments associated with pregnancy. Once more, she faced the dangers and pains of childbirth. A second son was born in July 1664. He died on 11 September. And so it went with the third child: Johanna was pregnant again within a few months, another child, another death. This one within less than two weeks. The year 1664 was a plague year in Amsterdam and this perhaps accounted for the death of one of the children.[35]

It is easy to imagine Johanna Timmers being devastated by the premature deaths of her three infant sons. The deaths were perhaps heartbreaking for their father, Lucas Wateringe, as well. But whatever his reaction, his grief would not have approached that experienced by his wife. This gender-related difference in reactions to the death of an infant seems to be universal.[36]

Children were the pride and joy of Dutch parents, perhaps especially those from the upper orders. Portraits of children on their deathbeds, of which more than thirty examples are known today, provide a moving testament to a parent's love.

Consider Illustration 7.1. Known today as the *Portrait of a Dead Child*, in 1645 the child's parents commissioned Bartholomeus van der Helst to paint this portrait. Judging by the close-cropped hair, the child is a little boy. He is dressed in a white linen shroud. Because it was feared that a person's soul might attach itself to the bed and render it unusable, the dead body was often placed on a layer of straw. Immediately after the funeral, the straw was burned.[37]

Some children survived infancy but then died within the next few years. In such instances, mothers and fathers may both have grieved deeply. Even so, a mother's grief would have been more consuming and longer lasting than the father's. After all, she was used to more intense and regular contacts with each of her children. Furthermore, she was usually isolated at home, with numerous daily reminders of the deceased child's absence: for example, a toy or a drawing tacked to the wall.[38] A father, on the other hand, usually had work outside the house that provided a respite from sorrow.

The death of an older child must have been a particularly heavy loss for both parents. An older boy or girl was a child with a distinct personality, a presence in the house, a child for whom the parents had expectations and plans for the future. Having survived its early and most vulnerable years, the death of an older child would have been unexpected.

Whatever their inner feelings about the death of a loved one, the seventeenth-century Dutch were expected not to show too much grief. Doing so could be seen as evidence of disagreement with what God had decided. In some instances at least, the bereaved found solace in believing that the deceased had been called to heaven and would enjoy peace in the hereafter. God's will was not to be questioned.[39]

A dead child sometimes left siblings behind. Depending on the ages of the surviving children and the nature of their relationships with the child who died, these siblings experienced shock, bewilderment, and uncertainty about how to react to the empty place in the family. Parents had to deal not only with their own reactions but also those of the remaining children. Bereavement and mourning were familiar to everyone.

Although some wealthy families were struck by multiple deaths, as we saw with Lucas Wateringe and Johanna Timmers, multiple deaths would have been most common among families from the city's lower echelons.[40] They were, after all, the families most familiar with the horrors of poverty, the terrors of sickness, and the lack of space and means to nurse their loved ones. But people from the lower orders lived anonymous lives on the margin and remain invisible to us today. Most left no trace on the historical record.

Continuing Sibling Relationships

Relationships that continued after the death of a sibling, like others in the familial context, were also influenced by the physical environment. In the homes of wealthy families, boys and girls either had bedrooms of their own or shared a bedroom with a sibling of the same sex. Under such circumstances, children were able to retreat from the view of other family members and surround themselves with their most cherished possessions. They experienced a degree of autonomy and privacy known to very few people at the time.[41] Servants surely saw this as a striking contrast to their own childhood experience.

In most families in Amsterdam no one had a room of his or her own, and the privacy and seclusion enjoyed by children in wealthy homes was completely lacking. The separation of the sexes for sleeping was in some instances virtually impossible. With just one room for sleeping, children went to bed in intimate propinquity to their siblings and parents.

Given the normal erotic component in sibling relationships between young boys and girls, this lack of physical privacy must have encouraged erotic fantasies and experiences.[42] After all, sexual curiosity among little boys and girls is completely normal. Children's fantasies and experiences stretch along a continuum from playing "doctor and nurse" or "mommies and daddies" all the way to incest.[43]

Biblical and legal prohibitions concerning sexual relations between kin were well known in the early modern period. They were formulated in terms of marriage and (implicitly) sexual relations between parents and children, brothers and sisters, nieces and nephews, and brothers- and sisters-in-law.[44] Still, among the wealthy elite, at least, it was not unusual for cousins or nieces and nephews to marry.[45]

Incestuous relationships within families were (and are) generally difficult to detect. But such relationships between brother and sister are known to have occurred in the Dutch golden age.[46] It is likely, however, that only a tiny fraction ever found their way into courts of law. This usually happened when a neighbor or someone else from outside the family brought the relationship to the attention of the authorities.

A lack of physical separation in sleeping arrangements in most Amsterdam homes also meant, of course, that opportunities for sexual misbehavior outside the surveillance of other members of the family were somewhat limited. Moreover, boys in most Amsterdam families lived apart from their siblings during the formative years, either serving apprenticeships or leaving the house to earn a living.

Things were different in wealthy families, where both boys and girls remained at home for much longer than did children from ordinary or poor families. But these children, of course, had rooms of their own or, at the very least, shared a room with another child of the same sex.

In the seventeenth century, family relationships took precedence over all others. It was widely believed that individuals acted for reasons of narrow self-interest, but that their interests were closely tied to those of other family members. For wealthy regents, this meant largely their biological kin. For other people, it meant the conjugal family (the family constructed by marriage). Partiality toward family members was considered a moral duty. When people spoke of "friendships," they usually meant relationships between family members.[47] Family solidarity was taken for granted.

At least among people born in Amsterdam, adult brothers and sisters often lived in the same neighborhood, visited one another regularly, served as witnesses at marriages, acted as godparents for one another's children, shared households, were partners in business, and provided emotional support in time of need. Only the rich were in a position to provide economic support, and to take on the guardianship of a sibling's children in the case of premature death. Even so, social support was enormously important to everyone.

Sibling relationships were the longest-lasting relationships that most people were likely to have, exceeding the length of their relationships with parents, husband or wife, sons or daughters. As when they had been children together, adult relationships had their ups and downs: love and mutual support, on the one hand; rivalry, jealousy, envy, and bitter discord, on the other.[48] Childhood alliances forged between siblings often lasted for life.

As with so much in the seventeenth-century Netherlands, evidence about sibling relationships is restricted almost entirely to the wealthy elite. Concerned with their family's history, its continuity, and the importance of allegiance, their loyalties were to the family of origin.

A handful of autobiographies, diaries, and family letters tell us most of what we know about social contacts, visiting patterns, business activities, friendships, and conflicts among brothers and sisters. They do not, however, provide much insight into how siblings actually felt about each other.[49]

Sibling Inequalities and Discontents

Siblings sometimes quarreled over family matters, including inheritances, and it is likely that some disliked one another intensely. But whatever their actual feelings about one another, sibling relationships were important to the lives of many people in the Dutch golden age.[50]

Even as adults, what had occurred in their early family relationships was central to their lives. After all, many had spent their childhoods in competition with siblings and must have had them in mind when thinking about their own well-being. This has been true of brothers and sisters through the ages.

Most children in seventeenth-century Amsterdam grew up expecting to live much as their parents had done. But there must have been exceptions: boys and girls who aspired to live a different kind of life, with different priorities, accomplishments, and experiences. Let me consider again the importance of autonomy for people's well-being and focus on the female sex in this regard.

The upbringing of boys and girls in the Dutch Golden Age focused on preparing them to occupy their proper places in society. Boys were taught that they were more intelligent than girls, more disciplined, more ambitious, and possessed of greater reasoning abilities. It was only fitting and proper, therefore, that they should enjoy a greater degree of autonomy and independence than their sisters. Girls were taught the same thing, and must have been fully aware of the low esteem in which they were held compared with boys.

But boys and girls were also brothers and sisters who grew up together in the same household, often spending a great deal of time in one another's company, and knowing intimately one another's strengths and weaknesses. Given such firsthand knowledge, some girls would have reached very different conclusions about the differences between themselves and their brothers.

More than one saw that she and her brother were equally matched in brains, equally determined, equally assertive, and had an equally active will. More than one saw that she was, in fact, superior to her brother in every way, that she knew all the things he knew along with all the things she knew herself. More than one wanted desperately to learn, to stretch her mind, to do something on her own, to give meaning to her existence, to have, in short, a life of her own, a life in which she could exercise autonomy and independence.[51]

A few girls grew up to be women who lived that life to some extent.[52] But most did not. It seems safe to assume, in any case, that the vast majority of women had less autonomy and independence than they desired. In growing up, jealousy, rivalry, and envy were common to sibling relationships, including those between brothers and sisters. So, too, were demands for equality and fairness, demands that seem to be characteristic of sibling relationships everywhere.

To varying extents, every female must have been aware that she suffered hardships as a result of arrangements between the sexes.[53] While some might have taken it for granted, others undoubtedly experienced flashes of blinding rage in this regard. Many males, who reaped the benefits of these arrangements, were probably also aware of male advantage. It is unlikely that members of the dominant sex would have chosen to bear the burdens associated with being a woman.[54]

In any case, feelings of discontent, dissatisfaction, resentment, bitterness, and anger about inequality and unfairness in relationships between the sexes were certainly not unknown among women in seventeenth-century Amsterdam. They saw that being a man was much the more promising route to well-being.

-V-

Just as gender, civic, and economic inequalities affected the everyday relationships, life chances, destinies, and wellness of being of individuals
in seventeenth-century Amsterdam families, so they affected individuals
in fractured families as well. In the following two chapters, I consider
the impact of these inequalities on the well-being of people in two types
of fractured families: widowed men and women, and orphaned boys and
girls.

Chapter 8

LOSING A SPOUSE AND A PARENT

On April 26, 1666, Christina Pelt is buried in Amsterdam's Lutheran Church. She is twenty-five years old. We met her in Chapter 6 as the wife of Arent van Deurs, a merchant who had come to the city from Haarlem. It is just fifteen months since the young couple married. Their infant daughter, Anna, survives her mother's death.

In January 1668, the widower remarries. He is now twenty-nine. His second wife, Christina Rulant, is twenty-two. A daughter, Johanna Maria, is born two years later, and a son, Aernout, four years after that. The three children from the two marriages grow up together in the same household.

-I-

In seventeenth-century Amsterdam, it was not uncommon for a husband or wife to die young. A great deal of female mortality, especially among women between the ages of twenty-five and fourty-five, was associated with childbirth. Male mortality was particularly high among soldiers and men who went overseas with the Dutch East and West India Companies, as well as among seafaring men in waters closer to home.

Second and third marriages were quite common (divorce was extremely rare). The duration of first marriages varied enormously, but given the mortality rates, the average would have been less than twenty years. In as many as a third of Dutch marriages, one or both partners had been married before. Widowhood had a profound affect on the well-being of the survivors and their children.

The Emotional Loss
The death of a spouse meant the emotional loss of someone with whom the survivor had experienced a privileged love and sexual relationship. According to Matthews Grieco, many women in early modern Europe welcomed the termination of the sexual aspects of the marital relationship. For most, she writes, "sexual relations were instrumental and manipulative, rather

than affective. They were a means to an end – marriage, money, or simply survival – rather than an end in themselves."[1]

Matthews Grieco may be exaggerating somewhat, but it was without doubt true that husbands did not hesitate to claim their conjugal rights, and that many wives must have associated sexual intercourse with the dangers and pains of childbirth. Sexual intercourse within marriage was expected. It seems to have been frequent as well.[2]

Whatever the sexual aspects of their relationship, the death of a spouse meant the loss of a partner in social relations with other married couples, of someone around whom time and daily routines had been organized, and, even in marriages characterized by joyless intimacy, of another person in the house. If nothing else, the absence of a warm human presence in the bed took some getting used to.

In loving relationships, the surviving partner would have responded with feelings of sadness, sorrow, despair, and other manifestations of grief. The nature and intensity of a widow or widower's grief response was, of course, not always the same, any more than it was on the death of a child, a sibling, or a parent. Many men and women who lost a spouse were left with no further focus than themselves.

A loss from sudden death was harder to accept than a death following a long illness. The more time that husband and wife regularly spent together, the more disruptive the loss. And the stronger their emotional attachment, the more deeply felt and intense the reactions to bereavement. Since the strongest affective bonds of married couples were usually with their spouse and children, the death of a spouse was a crisis for most husbands and wives.

Referring to the loss of a spouse in the early modern period, Plakans and Wetherell emphasize that it "was a crisis in which survivors *may or may not* have needed economic aid, but one in which survivors *almost certainly* needed, sought, and received emotional support."[3] For most people who were widowed, this emotional support came from their children, siblings, friends, and neighbors, and only secondarily, if at all, from extended kin.

A widowed man or woman's feelings of pain and loneliness could be somewhat alleviated by such emotional support. Men and women born in Amsterdam had more sources of support than those who had come to the city from elsewhere in the Dutch Republic, and the latter more than those from Germany, Norway, and countries even further away, most of whom had no relatives at all in the city.[4] For men, contacts with workmates, colleagues, or customers may have lessened their pain and loneliness.

For both sexes, however, the absence of physical contact was more difficult to assuage. It was not only a warm body in the bed that was missing, it was the comfort of physical touching, holding, caressing, embracing, and skin against skin. Missing, too, were a hand on the shoulder and a peck on the cheek. Whatever the depth of love and attachment in their marital relationship, the loss of physical intimacy affected widows and widowers alike.[5]

Along with the absence of physical intimacy, the widowed lost the affirming presence of their deceased spouse. For better or worse, husbands and wives are used to seeing themselves through the eyes of the other. With the death of a spouse, the survivor must learn to see himself or herself through the eyes of other people.[6] The longer a couple have been together, the more difficult this will be.[7]

For children, the death of their mother or father was a confusing and stressful experience, however common such deaths may have been.[8] Although the extent and nature of intimacy differed according to sex and age, children were used to at least a degree of intimacy with both parents. One child in four lost either its mother or father by the time it was ten.[9]

A child's experience following the death of its mother or father depended to a very significant extent on which parent died. Given the mother's role in childrearing, her premature death usually had a greater emotional impact on children than the death of their father. This would certainly have been the case in the many families where the father was away at sea.

Psychologically, the death of a child's mother was particularly devastating, giving rise to feelings of loss, intense grief, and often leaving a permanent scar. Financially, however, children suffered most when their father died prematurely: a consequence of the disadvantaged position of women in Dutch society.

-II-

Widowhood and the Gender Hierarchy
The death of a spouse had a different legal impact on a woman than on a man. A widow was no longer a "feme covert," a woman whose legal entity was covered by her husband. With his death, she now had control over her possessions, could enter into legal transactions, sign contracts, and appear before a court of law. She also had authority over her deceased husband's financial assets and possessions as well as over the goods acquired jointly by the couple during their years together. The extent and value of those assets and possessions reflected her husband's civic and economic standing.

In documents recording property transactions and the like, a widow's marital state was always recorded as a legal condition. She was identified as "the widow of...," while a widower was never so identified. This was the case even in newspaper reports. A woman offering a reward for the return of a diamond ring in the *Amsterdamse Courant*, for instance, was identified as the widow of so-and-so.[10] But a widower's marital status was never designated in written documents, newspaper articles, or anywhere else.[11]

In one respect, however, widows and widowers with minor children were on equal footing. The parent left behind with minor children immediately became their guardian by law. This meant that he or she was legally responsible for the children's upbringing and for the administration of their property. Whatever inheritance the children had been bequeathed was not distributed until they reached their majority.[12]

With or without children, widows and widowers were faced with establishing a life independent of their deceased spouse. Those with children had to find ways of dealing with the practical and emotional needs of their offspring. But widows and widowers differed enormously in the resources available for taking care of themselves and their sons and daughters. For many a widow, her husband's death meant the *death of her way of life*.

While both men and women suffered a personal loss with the death of a spouse, a wife's loss was material as well. We can only imagine a widow's worry and stomach-churning anxiety about what was going to happen. How, she must have asked herself, would she pay the rent, put food on the table, buy peat for warmth and cooking, clothe the children, and meet all the other expenses her deceased husband had taken care of?

The death of a husband and father could force a family to move into a smaller and more crowded house in a less desirable area of the city, so that it had consequences for their health and mortality. Accompanying this was a marked decline in the quality of their diet, clothing, and general standard of living. In short, the death of a husband and father often had a profound impact on the well-being, life chances, and individual destinies of other family members.

The death of a wife and mother only rarely had such consequences for a widower and his children. The reason for this discrepancy lay, of course, in a married woman's dependency on her husband's earnings. The greater a wife's financial dependency on her husband, the greater the disruption his death will cause in every aspect of life. As Hufton points out, "The loss of a husband in a society that defined a woman in terms of her relationship to a man was obviously an event that carried immense social, economic, and psychological consequences for a woman."[13] The Dutch Republic was such a society.

Following her husband's death, a widow's honor depended on exhibiting the proper level of grief and providing him with a proper funeral, an expense she could often ill afford.[14] The widow of a guild master, however, could usually rely on guild funds to cover burial expenses.

A widower was also expected to mourn as a demonstration of respect for his wife, and to provide her with an appropriate funeral. But his honor, in contrast to hers, depended on his quickly finding a new wife to do the housework and take care of the children. Such tasks were considered demeaning for a man.

The law required that both widows and widowers wait four to six months before contracting a new marriage. But a widow under the age of fifty was required to wait nine months to ensure that the paternity of a posthumous child was not mistakenly attributed to the second husband. A widow was also expected to observe a year of mourning after her husband's death.[15]

While it was considered dishonorable for a widow to remarry within a year, it was regarded as quite acceptable for a widower to do so.[16] In either case, the period of grieving appears short by today's standards when the duration of grief is considered to be between one and two years.[17] Assuming that the psychological mechanisms were the same in the seventeenth century, there were men and women who remarried before coming to grips with the death of their spouse.

The norms of mourning required both widows and widowers to wear clothes that were black and drab. This included such accessories as black headdresses, scarves, gloves, and even special mourning rings. The higher a family's social standing, the more expensive the mourning clothes they wore. Those of the rich were elaborate. Any sort of mourning clothes at all would have been an impossible luxury for poor people, some of whom dyed what they had black. Others wore a black armband or a black band on their hat. Children did the same.[18]

Illustration 8.1, a painting by Gerard ter Borch (1617-1681), shows a young woman peeling apples as a child watches. She is wearing what has been identified as a mourning veil. To viewers at the time, this signified the woman's status as a widow.[19] Wearing a veil or another item of mourning in public was more than a symbol of grief. It also identified someone as a widow or widower, and thus as a possible marital candidate for prospective suitors.

Although not all did so, a widow was expected to wear mourning clothes for at least two years. A woman who never remarried might wear mourning clothes for the rest of her life. A widower, on the other hand, usually wore his black clothes and black armband for just a few months.

Lacking the earning power of a man, a widow was in a seriously disadvantaged position. During her marriage, virtually every woman was financially dependent on her husband to one degree or another. With the disappearance of his earnings, economic deprivation was a distinct possibility. Few women were able to sustain a household on their own. Remarriage was consequently the aspiration of the vast majority of widows.

Economic survival was a widow's main concern in seeking a new husband, especially if she had young children. Fear and apprehension must have been common. The more children a widow had, the less likely she was to find a man willing to take on the burden of a new family.[20] Even a woman with just one child was in a disadvantaged position if she was poor.

Being poor was exhausting, and a poor woman's hard life made her prematurely old and an unattractive candidate for marriage.[21] Many widows never succeeded in remarrying, and there were far more widows than widowers all over early modern Europe.[22] With the large surplus of women in Amsterdam, the imbalance was even greater there than elsewhere.

Remaining a widow could be catastrophic, sometimes bringing permanent impoverishment for the woman and her children. Although the death of a wife could jeopardize the survival of a poor household, the consequences were generally far less devastating than when a husband died. For that reason, and because widowers were so much better off than widows in Amsterdam, I will now focus on the latter.

-III-

The Widows of Regents and Other Wealthy Men
A relatively small number of widows had the financial means to support themselves and their children. Some chose not to remarry, apparently preferring freedom from the patriarchal domination of a husband, including perhaps the sexual obligations connected with marriage, and unwanted pregnancies.

In fact, a few wealthy women exercised a great deal of individual control over their lives from the time they were young. Some chose not to marry, others married later than was the custom, bore just one child, and did not remarry after the death of their husband. One such was Clara Valkenier, a woman whose father had served as a burgomaster of Amsterdam on nine separate occasions.

Clara married the merchant and regent Gaspar Pellicorne in 1670, when she was thirty-eight and he was forty-one. Pellicorne occupied various high positions in the city government. A daughter, Clara Jacoba, was born to the couple in 1671. No other children followed. Portraits of husband and wife by the Amsterdam artist Wallerend Vaillant (1623-1677) are shown in illustrations 8.2 and 8.3. Each is fashionably dressed, reflecting their standing and wealth.

In 1674, the couple's wealth was estimated at 178,200 guilders. When Gaspar died in 1680, their daughter was nine. Clara never remarried; she raised the child herself – with, it should be noted, the help of one male and two female servants. She took over the responsibility of running the firm with which her husband had been associated: de Wede, Gaspar Pellicorne, & Pieter Pellicorne.[23] This highly capable business woman lived until 1710 and was seventy-eight when she died. No one knows how many women in such circumstances chose not to remarry and to run their own lives in the years they had remaining.[24]

Because of the couple's immense wealth, the death of Gaspar Pellicorne had no impact on the material well-being and way of life of his widow and her daughter Clara Jacoba. They continued to live in their fifteen-room house, surrounded by expensive furnishings, valuable silver, jewels, and porcelain, twenty family portraits, and eighty other paintings.[25]

Widows and children in other rich families went on enjoying lives of ease and comfort after the death of a husband and father. Alone or with siblings, the children remained in the same large, well-furnished houses, with bedrooms of their own, eating nourishing food, dressing in warm and fashionable clothes, and receiving the education deemed appropriate for the sons and daughters of the rich and privileged. One or more servants saw to their needs.

In wealthy families, being widowed gave a woman greater autonomy than she had experienced as a wife. Many a widow must have enjoyed having responsibility for her inherited property, as well as control over whatever proportion of the inheritance would eventually be passed on to the couple's children. Even if she remarried, her inherited possessions remained hers and were not relinquished to her new husband. But the situation of a wealthy widow and her children was highly unusual.

The vast majority of women were not so fortunate, being unable to support themselves and their children on the basis of an inheritance. Even while the husband and breadwinner was alive, many Amsterdam families had a hard time making ends meet. Building up a reserve for bad times was simply not possible. Because the bulk of jobs in Amsterdam paid so little, deceased husbands often left their heirs virtually nothing.

Most widows needed either to find a new husband to provide the necessary financial support or some means of generating an alternative source of income. If they did not succeed in remarrying, their ability to sustain themselves and their children depended more than anything on the civic and occupational status of their late husbands.

The Widows of Functionaries and Professionals

Middle-ranking city employees, lawyers, apothecaries, ministers, school-teachers, and other professionals were Amsterdam citizens and enjoyed high earnings. But, relatively speaking, the widows of such men were particularly hard hit by the death of their husbands. They had been accustomed to a high standard of living generated by their husbands' special training and knowledge.

Even though these men had been better off financially than most of the citizens of Amsterdam and far better off than the majority of the city's inhabitants, few left large enough inheritances for their wives and children to continue to live as they had done before.[26] These families often found themselves in a precarious situation. In the absence of a large inheritance and without their husbands' earnings, these widows were unable to sustain their standard of living.

Some were the daughters of reasonably well-off Amsterdam citizens. But the existing gender hierarchy had made it impossible for them to acquire the sorts of expertise and knowledge possessed by their deceased husbands. There was no possibility for the widow of, say, a lawyer or an apothecary to take over her late husband's business.[27] And it would have been considered beneath her dignity to seek any sort of menial employment.

With a limited inheritance and little opportunity of generating an income on her own, the widow of a professional man or minor city functionary must have found herself in seriously straitened circumstances, facing a real threat of poverty; she may well have experienced a powerlessness not felt since she was a child. Some remarried in desperation, making precipitous second marriages. Most would not again enjoy their previous way of life. Some, especially older widows, never did remarry.

Since these women had no special entitlement to financial assistance, they were condemned to the humiliation of applying for poor relief from the city or from the church to which they belonged.[28] This involved establishing that they were among the "deserving" poor.[29] All widowed applicants for charitable assistance were alike in having to establish that they were deserving. Strict rules determined the level of assistance that widows could receive; strict rules that were strictly ignored.

For whatever the rules, the widows of functionaries and professionals continued to be advantaged. It was not uncommon for them to be helped with discretion by the church to which they belonged, so that their middling way of life was safeguarded to some extent.[30] The rules were bent in a similar way by the municipal authorities. In both instances, the level of charitable assistance was the result of a process of negotiation between a widow and the responsible officials.[31]

Even when they received more than they were strictly entitled to, many widows of functionaries and professional men in Amsterdam lived in diminished economic circumstances. Mothers and children had to move to smaller and less comfortable dwellings in less desirable neighborhoods, leaving behind the social support of neighbors and the children's friends.

Plans for the education and training of young boys were altered radically. Girls would be sent out to work as servants at an earlier age than might otherwise have been the case. Families who employed servants had to let them go.

The Widows of Master Craftsmen

The widows of master craftsmen – the largest category of Amsterdam citizens – were in a more advantageous position. Their deceased husbands had contributed to guild funds that provided mutual aid in the event of serious difficulties. This constituted a unique form of social insurance. It was the most expensive and important form of mutual aid in Amsterdam.[32]

When a guild member, his wife, or his widow died, the guild's mutual fund paid for pallbearers, shrouds, and coffins. Sickness payments, and payments for old age and invalidism were other important benefits. So, too, were widow's benefits. A guild master who was unable to work usually received two or three guilders a week, or roughly 25-50 percent of a master's average weekly earnings. A retired guild member (there was no official age and this had to be negotiated) received three guilders a week.

Payments to widows were the largest financial burden on the city's guilds. These payments varied from one guild to another, with the widow of a surgeon, for example, receiving three guilders a week and the widow of a turf-carrier receiving one guilder and 12 stuivers per week. The differential in the benefits to which they were entitled was consistent with the differences in the financial backgrounds of the men in various Amsterdam guilds and with the amount they paid to enter them: 10 guilders for turf-carriers and more than 200 guilders for surgeons.[33]

A widow's benefit of even three guilders a week represented only a fraction of what a surgeon had earned. Many widows received less. Whatever the level of benefits received by the widow of a guild master, it was not enough to live on. All the same, payment of the funeral expenses for her husband and a weekly widow's pension were benefits not enjoyed by the widows of the vast majority of Amsterdam men who were not guild members.

A more important benefit for the widows of most master craftsmen was the fact that a widow who could establish that she had assisted her husband with his work was legally entitled to carry on his business when he died. Some widows took over their husband's guild membership (though not, for example, the widows of surgeons or turf-carriers).

The law did, though, require the presence of a journeyman able to guarantee the quality of the goods produced in what was now the widow's workshop. But her entitlement lasted only so long as she did not remarry. Once again, we see the city authorities' involvement in keeping women in a subordinate position.

Being able to take over her husband's workshop was advantageous to an artisan's widow in two ways. Most obviously, it provided a living for herself and her children and assured some stability and continuity in their lives, but her financial position and know-how also made her an especially attractive candidate for remarriage.[34]

She was in a much better position than the widow of a professional man to achieve financial independence and to avoid remarrying in haste. The same was true for the widows of men running taverns or other small businesses outside guild regulation. In both cases, a widow would be most likely to marry a man with an occupation similar to that of her late husband.

The Widows of Non-Citizen Residents and Temporary Inhabitants
As far as the economic well-being of a widow and her children was concerned, far and away the worst off were those women who did not get a widow's pension (the majority of women in Amsterdam), were unable to find a new husband, did not have an alternative source of income, and had not lived in the city long enough to have the status of a non-citizen resident.

Although the widows of non-citizen residents were considerably worse off than the widows of Amsterdam citizens, they were still better off than the widows of temporary inhabitants since they were sometimes granted charitable relief unavailable to the latter: large quantities of bread, some butter, peat for the fire, used clothing and shoes, and perhaps a small weekly allowance.[35]

Over the course of the seventeenth century, the rules changed, as did the criteria for receiving poor relief. Early in the century, an individual had to have been a resident for at least four years to qualify for assistance.[36] After 1650, however, applicants for assistance had to establish that they had lived in the city for six consecutive years.[37] Residence and membership requirements likewise became increasingly rigorous for people who sought assistance from the city's churches .

In some instances, poor-relief administrators interviewed the applicants themselves and made inquiries about them among their neighbors and other people. A good recommendation from neighbors or, even better, a member of the city's elite had a considerable influence on the amount of support a widow received from the poor relief board. The level of assistance consequently varied greatly from one family to another.[38]

Widows receiving charitable assistance from Amsterdam's English Reformed Church, for example, were visited twice a year and even more often if there was reason to question their entitlement to such relief. Later in the century, the church admitted as new members only those men able to support themselves and their families. The intention was to avoid having members who might become a burden on the church community.[39]

Whether from the city or the church, poor relief for non-citizens was minimal. A widow and her children might be placed in a multi-family house with other poor people, crowded into one or two sparsely-furnished rooms, and sharing a fireplace (for cooking and warmth) with another family. Mother and children often slept on straw mattresses and owned no more clothing than what was on their backs, wearing the same threadbare and faded garments day after day. Material hardship was the lot of most.

The authorities did not intend that a widow should be able to make ends meet from the charitable assistance she received.[40] Nevertheless, a poor widowed woman was subject to regular monitoring to assure that she behaved properly and that she really was in need of poor relief. Since families lived in close proximity to one another, neighbors kept the recipients of poor relief under close surveillance and did not hesitate to contact the relevant officials if they suspected fraud.[41] The need to control poor widows seems to have been widespread in early modern Europe.[42]

Not all Amsterdam widows qualified for charitable help from the city or a church. Some were unable to establish that their husbands had actually been residents or that they had been church members for the required number of years. But many more failed to qualify due to being the widows of immigrants who were temporary residents. Immigrant widows and their children often lived in the city's poorest neighborhoods: the Jordaan and the Eastern Islands areas.[43]

Little is known about exactly how they survived. A widow and her children might share board and lodgings with unmarried female friends or relatives, especially if she had a small inheritance. Sometimes a widow received help from other family members, usually brothers and sisters since her parents were seldom still alive. An older widow might be helped out by her adult children. But this was rare. Between 60 and 80 percent of widows in early modern Europe headed up their own household.[44]

In her study of widows in Leiden, Schmidt found that only 14 percent of widows lived in the households of others, and that an even lower percentage lived with their married children.[45] And van Wijngaarden remarks on the reluctance of relatives to take financial responsibility for members of their families who were poor. She notes further a lack of pressure for them to do so.

"Close relatives like children, parents and siblings could be approached for help," writes van Wijngaarden, but poor families could not count on their assistance. "Relations between parents and their adult children were usually very business-like... The poor relief administrators never urged the poor to ask their relatives for help, which tells us that people were not held responsible for the care of their poorer relatives."[46]

Whatever economic assistance relatives did provide was usually short-term and conditional, since most people had enough trouble assuring their own economic survival. Similarly with friends and neighbors; they might provide temporary assistance but nothing long-term. For those widows lacking an income or a new husband and failing to qualify for charitable assistance, the only (legal) alternative was some sort of menial work.

A poor widowed woman did whatever kind of menial work would provide some income. If she had young children, this meant work that she could do at home: sewing, spinning, weaving. If she found employment outside the home, it involved caring for the elderly and sick, hauling turf, selling used clothing, or doing other kinds of unskilled labor. Physical and emotional exhaustion would have been common. Since few kinds of employment were available to women and most work paid very little, it was virtually impossible for a working woman to earn enough to support herself and her children.[47]

Anyone in the family able to work was required to do so.[48] Sons and daughters were working when they were only seven or eight years of age. Some children combined two or three hours of school each day with their employment. Others labored ten or eleven hours per day, with no time off for schooling. Although paid a pittance, children usually earned more than their mothers. Their contribution was crucial to the family's survival.

Just as with single women, widows and their children not strictly entitled to charitable assistance from the city or the church did sometimes receive enough to survive. Religious convictions surely played a role here. As far as assistance from the city was concerned, the city father's recognized that both non-citizen residents and temporary inhabitants were important to Amsterdam's work force. The provision of relief, especially for wives and children left behind, was an important factor in terms of the city's attractiveness for married seamen and laborers.[49] Alms were thus distributed to their families in times of desperate need.[50]

The poor widow was a familiar figure everywhere in the early modern period as the object of charitable assistance. Material hardship was the lot of most. The poor widower, on the other hand, never occupied this position of dependency and vulnerability. While households receiving poor relief frequently consisted of a widow and children, it was rare for such a household to be made up of a widower and children.[51]

Poor widowers, in fact, hardly existed as a historical category in Amsterdam or elsewhere in early modern Europe. But it may be the case, as Cavallo and Warner suggest, that "less visible forms of aid and support directed to widowers prevented their pauperization and spared them the experience of public charity."[52]

This is, however, difficult to determine since marital status was not usually denoted for men. No mention is made of widowers in the Bible, which was often taken as the source of a Christian's duty to provide charitable help to widows.[53] In Amsterdam and elsewhere, poor relief for widows assured that they were under patriarchal control.

-IV-

Remarriage

Several generalizations apply to widows and widowers in the early modern period: a man was much more likely than a woman to remarry, did so sooner after the death of his spouse, and was in a position to remarry at an older age.[54] In Amsterdam, economic and civic status had an influence on the remarriage patterns of both.

The majority of widows and widowers sought to remarry, especially when they had young children. But the situation differed for the two sexes. As with so many other aspects of life, gender and age intersected in affecting the life prospects of the widowed. The younger the age of the surviving partner, the greater the likelihood that he or she would remarry. Even so, widows were disadvantaged in terms of finding a new partner.

Widowers everywhere had what has been termed a "studied avoidance" of being alone.[55] Most preferred a younger woman who had not been married before, although some ended up marrying a woman who was older, sometimes a widow. It was mainly wealthier widowers who were able to attract younger women as marital partners. Nevertheless, most widowers remarried and typically did so within a short period.

Like men elsewhere, widowers found youth a particularly important attribute of women.[56] They often married a woman several years younger than their first wife, preferring someone who had not been married previously and who had no children of her own. The appeal of a young female body and a woman's physical attractiveness helped make her a fitting candidate for marriage and remarriage alike. A young woman's beauty could compensate for relatively low social standing.

A man, by contrast, was more often judged by his power and economic position than by his looks. Thus, a widower's economic advantages could make up for his lack of attractiveness. Given that men were the ones with the earning power, widowers usually found willing partners. Widows were less successful. The difference between the situations of widowers and widows was much like that between single men and single women at the time. Once again, physical appearance counted more against women than against men.

Rich or poor, young or old, only a small minority of men in early modern Europe lived without a spouse.[57] It is difficult to be precise about the actual proportion of widowers who remarried, since men were never categorized as such. But it seems likely that at least three-quarters of widowers in seventeenth-century Amsterdam remarried, compared to less than a quarter of widows.[58] Widows with children were especially unlikely to remarry.

Among widowers, the imperative to remarry was strongest among laboring men and the poor. Especially when there were children in the home, these widowers needed someone to assume their deceased wife's domestic responsibilities. Most were unable to combine practical housekeeping and childcare with their work activities, a servant was beyond their means, and few had a daughter at home to take over household duties. Loneliness also played a role in a widower's search for a new wife.

Among widows, those who had been married to guild members and other widows with Amsterdam citizenship were most likely to receive and accept a proposal of marriage. Many wealthy women valued their independence too highly to consider remarriage, and poor women were viewed by men as an unwelcome economic burden.

When a widow did succeed in remarrying, it usually took her longer than a widower to find a partner. While a widower generally contracted a second marriage with a woman younger than his deceased spouse, the opposite was usually true for a widow; her second husband was often older than the first.[59] He was, in addition, sometimes located lower down in the economic hierarchy than her deceased husband. In such instances, a widow's remarriage involved a loss of social status.

If a widow remarried, her independent legal status reverted to its diminished capacity as a "feme covert." As when she married the first time, she suffered a loss of autonomy. In marked contrast, a widower's legal status in no way changed at the death of his wife or with his remarriage.

A newly married widow and her children usually moved into the house of her new husband. Even with no drastic changes in their standard of living, such a move was disruptive for children. If nothing else, it meant getting used to new surroundings. More significantly, it meant getting to know their mother's new husband and perhaps his children as well. The same was true for the children of remarrying widowers.

The remarriage of a surviving parent could radically alter a child's world, introducing strangers into the family constellation. Older children were especially likely to object to the remarriage of their father or mother. When this occurred, the surviving parent's loyalties were thus divided between his or her children and the new partner.

When a parent went ahead and married despite the children's objections, the children sometimes refused to accept the newcomer into the family. We can easily imagine a child's resentment of someone else sitting in its mother's (or father's) place at mealtime. And more than one child must have resisted what appeared to be counterfeit affection from an outsider.

Conflicts between stepmothers and stepdaughters and between stepfathers and stepsons occurred with some frequency. Physical violence was sometimes involved, usually with an older child attacking its step-parent. Younger children, on the other hand, were more likely to be the victims of violence from a step-father or step–mother.[60]

Relationships became still more complicated and disruptive when a remarried couple went on to have children of their own, thus bringing half-siblings into the picture. Jealousy, claims of preferential treatment and neglect, and familial intrigues could be the result. Questions about inheritances were also a source of conflict.

With the death of a stepfather or stepmother in a second marriage, the children might be taken into still another household. Some children thus grew up in three or four different households. Whatever the economic consequences when a widow or widower with children remarried, family tensions and emotional upheaval were not unusual.[61] Power struggles characterized many such living arrangements.

-V-

As if the early death of their mother or father were not disruptive enough, many children in seventeenth-century Amsterdam suffered the loss of both parents. In such instances, the orphaned child's destiny and well-being were determined largely by the position of its deceased parents in the city's civic and economic hierarchies. Here, too, the child's sex played a role. Amsterdam's orphans are the subject of Chapter 9.

Chapter 9

LOSING BOTH PARENTS: AMSTERDAM ORPHANS

A braham Peronneau, his wife, Maria Poniche, and their four children are living comfortably in a large house on the Warmoesstraat. The children's family life is shattered by the death of their father on November 27, 1691, followed shortly thereafter by their mother's death on December 7. The causes of death are not known, but the deaths of husband and wife within just ten days of one another suggests some sort of infectious disease.

-I-

Being Orphaned
In the previous chapter, I discussed the emotional and economic impact on a child of the premature death of its mother or father. Some children suffered the loss of both parents, with even greater consequences for their emotional and material well-being.

Although estimates vary, at least 2 percent of children in early modern Europe lost both parents before the children were ten, and at least 4 percent before they were fifteen.[1] The probability of a child being orphaned at a young age may seem quite low. Nevertheless, the *number* of orphaned boys and girls was often high.

This was certainly the case in seventeenth-century Amsterdam with its youthful population. During the 1680-1700 period, for instance, approximately 30 percent of its inhabitants were children under fifteen years of age. If 4 percent were orphaned before that age, approximately 2,500 orphans lived within the city's walls. Applying the same 4 percent figure to children over fifteen adds another 1,300 orphans to the total. In the last decades of the century, then, there must have been roughly 3,800 orphaned children in Amsterdam.[2] Given the many fathers away at sea, and the high percentage who never returned, the actual number was probably higher.

As well as the many children who suffered the death of both parents, there were hundreds of infants and young children who were abandoned by their impoverished mother or parents. Among them were the offspring of migrant women who had come to Amsterdam because of unwanted pregnancies.[3] Some infants had a note indicating their names. Others were given a last name related to the circumstances in which they were found: Rain and Wind (*Regen en Wint*) or Sunday (*Sondagh*), for example.[4]

The usual pattern for a child being orphaned was for one parent to die, its mother perhaps in childbirth or its father on a sea voyage or in some other type of work. When the surviving parent died, a child was legally an orphan. In cases where a child had been taken into a family with a step-mother or stepfather, it normally remained within that family constellation – sometimes with stepbrothers and stepsisters.

Emotional Loss and the Grieving Child

As with the death of a mother or father, the death of the surviving parent is a confusing and stressful experience for any child. A child's response and expression of grief depends partly on whether it is the mother or father who dies, with the death of the mother being particularly devastating.

The extent and character of a child's bereavement also depends on its age and level of development. Infants and children who can not yet talk express their grief physically: crying more than usual, refusing to eat, sleeping poorly, clinging to whoever gives them attention, and refusing to be comforted. They may also have difficulties in learning to talk, to walk, and with other kinds of learning. Children who can talk react similarly. But they are able to ask why their father or mother died or where he or she is. Some may act younger than they actually are: having, for example, their sleep disturbed by nightmares or wetting the bed.

School-age orphans grieve as adults do, with manifestations of sadness, sorrow, despair, and apathy. Adolescents – particularly males – are less likely to express grief openly. They are expected to show self-control and restraint, and so find it difficult to show their grief.[5]

-II-

Economic and Social Support

Whatever the ages at which boys and girls in seventeenth-century Amsterdam were orphaned, all were in need of emotional support to get through the difficult period of mourning: from relatives, family friends, or other adults. The majority needed financial and social support as well. The death of both parents left them dependent on other adults for shelter, a place to sleep, food to eat, clothing, and their education and training. This assistance was necessary until such time as an orphaned child became financially self-sufficient.

The Children of the Wealthy Elite

The sons and daughters of wealthy parents continued to be advantaged. Their parents had been embedded in tight social networks of well-to-do relatives and close friends, some of whom had been legally designated as the guardians of dependent children in the event of the premature deaths of both parents. These orphans could consequently be sure that another wealthy family would see to their upbringing and education.

In regent families, kin were usually ready to take responsibility for an orphaned child's welfare. This was, in fact, generally the case whenever someone in the family of birth needed help: parent, child, brother, or sister. Wealthy relatives were, of course, *able* to help should the need arise. But their kinship orientation – to the family into which they had been born – also played a role in their readiness to take in relatives' orphaned children. This was true not only of regent families, but of other wealthy families as well.

It was not, however, the fate of the four orphaned children of Abraham Peronneau and Maria Poniche. Originally from The Hague, Peronneau was a wealthy Amsterdam merchant who dealt in silk and other materials. He and Maria Poniche married in 1666 when he was thirty-four years of age and she was eighteen. In the course of the next twenty-three years, Maria gave birth to eight children, the last when she was age forty-one. Four of the eight died prematurely.

Although wealthy, the couple did not designate relatives as legal guardians. In their wills, they named Benjamin Philips and Reene Hourrays as guardians of the children. Presumably these were friends who had agreed to take in the children should both Abraham and Maria die before their offspring reached legal maturity. The oldest of the four Peronneau children was twelve and the youngest just two when their parents died.

The Peronneaus had been living a comfortable life. This is evident from the detailed inventory of the family's material possession made on January 6, 1692. As was usual with inheritances, bankruptcies, or the guardianship of orphans, such an inventory was the joint product of several people working together: a public notary, a clerk, and one or more women who were household appraisers (*schatsters*) licensed by the city.[6]

In the Dutch Republic, as throughout much of Europe, public notaries were responsible for administering oaths, taking affidavits and dispositions, and preparing and certifying the authenticity of contracts, wills, and other important documents. Unlike the English, who favored informal agreements based on the good faith of those involved, the Dutch wanted a formal public document for practically every agreement they entered into.[7]

Household inventories were included among these documents.

Notaries in the Netherlands also often acted as financial go-betweens for people lending and borrowing money.[8] They were expected to be of high moral character and have the technical knowledge needed to carry out their duties.[9]

The city fathers appointed three sets of special appraisers in addition to the usual household appraisers to inventory Abraham Peronneau and Maria Poniche's material possessions. They were responsible for establishing the monetary value of the couple's many paintings, their books and atlases, and the large quantity of expensive silk, wool, and other materials that the merchant had in the house.[10] Peronneau was a well-known collector of art.

The paintings were valued at 4,371 guilders. Three family portraits were among them. None survives today. The family's furniture was valued at 1,983 guilders, and their atlases and books at 498 guilders. They also owned valuable porcelain. The rich merchant's silks and other fabrics were assessed at 10,269 guilders. Almost 54,000 guilders was owed to Abraham Peronneau at the time of his death.

The disposition of their possessions upon death was a sacred responsibility in every family.[11] The notary's certification ensured that the assets and debts were specified and that the rights of inheritance of the children of Abraham Peronneau and Maria Poniche were protected and guaranteed.

The early and almost simultaneous deaths of both parents must have been a traumatic experience for the four children, as was having to leave home to go to live with their guardians. But, like orphans from other wealthy families, they enjoyed a considerable advantage over the vast majority of orphaned children in Amsterdam.

For one thing, the Peronneau children were in a position to receive the emotional support they needed following the deaths of their mother and father. Their guardians, Benjamin Philips and Reene Hourrays, were available to provide care and individual attention: to hold and comfort the two-year-old, and to support the three older children through their period of grieving. Of course there is no way of knowing whether they actually did so. The children also continued to live a comfortable material existence and could look forward to virtually the same bright future as when their parents were alive.

The Children of Other Amsterdam Citizens

With the notable exception of the city's many immigrant families, most orphaned children had relatives living in Amsterdam: an aunt, an uncle, a grandparent, an older sibling, or a surviving step-parent.[12] But for financial or other reasons, relatives usually chose not to take in the orphaned children of their deceased kin. They had no legal responsibility to do so.

When a relative did so, financial considerations were often involved. An older orphan taken in by, say, an aunt or uncle was expected to pay room and board.[13] Since most orphans were not taken in by relatives, they spent the rest of their childhood in an institutional setting: an Amsterdam orphanage. Others, especially infants and young children, were usually placed with wet-nurses or foster families.

Amsterdam had two municipally-managed orphanages.[14] One, the Burgerweeshuis, was set up in 1523 to care for the orphaned children of economically stable citizens.[15] The children's fathers were, writes Anne McCants, "men of modest, but respectable means – shopkeepers, traders, and artisans, to name only the most important groups."[16] In the late seventeenth-century, they constituted between a quarter and a third of the city's families.[17]

As with membership in Amsterdam's guilds and entitlement to charitable assistance, citizenship was a prerequisite for admission to the Burgerweeshuis. The children of non-citizen residents and temporary inhabitants were excluded. And admission to this municipal orphanage involved a further requirement: that a child's deceased parents had been citizens for at least seven years.

The regents of the Burgerweeshuis required that inventories be drawn up for the estates of all deceased citizens who had minor children and who met the requirements for admission. This enabled the regents to determine the extent to which the estates could contribute to the cost of maintaining the orphaned children.

The Burgerweeshuis had temporary access to the inheritances of the orphaned children, which provided the institution with working capital to invest.[18] The proceeds from the investments went to the orphanage, and the inheritances were eventually returned to the orphans when they left the orphanage. This was usually when they were anything from twenty to twenty-five.[19]

The vast majority of Amsterdam families did not meet the requirements for admission to the Burgerweeshuis. Consequently, orphans whose parents had either been citizens for less than seven years, non-citizen residents, or temporary inhabitants were denied admittance. They ended up either in the second municipal orphanage, the Aalmoezeniersweeshuis, or in one of several orphanages established by religious groups.

Of those orphans who were eligible for the Burgerweeshuis, only boys fourteen or younger and girls twelve or younger were admitted. Older boys and girls had to find other living arrangements (perhaps paying rent to a relative) and often go out to work as well. Infants were not admitted to the Burgerweeshuis, and orphaned babies were farmed out to wet-nurses until they were four or five years of age.

Also excluded from the Burgerweeshuis were illegitimate children, foundlings and abandoned children, orphans under school age, and the physically and mentally handicapped. All became wards of the city and were placed in fostercare with poor families.[20] Many of these families took in orphaned children as a way of supplementing their earnings. The level of care was not always high.

The number of children living in the Burgerweeshuis varied during the course of the seventeenth century: 500 in 1611, around 1,000 in 1660, and roughly 600 at the end of the century.[21] This decline was due primarily to changes in Amsterdam's policy of poor relief in the second half of the century.

Boys and girls were housed in separate buildings, and the two sexes were kept rigidly segregated except during lessons; boys and girls were taught together until they were ten. Brothers would have been together in one building and sisters in the other. Many of the orphaned boys and girls must have craved the companionship and support of a sibling of the opposite sex who lived in the other building.

The quality of care received by the children of citizens was far superior to that received by the children of non-citizen residents and temporary inhabitants.[22] In fact, the two municipal orphanages – the Burgerweeshuis and the Aalmoezeniersweeshuis – were intended to emulate the family backgrounds of the orphans in each: what McCants terms the middling classes in one, the lower orders in the other.

Since the Amsterdam city governors controlled the budgets of both orphanages, they were able to make sure that differences in the quality of the two were maintained. They did so by appointing boards of directors with responsibility for seeing to the food, clothing, and living standards in each. At the Burgerweeshuis, the board of directors (*regenten* and *regentessen*) consisted of men and women from the city's most elite families. At the Aalmoezeniersweeshuis it contained highly placed people but no one from the very top.[23]

Both orphanages had a division of labor between *regenten* and *regentessen*. The male regents had responsibility for the upkeep of the buildings, the accounts, educational matters, the provision of foodstuffs, discipline, and the hiring of male personnel. Their female counterparts saw to the cleanliness of the orphans, their upbringing, the production and care of textiles, the hiring of maids, and daily shopping.[24]

Serving as a regent or regentess in the Burgerweeshuis – i.e., as a member of the board of directors – was a clear indication of membership of the highest echelon of Amsterdam society. Appointment was determined by kinship and patronage. In the case of a regentess, helping the less fortunate allowed a woman to establish and confirm her elite status.[25] One such woman was Debora Blaeuw who served as regentess during the 1668-1702 period. She had no children of her own.

A surviving portrait (Illustration 9.1) by Adriaen Backer (1635/36-1684) allows us to see what Debora Blaeuw looked like.[26] Over the fifty-year period between 1633 and 1683, four large group portraits were made: two of the regents and two of the regentesses of the Burgerweeshuis.[27] The portraits probably hung together in the boardroom where the regents and regentesses held their meetings.

Like the exterior of the orphanage itself, the boardroom was grand and luxurious – as was fitting for these wealthy men and women. Orphanage personnel and other people entered only when summoned.[28] The boardroom was a very different world from that in which the orphaned boys and girls spent their everyday lives.

Backer's large portrait (193 x 282cm) from 1683 shows four fashionably-dressed regentesses sitting at a table. All have their hair in ringlets, a popular fashion at the time. Debora Blaeuw sits at the end on the left. Twice widowed, her third marriage was to Johan Hudde, an influential regent who served in the highest positions in the city government, sat on the board of directors of the East India Company, and was a board member of various church organizations. Hudde was a man of great erudition, enormous power, and elevated social standing. As we saw in an earlier chapter, he served as an Amsterdam burgomaster a total of twenty-one times.[29]

In Backer's portrait, the orphanage house-mother (*binnenmoeder*) is shown introducing two recently arrived orphans to the four regentesses. Behind Debora Blaeuw at the left, a servant holds clean uniforms for the young boy and girl.[30] It may seem surprising that children of Amsterdam citizens, hardly the city's poorest residents, are portrayed wearing such shabby clothing. But since the regentesses commissioned and paid for the group portrait themselves,[31] they must have agreed to this depiction of the two orphans as bedraggled and untidy.[32]

If nothing else, the portrait serves as a visual expression of the social distance between the rich elite and the children of ordinary citizens. As we have seen, the widest gulf in Amsterdam society was that between the rich and the rest. Although children sent to the Burgerweeshuis were from a more advantaged background than those sent to the Aalmoezeniersweeshuis, they were nonetheless part of the "rest." The rich took care of their own.

This is not to minimize the wide differences between the two municipal orphanages. To begin with, the ratio of children to personnel differed dramatically: at a somewhat later time, it was 9:1 in the Burgerweeshuis as compared to 32:1 in the Aalmoezeniersweeshuis.[33] There were also differences in the clothes the children wore, their diets, the amount of living space they had, their sleeping arrangements, and the quality of schooling and training they received. This was, of course, the intention of the city governors: the existing social hierarchy had to be maintained. Even young children were to be kept where they belonged.

Since clothing provided a direct indication of a person's social position, children in the two orphanages were dressed in ways that set them apart. Orphans from the Burgerweeshuis wore a vertically-divided red and black uniform, the city colors of Amsterdam (see the uniforms held by the servant in Illustration 9.1).

The uniforms of boys and girls had the same color combinations of red and black, but otherwise differed. Both, however, were in line with the dress fashionable for people like their deceased parents. Orphans from the lower strata of society wore uniforms with a red and black *bragoen*, a raised seam at the shoulders of a neutral-colored uniform.[34]

Debora Blaeuw and the other directors of the Burgerweeshuis saw to it that their charges had a plentiful and healthy diet. It was, in fact, a diet that could have been afforded only by middling (and, of course, wealthy) Amsterdam families. Meat, fish, cheese, and sugar with their evening porridge were a regular part of the children's diet. All were expensive and beyond the means of most families in the city.[35]

Consistent with other differences between the two orphanages, the boys in the Burgerweeshuis received a better quality of schooling and were prepared for higher levels of employment than their counterparts in the other municipal orphanage. Children in both orphanages were taught reading, writing, and arithmetic, and were given religious instruction. They attended classes for seven or eight hours a day on six days of the week.

Great care was taken to assure that orphans, like other people in Amsterdam (and Dutch society more generally), should know their place and not aspire to better it. Because the fathers of the orphans at the Burgerweeshuis had been citizens of a middling rather than high level, their sons were forbidden to follow the elite schooling that would have prepared them for university study.[36]

In 1652, the city governors instructed the regents of the Burgerweeshuis not to send any orphan boys to the Latin school. Instead, the burgomasters noted in their deliberations, the boys should be restricted to particular trades in accordance with their capacities.[37] It was important to avoid educating the boys above their station.

The boys were to be trained in the sorts of trades suitable for boys of their background and (presumed) abilities. Few were given the opportunity to prepare for higher-status and more specialized trades such as surgery, diamond-cutting, map-making, or painting.[38] There were, however, exceptions.

On February 4, 1662 Erick van den Weerelt, identified in the apprenticeship contract simply as "orphan," was placed in an apprenticeship for three years with the master painter, Jan Lievensz [Lievens]. The regents of the Burgerweeshuis agreed to pay the master the sum of 50 guilders a year. In 1665 the apprenticeship was extended for another three years. And in 1669 the regents signed a contract with a second master painter, Karel Dujardin, for a further year at a cost of 80 guilders.[39] The total length of the boy's apprenticeship was longer than the average at the time.[40]

Somewhere between the ages of ten and fourteen, boys from the Burgerweeshuis were apprenticed to master craftsmen. This was, of course, what would have happened were their parents still alive. Formal employment contracts were drawn up between the orphanage and the individual master. A boy was not permitted to leave the confines of the orphanage until a contract of this kind had been signed.

Although most apprentices in Amsterdam resided in the homes of their masters, boys from the Burgerweeshuis were required to return to the orphanage in the evening. All the same, they were able to leave the premises each day and could establish outside contacts in a way that girls could not. Such contacts are important to adolescent boys and girls alike.

Once they turned twelve, the girls in the Burgerweeshuis divided their time between acquiring "typical" female skills (sewing, knitting, cleaning, cooking) and performing related tasks in the orphanage. They were not usually allowed to work outside the orphanage, and spent their time in the orphanage workshop until they were discharged at the age of twenty. The only time the girls left the orphanage was to attend church. As in so many other areas of life, females were systematically disadvantaged.

Children of Non-Citizen Residents and Temporary Inhabitants
The second city orphanage, the Aalmoezeniersweeshuis, was established in 1664 to care for children whose parents met neither the citizenship requirements nor those for church membership and admittance to church-run orphanages. It had a population of about 1,300 orphans in 1682 and around 800 at the end of the century.[41]

The Aalmoezeniersweeshuis was intended for orphans over the age of four, but also took in orphaned infants and toddlers, and some abandoned children. Infants not yet weaned were relegated to the homes of nonresident wet-nurses. In a later period, 58 percent of the children were residents in the orphanage itself, around 31 percent lived in the homes of wet-nurses in Amsterdam, and roughly 10 percent lived with families in the countryside.[42]

Mortality was especially high for infants living in the homes of wet-nurses. McCants presents no figures for the seventeenth century, but indicates that a century later 51.5 percent of the infants sent out to a wet-nurse died before reaching their first birthday.

The regents attributed this high figure, she writes, to "the poor quality of care being given the infants by the wet-nurses in their employ. In particular the regents complained about the lack of tenderness; improper heating, food, and shelter; and the dilatory responses to illnesses."[43] Since wet-nurses often had several infants in their care, this is not surprising. Even the infants who survived must have been physically and emotionally damaged.

Many Amsterdam orphans had never known their father. He was perhaps a soldier or away at sea and they were raised solely by their mother. If she died prematurely, the child or children often ended up in the Aalmoezeniersweeshuis. In many cases, the father was already dead, his identity was not known, or he had run away. In such instances, orphans aged between ten and twelve were taken into the orphanage temporarily until an employer was found with whom they could live.[44] A disproportionate number were the children of foreign-born parents.

Children at the Aalmoezeniersweeshuis received only two-thirds of the per capita resources enjoyed by their counterparts in the Burgerweeshuis. Their diet included less meat and no fish at all, and was generally deficient in nutritional value. It is likely that they were of smaller stature than the orphaned sons and daughters of the city's citizens.

The children also had significantly less living space. A bed in the Aalmoezeniersweeshuis, for example, was shared by as many as five of the smaller and three of the larger children.[45] In the Burgerweeshuis, by contrast, a child usually shared a bed with just one or two others.[46]

Even so, the latter were in no way as well-off as orphans who were the children of the wealthy elite. Now living in the large homes of relatives or family friends, they often had their own bedrooms and their own individual beds as well. With a bed to itself, a child could enjoy the pleasure of lying in bed and stretching its limbs as it pleased.

As is to be expected, the mortality rate in the Aalmoezeniersweeshuis was much higher than in the orphanage which cared for the children of Amsterdam citizens. Figures are not available for the seventeenth century, but in the eighteenth century orphans in the former were five times more susceptible to childhood mortality than the orphans in the Burgerweeshuis.[47] Similar differences would have existed a century earlier.

Unlike boys in the Burgerweeshuis, who were placed in apprenticeships so that they could eventually earn their living as skilled artisans, boys in the Aalmoezeniersweeshuis were expected to seek unskilled and poorly-paid employment. Many were sent out to work, "left," in McCants' words, "to the mercy of the casual labor market."[48]

When they were fifteen or sixteen, boys were encouraged to enter employment with the Dutch East India Company as "ship's boys."[49] Although this meant low wages, years away from Amsterdam, and a good chance of dying en route or in the Far East, such employment was seen as perfectly suitable for boys from the lower orders.

Amsterdam's municipal orphanages and other charitable institutions, notes McCants, were considered to be in the interests of everyone: the wealthy elite, ordinary citizens, the lower orders, and the poor alike. With orphanages, as with other institutional arrangements, the city governors took it for granted that hierarchy and inequality were natural and necessary.

We have seen that an important aspect of citizenship was the access it provided to the Burgerweeshuis. It provided, writes McCants, a kind of "social insurance against the deleterious effects of parents' premature death." It "guaranteed that the children of the reasonably prosperous would not end up as paupers through the accident of their parents' death." And the existence of the Burgerweeshuis "protected the social hierarchy not only from the usually hypothesized fear of social insurrection from below but also from the potentially destabilizing effects of downward social mobility."[50]

The same system that prevented boys from the Burgerweeshuis "from obtaining high-status jobs," writes McCants, "also protected them from having to scramble for the unsteady employment offered in the casual labor market."[51] The board of directors saw that they were apprenticed for trades requiring a degree of skill, thus ensuring that they would not have to take low-skilled, poorly-paid laboring jobs. Many boys were later employed in the building industry, shipbuilding, and in crafts connected with woodworking.[52] None had to toil as a common laborer, the fate of most orphans in the Aalmoezeniersweeshuis.

The two-tier arrangement under which boys in the Burgerweeshuis were generally forbidden to undertake schooling or training that might have allowed them to rise above their appointed station also protected them from falling below their position in Amsterdam's civic and economic hierarchies.

In maintaining the two-tier system of care for orphans, the city governors required a rationale or justification for the privileged position of the children of Amsterdam citizens and the superior quality of the Burgerweeshuis. This justification, argues McCants, rested on the financing of municipal institutions.[53]

These institutions were usually financed by excise taxes imposed on ordinary consumption items rather than by taxes that targeted wealth. The rich elite, making up only a tiny minority of Amsterdam residents, had little need for institutional assistance. Although the lower orders and the poor constituted the largest segment of the population, their tax burden was much lower than that of middling citizens. It was the latter who paid the bulk of tax revenues in the city. Should a husband and wife die prematurely, their orphaned children were thus entitled to a level of institutional care superior to that received by the children of non-citizens.

A more generous level of charity, argues McCants, was one way of securing the acquiescence of middling citizens to the existing hierarchy and inequalities between themselves and the wealthy elite. At the same time, a less generous level for the lower orders was consistent with their lesser tax burden.[54] Consequently, they had nothing to complain about.

Amsterdam also had orphanages established by religious groups: two Roman Catholic orphanages, one for girls (1629) and one for boys (1672); a French Reformed orphanage (1631, enlarged 1669); an English Presbyterian orphanage (1651), an orphanage for children from the Reformed Church (1657), orphanages for three different Mennonite communities (1672, 1675, 1677), and a Lutheran orphanage (1678).[55] Like the Aalmoezeniersweeshuis, they were intended primarily for poor children.

Boys and girls in these orphanages, usually the children of parents who did not hold citizenship, also received a level of care below that received by the orphans in the Burgerweeshuis. Boys over fourteen and girls over twelve had to find somewhere else to live. They often had to find employment as well. Some boys suffered the loss of an opportunity to follow an apprenticeship, while the girls had to go out to work sooner than would otherwise have been the case.

The two municipal orphanages and the religious orphanages were between them taking care of roughly 3,400 children in the last decades of the seventeenth century.[56] The actual number of orphans in Amsterdam must have been greater. How much greater is not clear.

Children were separated from their parents in other ways than through death. Foundlings were left by their mother or their parents, and older children were also abandoned. Kuijpers estimates that at least a third of the children cared for by the Aalmoezeniersweeshuis were foundlings or abandoned children, and thus not actually orphans.[57] Nevertheless, they needed care.

In an effort to avoid the expenses involved in caring for such children, orphanage authorities in 1690 began placing notices in the *Amsterdamse Courant* offering a 25 guilder reward for information about the person or persons who had left or abandoned children. Some of the religiously-supported orphanages did the same. This notice appeared on June 5, 1696:

> The poor-relief board of the Dutch Reformed community in this city makes known that the widow of Claes Hermans and later of Jan Pool, 36 years of age, of long stature, with a wide face, born in Cortenhoef, living in the Utrechtse

Dwarsstraat, across from the Red Lion [an inn] in a basement, in April 1696 has run away unfaithfully and without love, abandoning her 5 children. As has Philip Carels, 36 or 37 years old from Rotterdam, tall and thin, a lace-maker by profession, with a brown face, straight black hair, a brown cloth coat, and black stockings, and wearing a black hat, run away from his wife and 4 children more than six weeks ago, residence in the Egelantiersstraat. Anyone pointing out either or both of the above-named persons will be fairly rewarded by the poor relief board and their name kept secret.[58]

Given that this notice was placed in the *Courant* by the board of the Reformed Church, the church must have been caring for the nine children in the absence of their runaway parents. If they were eventually apprehended, it is likely that both the man and woman would have been sent to the workhouse and their meager earnings would have been taken and put toward the upkeep of the abandoned children. As for the nine children, there is a good chance they spent the rest of their childhood in the orphanage of the Reformed Church.

-III-

The Orphanage Experience
Despite the many differences in the quality of care received by children in the Burgerweeshuis and the other Amsterdam orphanages, the experiences of orphaned children were in some ways strikingly similar. On admission, children were given a thorough wash all over and their hair was cut short and deloused. This was a precaution against infectious diseases. Cropping their hair short also diminished their individuality.

The young boy or girl was then dressed in the orphanage's easily recognizable uniform – another way of suppressing individuality – which proclaimed the child's status as an orphan. The first days and weeks in the orphanage must have been a time of uncertainty and fear. Every child must have retained a vivid memory of its arrival and early days in an orphanage.

We have no way of knowing whether and how often orphans, especially older ones, talked about their parents. Nor do we know how the orphanage staff dealt with such symptoms of grief and distress as nightmares and bedwetting (in a bed shared with other children). In any case, a child in an orphanage certainly received far less emotional support than one living in the household of a guardian.

Within their segregated accommodation – boys in one house, girls in another – orphaned children ate together, played together, and attended school together. They slept together, shared the same chamber pots and the same privies in the garden, and inhaled the same foul odors when the windows were closed against the so-called bad air at night.[59] They were marched to church together, two by two, with no talking on the way. Privacy was virtually nonexistent.[60]

From the time they got up at 5:30 in the morning until they went to bed after their evening meal, orphans were closely regimented and subject to strict discipline from members of the orphanage staff. There are no personal accounts of being an orphan in seventeenth-century Amsterdam. But it is likely that the experience resembled the following short account of being an orphan early in the twentieth century:

> We had not known what it was...to take medicine in a gulp because someone could not be bothered to wait for us, to have our arms jerked into our sleeves and a comb ripped through our hair, to be bathed impatiently, to be told to sit up or lie down quick and no nonsense about it, to find our questions unanswered and our requests unheeded.[61]

Given the large number of children in Amsterdam orphanages, especially the two municipal ones, relations between the staff and individual boys and girls must have been quite impersonal. The staff probably knew no more about the children than their first names.

In fact, dozens had the same first names: Johannes, Willem, Pieter, and Jan, among the boys; Anna, Cornelia, Catharina, and Elizabeth, among the girls. Some boys in the orphanage may have been called Willem M, Willem P, little or big Willem; and some girls Anna H, Anna the redhead, or Anna blue-eyes. Although bearing Dutch names, many of these children had been called something else in the place they migrated from.

Orphanages in the Dutch Republic were modeled on the family household, although they were obviously much larger and more complex than actual households. Ideally at least, the orphanage took over the functions ordinarily performed by the children's deceased parents. As in the family, there was a hierarchy of functions.

The terms "father" and "mother" were applied to the leading couple who supervised the activities of the rest of the staff. Whatever their efforts, they could not possibly have reproduced life in the parental home. How could they? Orphans must have constantly compared the way things were with the way they used to be. Unavoidably, then, the orphanage household was a poor substitute for the real thing. For other children, the orphanage was the only home they ever knew.

Every orphanage would have had children who made friends easily and others who found it difficult, loving friendships and bitter hatreds, bullies and children quick to stand up for others. Lacking the sheltering presence of their parents, orphaned boys and girls had to find their own way in reacting to life in an orphanage. There can be no doubt that it was very hard for orphans to get on with their lives.

An older child must have had an aching need for the love it once had, while an abandoned infant experienced an aching need for a love it had never known. An endless hunger for love and affection would have been common to these boys and girls. It was a hunger seldom satisfied, for demonstrations of affection were probably rare in the world of orphanages, foster parents, and wet-nurses. Emotional deprivation was the lot of most.

The psychotherapist and writer Eileen Simpson, who grew up as an orphan herself, writes with compassion and insight about the situation of orphaned children. "To be reasonably lucky," she writes, "an orphan should have a brother or sister close in age, a modest inheritance ... and hospitable relatives."[62] By these criteria, only a minority of orphans in Amsterdam's golden age would have been reasonably lucky.

A SUMMING UP

S tudies of Amsterdam's golden age give little systematic attention to people's well-being and none at all to differences among groups and within households. As with other aspects of people's lives in the past, questions should always be posed about any period represented as a "golden" age. For it need not have been so for everyone. A culture or society is not a unitary entity. Nor is a city. What is true of the whole may not be true of its constituent parts.

Any assessment of life in a particular time and place must distinguish among different groups and social strata. Moreover, it is always better to explore the past in terms of what divided people rather than as a single, homogeneous culture, shared community of interests, or the like. Only by doing so is it possible to uncover differences concealed by focusing on the whole. It may increase our understanding of the whole as well.

In that connection, this book's major aim is to assess the well-being of people who differed in civic status, economic standing, and gender during Amsterdam's golden age. Toward that end, I have conceptualized the wellness of being in terms of people's biological, physical, social, and emotional functionings; discussed several important dimensions of well-being; specified various indicators relevant to assessing those dimensions; and examined the relevant historical evidence concerning people's well-being.

My analysis shows that, alone and in combination, people's positions in the three systems of hierarchy had an impact on the most important dimensions of human well-being: staying alive, which involved having the means necessary to do so (food, water, adequate housing, etc.), access to economic resources, relationships with others, self-esteem, and autonomy or personal control over their lives. Other dimensions of people's lives were affected as well.

Differences in people's levels of well-being cannot, however, be summed up in a composite index. There is no way to aggregate the various indicators in order to arrive at an assessment for each dimension. Consequently, the dimensions cannot be added up to reach an overall assessment. This is a problem common to all empirical assessments of the wellness of people's being. It is an even greater problem in a historical study that relies heavily on secondary sources.

Even if it were possible to assess the impact of civil status, economic standing, and gender in a composite index, much valuable information would be excluded. Consider just one dimension of well-being, relationships with others: between master artisans and journeymen, servants and their employers, husbands and wives, and brothers and sisters. A composite index of the impact of inequalities on people's interpersonal relationships would convey nothing about the quality of these relationships.

Measurement is not everything. Descriptive richness is far more important in assessing the goodness of people's lives in a particular time or place. I have tried to provide such richness in considering the impact of people's positions in Amsterdam's three systems of inequality on their functioning during infancy, childhood, adolescence, adulthood, and old age, for the unmarried, the never married, the married, the widowed, and the orphaned.

As well as assessing well-being, this book has a second aim: to identify, describe, and explain the intervening mechanisms linking people's positions in the different systems of hierarchy to the wellness of their being. Two mechanisms constituted the most fundamental links in this regard: (1) inherited entitlements and their accompanying constraints, and (2) the coercive power of the ruling regent elite in assuring that entitlements and constraints were maintained.

With the first mechanism, these inherited entitlements and constraints arose from civic status, economic standing, and gender. Entitlements for some people created obstacles and barriers for others. People without entitlements of their own lived at the discretion of those who did. Dependence and vulnerability were the result.

Entitlements and constraints played a mediating role in virtually every aspect of people's lives in Amsterdam's golden age: the social recognition they received, their schooling and training, the kinds of work they did, the conditions of their labor, their earnings, their chances of marrying, the rights and obligations of husbands and wives, the remarriages of the widowed, the life chances of orphans and foundlings, charitable assistance in cases of dire need, and even the clothing that people were entitled to wear.

Hierarchy was regarded as natural, and entitlements arising from civic status, economic standing, and gender were viewed as the inevitable result of innate superiority. Consider in this regard some of the entitlements that were derived from a person's biological sex. A mere accident of birth entitled a boy to greater autonomy, and to a level of training and education unavailable to a girl. It entitled a male to greater access to economic resources, and to higher wages than a female doing the same work. And it entitled a husband to a superior legal status and to the right to claim public space.

The other side of a male's entitlements were the constraints or obstacles they created for a female. Most notable perhaps was that a married woman's identity was subsumed by law into the identity of her husband. Upon marriage, he took over control of her property, appeared as her guardian at court, and contracted agreements in her name. Women could not but have been aware of the ever-present relevance of having been born female.

The entitlements and accompanying constraints arising from civic status and economic standing had similar consequences for people's well-being. The majority of people with citizenship had acquired it by birth, and thus enjoyed a privileged position from the beginning. Similarly with the privileges connected with having "chosen one's parents well," i.e., having been born into a rich or well-to-do family. These inherited privileges provided a minority of individuals with a head start in life.

With the second mechanism intervening between people's positions in the different systems of inequality and the wellness of their being, the coercive power of the ruling political elite had an enormous impact. Also playing a role were religious doctrines, treatises on good conduct, and the norms and values engraved in social consciousness and embedded in the city's dominant institutional arrangements. Relationships in guilds, the workplace, and the neighborhood had an influence as well.

But the power of the regent elite was especially important. For the city fathers functioned as the guardians of hierarchy and deference. It was they who formulated, enacted, and enforced the laws, policies, and practices that upheld the numerous entitlements (and consequent constraints) arising from inequalities in civic status, economic standing, and gender.

From the perspective of the political elite, the maintenance of existing inequalities and structures of privilege was crucial. Even with no overt threats to the positions of the regents themselves, it was imperative that subordinate groups maintain their positions *relative* to one another. Any change in the existing relations of hierarchy and power was a potential source of instability and was to be avoided if possible. Social order required hierarchy and subordination. All should be in their proper place.

In some ways, things are not all that different today. Just as they did in the seventeenth century, group-based hierarchies occupy a prominent place in Amsterdam, in the Netherlands more generally, and, in fact, in most places in the world. Resting on gender, civic status, economic position, race, ethnicity, caste, tribe, lineage, and other biological or group attributes, these hierarchies give rise to entitlements and constraints affecting the well-being of virtually everyone.

Moreover, similar mechanisms are involved. No more than in Amsterdam's golden age are differences in the wellness of people's being a consequence of inexorable or inevitable natural processes. Instead, they are generally (though by no means always) the result of inherited entitlements and the power of the political elite in assuring that they are maintained.

Without any intent or effort of their own, individuals acquire entitlements associated with the privileges of male sex, skin color, citizenship, or whatever. Although being born male, with a particular skin color, or with citizenship is *not* of one's own doing, entitlements automatically follow. And as is always the case, entitlements for some result in disadvantages and vulnerabilities for others.

Now, as in the past, the coercive power of the political elite has consequences for the maintenance of inherited entitlements. Government decisions, laws, and policies affect the private and public realms alike, penetrating far beyond the political sphere into the economic, educational, religious, and family arrangements that constitute the basic structure of every society. In fact, the private/public distinction often disappears as personal matters become a matter of political concern. Individual interests are then subordinated to the maintenance of social order.

The power of the state (the ruling elite) can be harnessed for human welfare or corrupted by misuse. All too often, it functions to maintain hierarchies of inherited entitlements. These concern virtually every aspect of an individual's life: education and training, the availability of jobs, the incomes associated with different kinds of work, relationships in the workplace, the distribution of wealth, the tax structure, the regulation of marriage and divorce, births and deaths, health care, welfare benefits, and public services.

To take just one example, a double standard of education, employment opportunities, and pay for the two sexes exists almost everywhere. The same is true of race, ethnicity, and nationality. As always, inherited endowments have consequences for the wellness of people's being. The state is complicit in their continuing influence.

Perhaps I exaggerate the extent to which the mechanisms linking hierarchy and well-being are the same now as they were in Amsterdam's golden age. But I think not. Inherited privilege shapes people's lives in all times and places. An individual who is born male is the beneficiary of a history of entrenched advantage. So, too, is someone born with the right skin color, with citizenship, or with well-to-do parents.

Although sometimes unintended and unrecognized, the coercive power of the state assures the continuance of hereditary privileges as a basis for social order. Together, inherited privilege and the actions of the political elite solidify structures of hierarchy that affect people's well-being in every society. It is this I have pointed to in my discussion above.

In any case, I hope to have accomplished the book's two major aims: to examine the nature and impact of inequalities in the city's main systems of hierarchy on people's well-being in Amsterdam's golden age; and to identify, describe, and explain the social mechanisms linking these inequalities to the wellness of their being.

I also hope to have reminded readers of the extent to which human beings in all times and places have characteristics in common and react in predictable ways. This allows us to read Homer, Ovid, or Shakespeare and feel that we are reading about ourselves. All three emphasize our common humanity. Consider *The Merchant of Venice* (Act III, Scene I), where Shakespeare has Shylock ask:

> Hath not a Jew eyes? Hath not a Jew hands, organs, dimensions, senses, affections, passions: fed with the same food, hurt with the same weapons, subject to the same diseases, healed by the same means, warmed and cooled by the same winter and summer as a Christian is? If you prick us, do we not bleed? If you tickle us, do we not laugh? If you poison us, do we not die? And if you wrong us, shall we not revenge?

So it is with all of us, and so it has always been.

NOTES

INTRODUCTION

1   James Griffith, *Well-Being*. Oxford: Clarendon Press, 1986; Thomas Scanlon, "Value, Desire, and Quality of Life" in Martha Nussbaum and Amartya Sen, eds., *The Quality of Life*. Oxford: Clarendon Press, 1993, 185-200; Julia Annas, "Women and the Quality of Life: Two Norms or One?" in Ibid, 287-291; and discussions in earlier books of my own, Derek L. Phillips, *Toward a Just Social Order*. Princeton: Princeton University Press, 1986, especially chapter 8; and *Looking Backward: A Critical Appraisal of Communitarian Thought*. Princeton: Princeton University Press, 1993, 18-19.

2   Especially relevant in this regard are Nussbaum and Sen, *Quality of Life*; Amartya Sen, *On Economic Equality*. Expanded edition. Oxford: Clarendon Press, 1997; Sudhir Anand and Amartya Sen, "The Income Component of the Human Development Index," *Journal of Human Development* 1 (2000):83-106; Martha Nussbaum, *Women and Human Development: The Capabilities Approach*. Cambridge: Cambridge University Press, 2000; Michele M. Moody-Adams, "The Virtue of Nussbaum's Essentialism," *Metaphilosophy* 29 (October 1998):263-272; Susan Moller Okin, "Poverty, Well-Being, and Gender: What Counts, Who is Heard?" *Philosophy and Public Affair* 31 (2003):280-316; Alison M. Jaggar, "Reasoning about Well-Being: Nussbaum's Methods of Justifying the Capabilities," *Journal of Political Philosophy* 14 (September 2006):301-322; and Mark McGillivray, ed., *Human Well-Being: Concept and Measurement*. Basingstoke: Palgrave McMillan, 2007.

3   See, for example, Karel Davids and Jan Lucassen, *A Miracle Mirrored: The Dutch Republic in European Perspective*. Cambridge: Cambridge University Press, 1995; Lee Soltow and Jan Luiten van Zanden, *Income and Wealth Inequality in the Netherlands, 16th-20th Century*. Amsterdam: Spinhuis, 1998; Mark Rapley, *Quality of Life Research: A Critical Introduction*. London: Sage Publications, 2003; Tommy Bengtsson, Cameron Campbell, and James Z. Lee, eds., *Mortality and Living Standards in Europe and Asia*. Cambridge: MIT Press, 2004; and Robert C. Allen, Tommy Bengtsson, and Martin Dribe, eds., *Living Standards in the Past: New Perspectives on Well-Being in Asia and Europe*. Oxford: Oxford University Press, 2005. Although less explicitly concerned with well-being as such, two important earlier works are Leo Noordegraaf, *Hollands welvaren? Levensstandaard in Holland 1450-1650*. Bergen: Octavo, 1985; and Hubert Nusteling, *Welvaart en werkgelegenheid in Amsterdam, 1540-1860*. Amsterdam: De Bataafsche Leeuw, 1985.

4   A recent comparative study of well-being in the United States focuses mainly on people's health. Orville Gilbert Brim, Carol D. Ryff, and Ronald C. Kessler, *How Healthy Are We? A National Study of Well-Being at Midlife*. Chicago: University of Chicago Press, 2004.

5 A recent exception is Jan Luiten van Zanden, "What Happened to the Standard of Living Before the Industrial Revolution? New Evidence from the Western Part of the Netherlands" in Allen, Bengtsson, and Dribe, *Living Standards*, 173-194. This interesting and informative study focuses mainly on economic aspects of the quality of life.

6 This analysis represents an extension of my earlier transdisciplinary approach to the realization of well-being in a just and humane society. See Phillips, *Just Social Order*; and Phillips, "Work, Welfare, and Well-Being" in Hans Bak, Frits van Holthoon, and Hans Krabbendam, eds., *Social and Secure? Politics and Culture of the Welfare State: A Comparative Inquiry*. Amsterdam: VU University Press, 1996, 19-46.

7 My approach to well-being bears a family resemblance to the capability approach of Sen and Nussbaum (footnote 2). But the capability approach focuses on conceptualizing and assessing well-being, while I also want to show how it is affected by people's positions in a society's major systems of hierarchy. My concern with locating the mechanisms intervening between inequalities and well-being parallels that of Brim and his associates, *How Healthy Are We?*

8 Inequality was taken for granted by the powerful and privileged. This is made abundantly clear in the literature of the time considered in Maria A. Schenkeveld, *Dutch Literature in the Age of Rembrandt: Themes and Ideas*. Amsterdam and Philadelphia: John Benjamin Publishing Company, 1991.

9 Dutch cities continued to have this autonomous character well into the eighteenth century. Useful discussions can be found in Maarten Prak, *Republikeinse veelheid, democratische enkelvoud: Sociale verandering in het Revolutietijdvak 's-Hertogenbosch 1770-1820*. Nijmegen: Uitgeverij SUN, 1999; and Jan Luiten van Zanden and Arthur van Riel, *The Strictures of Inheritance: The Dutch Economy in the Nineteenth Century*. Princeton: Princeton University Press, 2004, 32-33.

10 For a description of the situation in Amsterdam, see Renee Kistenmaker and Roelof van Gelder, *Amsterdam: The Golden Age: 1275-1795*. New York: Abbeville Press, 1983, 58-69.

11 Marc Boone and Maarten Prak, eds., *Individual, corporate, and judicial status in European Cities (late middle ages and early modern period)*. Leuven-Apeldoorn: Garant Publishers, 1996; and Henk van Nierop, "Popular participation in politics in the Dutch Republic" in Peter Blickle, ed., *Resistance, Representation, and Community*. Oxford: Oxford University Press, 1997, 272-290.

12 For an informative discussion of citizenship, see Charles Tilly, "Identity and Social History," *International Review of Social History*, 40, Supplement 3 (1995):1-17.

13 Although the regents were closely connected through ties of blood and marriage, factions existed among them. Nonetheless, they were united in seeing themselves as the political elite.

14 For what he calls "organizational entwining" in the Dutch Republic more generally, see Philip S. Gorski, *The Disciplinary Revolution: Calvinism and the Rise of the State in Early Modern Europe*. Chicago: University of Chicago Press, 2003.

15 Erika Kuijpers, *Migrantenstad: Immigratie en Sociale Verhoudingen in 17e-Eeuws Amsterdam*. Hilversum: Verloren, 2005.

16 What I refer to as economic standing is sometimes spoken of in terms of "class." But the concept of class has always resisted clear definition. As the authors of an article on class analysis note: "many centuries of debate have left academics no closer to consensus on the basic structure of social classes, let alone the underlying principles by which such classes are generated and maintained." David B. Grusky and Jesper B. Sorensen, "Can Class Analysis Be Salvaged?" *American Journal of Sociology*

103 (March 1998):1199. Hacker makes the same point in an extended review of five books focusing on economic inequality in the United States today. Andrew Hacker, "The Rich and Everyone Else," *The New York Review of Books*, May 25, 2006:16-19.

17 Soltow and van Zanden, *Income and Wealth Inequality*, 38.

18 Ibid.; van Zanden, "What Happened to the Standard of Living?" and Maarten Prak, *The Dutch Republic in the Seventeenth Century*. Cambridge: Cambridge University Press, 2005, chapter 9, "Toil and Trouble."

19 See van Nierop, "Popular participation." In Blickle, ed., *Resistance*, 277-290; Harald Hendrix and Marijke Meijer Drees, eds., *Beschaafde Burgers: Burgerlijkheid in de vroeg moderne tijd*. Amsterdam: Amsterdam University Press, 2001; and the discussion in Klaske Muizelaar and Derek Phillips, *Picturing Men and Women in the Dutch Golden Age: Paintings and People in Historical Perspective*. New Haven and London: Yale University Press, 2003.

20 See, for example, Els Kloek, Nicole Teeuwen, and Marijke Huisman, *Women of the Golden Age: An international debate on women in seventeenth-century Holland, England and Italy*. Hilversum: Verloren, 1994.

21 Earle was one of the first to make this clear. See Peter Earle, "The Female Labour Market in London in the Late Seventeenth and Early Eighteenth Centuries," *Economic History Review* (2d ser.) 42 (1989):328-353. For working women in the Dutch golden age, see the special journal number on "Themanummer Vrouwenarbeid in de Vroegmoderne tijd in Nederland," *Tijdschrift voor Sociale en Economische Geschiedenis* 3(2005); and Elise van Nederveen Meerkerk, *De draad in eigen handen: Vrouwen en loonarbeid in de Nederlandse textielnijverheid, 1581-1810*. Amsterdam: Aksant, 2007.

22 The estimate for the number of servants is based on Table 3 in Lee Soltow, "Income and Wealth Inequality in Amsterdam, 1585-1805," *Economisch-En-Sociaal-Historisch Jaarboek* 52 (1989):72-95. The figures for the number of guilds and guild membership come from Jan Lucassen, "Labor and Early Economic Development" in Davids and Lucassen, *A Mirror Mirrored*, 406; and Sandra Bos, *"Uyt Liefde tot Malcander:" Onderlinge hulpverlening binnen de Noord-Nederlandse gilden in internationaal perspectief (1570-1820)*. Academisch Proefschrift, Vrije Universiteit, Amsterdam, 1998, 51.

23 For those who do not recall the tale, a short summary. Together with his father, Daedalus, Icarus was imprisoned on the island of Crete, shut in by the sea. The only hope of escape was flight, and Daedalus used feathers to construct a pair of wings for himself and his son, attaching the wings to their shoulders with wax. "I warn you, Icarus," said Daedalus, "you must follow a course midway between earth and heaven, in case the sun should scorch your feathers, if you go too high, or the water makes them heavy if you are too low. Fly halfway between the two." But Icarus disobeyed his father by flying too close to the sun, the wax melted, his wings dropped off, and he fell into the sea and drowned. Too ambitious, too prideful, Icarus met with disaster. Ovid, *Metamorphoses*. Translated with an introduction by Mary M. Innes. London: Penguin Classics, 1955, 184.

24 Cited in Marijke Meijer Drees, "Zeventiende-eeuwse literatuur in de Republiek: burgerlijk?" in Hendrix and Meijer Drees, *Beschaafde Burgers*, 67-75.

25 For an idea about legal regulations in the Dutch Republic, see Henk van Nierop, "Private Interests, Public Policies: Petitions in the Dutch Republic" in Arthur K. Wheelock, Jr. and Adele Seeff, eds., *The Public and Private in Dutch Culture of the Golden Age*. Newark: University of Delaware Press, 2000, 33-39; and, for pre-industrial Europe more generally, Sheilagh Ogilvie, "How Does Social Capital Affect Women? Guilds and Communities in Early Modern Germany," *The American Historical Review* 109 (April 2004):325-359.

26   Peter Glick and Susan T. Fiske, "The Ambivalent Sexism Inventory: Differentiating hostile and benevolent sexism," *Journal of Personality and Social Psychology* 70 (1996):491-512.

27   Sennett and Cobb refer to "the hidden injuries of class" in this regard. Richard Sennett and Jonathan Cobb, *The Hidden Injuries of Class*. New York: Vintage Books, 1972.

28   Onora O'Neill, a philosopher, and Mary Jackman, a sociologist, are particularly attentive to the harms ensuing from unequal social relations. See, Onora O'Neill, "Justice, Gender, and International Boundaries" in Nussbaum and Sen, *Quality of Life*, 303-335; Mary R. Jackman, "Gender, Violence, and Harassment" in Janet Chafetz Saltzman, ed., *Handbook of the Sociology of Gender*. New York: Kluwer Academic/Plenum Publishers, 1999, 45-61; and Mary R. Jackman, "License to Kill: Violence and Legitimacy in Expropriative Social Relations" in John T. Joost and Brenda Major, eds., *The Psychology of Legitimacy*. Cambridge: Cambridge University Press, 2001, 437-467.

29   Muizelaar and Phillips, *Picturing Men and Women*.

30   The capabilities approach represented in the writings of Sen and Nussbaum (footnote 2) rejects the inclusion of economic resources as a dimension of well-being. This is because they regard economic resources as only a *means* of enhancing people's well-being, which concerns what matters "intrinsically": their functionings and capabilities. As noted by Robeyns, however, an adequate analysis of the impact of inequalities on people's well-being requires the inclusion of people's access to economic resources. Ingrid Robeyns, "Sen's Capability Approach and Gender Inequality: Selecting Relevant Capabilities," *Feminist Economics* 9 (2003):64.

31   In a comparison of the life expectancy of a newborn child in 171 countries, variations in income explained more than two-thirds of the differences among them. Steve Dowrick, "Income-based Measures of Average Well-Being" in McGillivray, *Human Well-Being*, 70.

32   Some psychologists speak of relatedness as an innate psychological need. See, for example, Richard M. Ryan and Edward L. Deci, "On Happiness and Human Potentials: A Review of Research on Hedonic and Eudaimonic Well-Being." *Annual Review of Psychology* 52 (2001):141-166. It is, in any case, an inescapable social need. No one survives without the help of other people.

33   Marmot summarizes recent evidence concerning the health-related benefits of social involvement and support. Michael Marmot, *Status Syndrome*. London: Bloomsbury, 2004. See also, Brim, Ryff, and Kessler, *How Healthy Are We?*

34   See, for example, Alan Gewirth, *Self-Fulfillment*. Princeton: Princeton University Press, 1998, 94-96, 126.

35   In the psychological literature, this is often described as a sense of control or self-efficacy. See, for example, A. Bandura, *Self-efficacy: The exercise of control*. New York: Freeman, 1997. An emphasis on autonomy is central to moral theorizing. See, for example, David Richards, "Rights and Autonomy," *Ethics* 92 (1981): 3-20; and Diana Meyers, "Personal Autonomy and the Paradox of Feminine Socialization," *Journal of Philosophy* 84 (1987):619-628. This emphasis is reflected in writings about well-being today.

36   As far as well-being in contemporary societies is concerned, studies of subjective well-being or happiness are dominant. Prominent among such studies is Richard Layard, *Happiness: Lessons from a New Science*. London: Allen Lane, 2005. Although some of my own early research concerned self-reports of happiness, I soon came to be highly critical of studies based on interviews and questionnaires. See, for example,

Derek L. Phillips and Kevin J. Clancy, "Modeling Effects in Survey Research, *Public Opinion Quarterly* 36 (Summer 1971):246-253; Derek L. Phillips, *Knowledge from What? Theories and Methods in Social Research*. Chicago: Rand McNally, 1971; and Derek L. Phillips and Kevin J. Clancy, "Some Effects of 'Social Desirability' in Survey Studies," *American Journal of Sociology* 77(March 1972):921-940. With all their inadequacies, interviews and questionnaires continue to have a dominant influence in social science research. Despite my reservations about self-reports in studies of well-being, there is much to be learned from the telephone interviews and self-administered questionnaires used in Brim, Ryff, and Kessler, *How Healthy Are We?*

37 Good discussions of problems regarding the location of suitable indicators are found in Leo Noordegraaf and Jan Luiten van Zanden, "Early modern economic growth and the standard of living: did labour benefit from Holland's Golden Age?" in Davids and Lucassen, *A Miracle Mirrored*, 410-437; Van Zanden, "What happened to the Standard of Living"; Enrica Chiappero Martinetti, "A Multidimensional Assessment of Well-Being Based on Sen's Functioning Approach," *Revista Internazionale di Scienze Sociali* 108 (2000):207-239; and Susan Harkness, "Social and Political Indicators of Human Well-Being" in McGillivray, *Human Well-Being*, 88-112.

38 For a somewhat different concern with emotions in past times and places, see Barbara H. Rosenwein, "Worrying about Emotions in History," *American Historical Review* 3 (June 2002):821-845.

39 Many of these "ego-documents," as they are called, have been published in R. Lindeman, Y. Scherf, and R.M. Dekker, *Egodocumenten van Noord-Nederlanders uit de zestiende tot begin negentiende eeuw. Een chronologische lijst*. Haarlem: Stichting Egodocumenten, 1993. Dekker has done pioneering work on the importance, strengths, and weaknesses of ego-documents in the Netherlands. Other scholars have also utilized such sources. For comments on daily life by three well-placed men in Dutch society, see Mieke B. Smits-Veldt, "Images of Private Life in Some Early-Seventeenth-Century Ego-Documents" in Wheelock and Seeff, *The Public and Private*, 164-177.

40 Lindeman, Scherf, and Dekker, *Egodocumenten*. Among the 125 ego-documents, only nine were written by women. A more recent publication shows a limited correspondence from women in the Dutch seventeenth century. Annemarie Armbrust, Marguérite Corporaal & Marjolein van Dekken, eds., *'Dat gy mij niet vergeet'. Correspondentie van vrouwen in de zeventiende en achttiende eeuw*. Amsterdam: Aksant Academic Publishers, 2006.

41 Such feelings are expressed in the correspondence of the wealthy Van der Meulen and Huydecoper families discussed in Luuc Kooijmans, *Vriendschap en de Kunst van Het Overleven in de Zeventiende en Achttiende Eeuw*, Amsterdam: Uitgeverij Bert Bakker, 1997. With grief, poems were a medium for some people to express their bereavement. See, for example, Rudolf Dekker, *Uit de schaduw in 't grote licht: Kinderen in egodocumenten van de Gouden Eeuw tot de Romantiek*. Amsterdam: Wereldbibliotheek, 1995, 215.

42 As pointed out by two experts on the use of "ego-documents," they are sometimes a highly misleading source of evidence. See Arianne Baggerman and Rudolf Dekker, "'De Gevaarlijkste van Alle Bronnen: Egodocumenten, nieuwe wegen en perspectieven,'" *Tijdschrift voor Sociale en Economische Geschiedenis* 1 (2004):3-22.

43 Dekker says that introspection in ego-documents occurs only after the middle of the eighteenth century. Rudolf Dekker, "Egodocuments in the Netherlands from the Sixteenth to the Nineteenth Century" in Erin Griffey, ed., *Envisioning Self and Status: Self-Representation in the Low Countries, 1499-1700*. Hull: Association for Low Countries Studies in Great Britain and Ireland, 1999, 271.

44 For a critical look at the historical profession in this regard, see Bonnie G. Smith, *The Gender of History: Men, Women, and Historical Practice*. Cambridge: Harvard University Press, 1998.

45 Valuable exceptions are Dekker, *Uit de schaduw*; and Smits-Veldt, "Images of Private Life." Amelang has uncovered a fairly large number of artisan autobiographies in early modern Europe. Most, however, are characterized by an absence of reflection about personal feelings and sentiments. James S. Amelang, *The Flight of Icarus: Artisan Autobiography in Early Modern Europe*. Stanford, California: Stanford University Press, 1998.

46 This is discussed with considerable insight in Ludmilla Jordanova, *History in Practice*. London: Arnold, 2000:94-100.

47 See, in this regard, J.M. Barbalet, *Emotion, Social Theory, and Social Structure: A Macrosociological Approach*. Cambridge: Cambridge University Press, 2001.

48 For examples of feelings of both humiliation and pride arising from relationships working as a waitress, hotel maid, house cleaner, nursing home aide, and salesperson, see Ehrenreich, and from working on the bottling line in a pickle factory, and as a care assistant in a private old people's home, Adams. Barbara Ehrenreich, *Nickel and Dimed: On (Not) Getting By in America*. New York: Henry Holt and Company, 2001; and Fran Adams, *Below the Breadline: Living on the Minimum Wage*. London: Profile Books, 2002. Anyone who has ever done low-wage work knows such feelings. See also James C. Scott, *Domination and the Arts of Resistance: Hidden Transcripts*. New Haven and London: Yale University Press, 1990; Sandra Lee Bartky, *Femininity and Domination*. New York and London: Routledge, 1990; William Ian Miller, *Humiliation*. Ithaca and London: Cornell University Press, 1993; and Mia Bay, *The White Image in the Black Mind: African-American Ideas about White People, 1830-1925*. New York: Oxford University Press, 2000.

49 Once the province of psychology, a concern with feelings and emotions has become a focus of attention for historians, sociologists, and other scholars in recent years. For a useful overview, see Scott McLemee, "Getting Emotional," *The Chronicle of Higher Education*, February 21, 2003:1-12.

50 I discuss emotions at some length in Phillips, *Just Social Order*, 156-157, 208-223. For critical overviews by two historians of the main currents in research on emotions today, see Jeroen Deploige, "Studying Emotions: The Medievalist as Human Scientist;" and Walter Prevenier, "Methodological and Historiographical Footnotes on Emotions in the Middle Ages and the Early Modern Period" in Elodie Lecuppre-Desjardin and Anne-Laure Van Bruaene, eds., *Emotions in the Heart of the City (14th-16th century)*. Turnhout, Belgium: Brepols, 2005, 3-24, and 273-293, respectively.

CHAPTER 1

1 Knowledge of this hierarchical order of dignitaries entering the new Town Hall comes from Hans Bontemantel. Himself a member of Amsterdam's city council from 1652-1672, he kept systematic notes concerning the affairs of the city government. Hans Bontemantel, *De Regeeringe van Amsterdam, Soo in 't Civiel als Crimineel en Militaire (1653-1672)*. Published by G.W. Kernkamp. 's-Gravenhage, 1897. Vol. two, 61. The translation is mine.

2 Katherine Fremantle, *The Baroque Town Hall of Amsterdam*. Utrecht: Haentjens

Dekker & Gumbert, 1959, 19, and Illustration 15; and Sjoerd Faber, Jacobine Huisken, and Friso Lammertse, trans. Michael Hoyle, *Van heeren, die hunn' stoel en kussen niet beschaermen: het stadsbestuur van Amsterdam in de 17e en 18e eeuw*. Trans. in English as *Lords, who seat nor cushion do ashame: the government of Amsterdam in the 17th and 18th centuries*. Amsterdam: Stichting Koninklijk Paleis, 1987.

3   Maarten Prak, "Velerlei soort van volk: Sociale verhouding in Amsterdam in de zeventiende Eeuw," *Amstelodamum* (1999):29-54; and Erika Kuijpers and Maarten Prak, "Burger, ingezetene, vreemdeling: burgerschap in Amsterdam in de 17e en 18e eeuw" in Joost Kloek and Karin Tilmans, *Burger*. Amsterdam: Amsterdam University Press, 2002, 113-132.

4   Israel presents a clear and extended discussion of the *regenten*. Jonathan Israel, *The Dutch Republic: Its Rise, Greatness and Fall, 1477-1806*. Oxford: Clarendon Press, 1995. For the activities, responsibilities, and power of the city government, see J.L. Price, *Holland and the Dutch Republic in the Seventeenth Century: The Politics of Particularism*. Oxford: Clarendon Press, 1994.

5   Antonio Porta, *Joan en Gerrit Corver: De politieke macht van Amsterdam (1702-1748)*. Assen: van Gorcum, 1975, 26.

6   The power of the regents far exceeded that of the nobility, who consisted of some two or three hundred families living mostly around The Hague. The nobility counted for little in Amsterdam. Thera Wijsenbeek-Olthuis, "Noblesse Oblige: Material Culture of the Nobility in Holland. in Anton Schuurman and Pieter Spierenburg, eds., *Private Domain, Public Inquiry: Families and Life-Styles in the Netherlands and Europe, 1550 to the Present*. Hilversum: Verloren, 1996, 112.

7   Porta, *Joan and Gerrit Corver*, 377, says that in 1747 this circle consisted of 80 men at the most. If anything, even fewer men would have been involved fifty or a hundred years earlier.

8   Tilly speaks of Amsterdam and other cities at the time as "largely autonomous city-states." Charles Tilly, *Coercion, Capital, and European States, AD 990-1990*. Cambridge: Basil Blackwell, 1990, 30.

9   Kistemaker and van Gelder, *Amsterdam*, 108.

10 Van Nierop, "Popular participation," 273.

11 Elizabeth Edwards, "Roles, Status and Power: Amsterdam Regents in the Later Part of the Seventeenth Century" in Griffey, ed., *Envisioning Self*, 218-237.

12 Porta, *Joan en Gerrit Corver*, 23.

13 I draw here on Kuijpers and Prak, "Burger, ingezetenen, vreemdeling." Also informative is Lotte van de Pol, *Amsterdams hoerdom: Prostitutie in de zeventiende en achttiende eeuw*. Amsterdam: Wereldbibliotheek, 1966, chapter 3, in which she discusses people losing their citizenship when acting dishonorably.

14 See the discussion in Craig E. Harline, *Pamphlets, Printing, and Political Culture in the Early Dutch Republic*. Dordrecht: Martinus Nijhoff, 1987.

15 Prak, "Velerlei soort," 43-44.

16 The definitive work in this regard is Bos, "*Uyt Liefde*. See also Sandra Bos, "A tradition of giving and receiving: Mutual aid within the guild system" in Maarten Prak, Catharina Lis, Jan Lucassen, and Hugo Soly, eds., *Craft Guilds in the Early Modern Low Countries: Work, Power, and Representation*. Aldershot and Burlington: Ashgate, 2006, 174-193.

17 Maarten Prak, "The politics of intolerance: citizenship and religion in the Dutch Republic (seventeenth to eighteenth centuries)" in R. Po-Chia Hsia and Henk van Nierop, eds., *Calvinism and Religious Toleration in the Dutch Golden Age*. Cambridge: Cambridge University Press, 2002, 161-162.

18 A woman who married a male citizen also acquired citizenship automatically. Kuijpers and Prak, "Burger, ingezetene, vreemdeling," 120, 130.

19 In the period 1681-1685, however, the regents intervened in regard to the settlement of French Protestant refugees from France. In an attempt to attract lucrative manufacturing to Amsterdam – and prevent it going to Rotterdam, Delft, or elsewhere – the city governors provided the refugees with citizenship of the city as a gift, exempted them from all city taxes and responsibilities for a period of three years, and assured them immediate admittance to the relevant guilds. In addition, they proposed providing them with places to work and to live. A total of 704 refugees came to the city in the 1681-1685 period. I draw here on Cees Cruson, "De vluchtelingenpolitiek van de Amsterdamse magistraat in de periode 1681-1685" in C.I. Cruson and J. Dronkers, eds., *De Stad: Beheersing van de stedelijke ruimte*. Bohn Stafleu Van Loghum, 1990:89-109.

20 Maarten Prak, "Armenzorg 1500-1800" in Jacques van Gerwen and Marco H.D. van Leeuwen, eds., *Studies over Zekerheidsarrangementen: Risicos, risicobestrijding en verzekeringen in Nederland vanaf de Middeleeuwen*. Amsterdam/The Hague: Nederlandsch Economisch Historisch Archief Verbond van Verzekeraars, 1998, 69.

21 Kuijpers, *Migrantenstad*, 338.

22 Jan de Vries and Ad van der Woude, *The First Modern Economy: Success, Failure, and Perseverance of the Dutch Economy, 1500-1815*. Cambridge: Cambridge University Press, 1997, 679.

23 Utilizing a list of the occupations and incomes of household heads assessed for taxes at a somewhat later period, they counted all the men in Amsterdam who received a salary from the city, the VOC (Dutch East Indies Company), the WIC (West Indies Company), or from institutions for the care of the poor, as well as all the men working as lawyers, surgeons, bookkeepers, and in other "free" professions. A total of 1,248 men were found to occupy such positions. Lee Soltow and Jan Luiten van Zanden, *Income and Wealth Inequality in the Netherlands, 16th-20th Century*. Amsterdam: Het Spinhuis, 1998, 45-46.

24 Kuijpers and Prak, "Burger, ingezetene," 116. Lucassen suggests a figure of 25-30 percent. Jan Lucassen, "Labour and Early Economic Development" in Davids and Lucassen, *A Mirror Mirrored*, 406.

25 Nusteling, *Welvaart en werkgelegenheid*, 239.

26 Maarten Prak, "Het oude recht der burgeren: De betekenis van burgerschap in het Amsterdam van de zestiende en zeventiende eeuw" in Hendrix and Meijer Drees, *Beschaafde Burgers*, 26.

27 Kuijpers and Prak, "Burger, ingezetene," 127-128.

28 Ibid., 130.

29 My estimate is in line with the conclusion offered by van Zanden and Prak. "Although exact figures are lacking, it can safely be assumed that between a quarter and a third of the urban population had formal citizenship rights." Jan Luiten van Zanden and Maarten Prak, "Towards an economic interpretation of citizenship: The Dutch Republic between Medieval communes and modern nation states." Unpublished manuscript, 2004, 17.

30 Van Nierop, "Popular participation," 278.

31 In 1664 one in every eight Amsterdammers died. Nusteling, *Welvaart*, 39.

32 Prak, *The Dutch Republic*, 144.

33 Jan de Vries, *European Urbanization, 1500-1800*. London: Methuen, 1984, 210.

34 Israel, *The Dutch Republic*, 622-627.

35 Kuijpers, *Migrantenstad*, 379, Table 2.18.

36 Ibid., my calculations.
37 Peter Clark, "Migration in England during the late seventeenth and early eighteenth centuries," *Past and Present* 83 (1979):57-90.
38 Jan Lucassen, *Migrant Labour in Europe 1600-1900*. Trans. Donald A. Bloch. London: Crown Helm, 1987, especially 42-51.
39 Jan Lucassen, "The Netherlands, the Dutch, and long distance migration in the late sixteenth to early nineteenth centuries" in N. Canny, ed., *Europeans on the Move. Studies on European Migration, 1500-1800*. Oxford: Oxford University Press, 1994:153-191.
40 Kuijpers, *Migrantenstad*, 84.
41 Lotte van de Pol and Erika Kuijpers, "Poor Women's Migration to the City: The Attraction of Amsterdam Health Care and Social Assistance in Early Modern Times," *Journal of Urban History* 32 (November 2005):45.
42 S. Hart, *Geschrift en Getal: Een keuze uit de demografisch-economisch-en sociaal-historische studiën op grond van Amsterdamse en Zaanse archivalia, 1699-1800*. Dordrecht: Hollandsche Studien, 1976, 128.
43 Ibid., 195.
44 Ad Knotter, "Vreemdelingen in Amsterdam in de 17e eeuw: groepsvorming, arbeid en ondernemerschap," *Historisch Tijdschrift Holland* 27 (February 1995):219-235.
45 Kuijpers. *Migrantenstad*, 336.
46 Ibid., 99-100.
47 This is suggested by Rudolf Dekker, "Labour Conflicts and Working-Class Culture in Early Modern Holland," *International Review of Social History* 35 (1990):385.
48 I consider this in later chapters.
49 For discussions of migrants finding work and a place to stay in Amsterdam, see Marc A. van Alphen, "The Female Side of Dutch Shipping: Financial Bonds of Seamen Ashore in the 17th and 18th Centuries" in Jr. Bruijn and W.F.J. Mörzen Bruyns, eds., *Anglo-Dutch Mercantile Marine Relations, 1700-1850*. Amsterdam: Rijksmuseum, 1991, 125-133; and Roelof van Gelder, *Het Oost-Indisch avontuur: Duitsers in dienst van de VOC (1600-1800)*. Nijmegen: Uitgeverij SUN, 1997, 133-143.
50 See Noordegraaf, *Hollands welvaren?*, 52-55.
51 R. van Gelder, "De VOC en de WIC: De invloed van de wereldhandel, 17e-18e eeuw" in W.F. Heinemeijer et al, eds., *Amsterdam in Kaarten: Verandering van de stad in vier eeuwen cartografie*. Ede/Antwerp: Zomer & Keuning, 1987, 73.
52 De Vries and van der Woude, *First Modern Economy*, 643.
53 Lucassen, *Migrant Labour*, 156.
54 Jaap R. Bruijn, *The Dutch Navy of the Seventeenth and Eighteenth Centuries*. Columbia, South Carolina: University of South Carolina Press, 1993, 124, 129; and C.A. David, "De Zeeman" in H.M. Beliën, A.Th. van Deursen, and G.J. van Setten, eds., *Gestalten van de Gouden Eeuw*. Amsterdam: Bert Bakker, 1995, 108-109, 125.
55 H.L. Switzer, "De Soldaat" in Ibid., 174-179.
56 J.L. van Zanden, *The Rise and Decline of Holland's Economy: Merchant Capitalism and the Labor Market*. Manchester and New York: Manchester University Press, 1993, 62-63.
57 Kuijpers, *Migrantenstad*, 217.
58 The holdings of the general library at the University of Amsterdam include a guide to help native English speakers learn Dutch. Wm. Sewel, *A Compendious Guide to the Low-Dutch Language. The second edition, with Some Additions*. Amsterdam. Printed for the Widow of Stephen Swart, Bookseller, on the West-side of the Exchange, at the sign of the Crowned Bible, 1706. For the problem of the Dutch learning English, see

P.L.M. Loonen, *For to Learne to Buye and Sell: Learning English in the Low Dutch Area Between 1500 and 1800, A Critical Survey*. Grongingen: Universiteits-drukkerij, 1990. Proefschrift [dissertation], University of Nijmegen.

59   E.H. Lennenberg, *Biological Foundations of Language*. New York: Wiley, 1967.

60   Kuijpers presents figures for age at the time of migration for men and women marrying for the first time in the year 1600. Roughly two-thirds of both had been older than 14 when they migrated and may have had some problems learning the language. *Migrantenstad*, 363, Table 2-5. She indicates an absence of similar evidence for later periods.

61   Maarten Schneider and Jan Hemels, *De Nederlandse krant 1618-1978*. Baarn: Wereldvenster, 1979, 78-82.

62   Collections of the *Amsterdamse Courant* can be found in several libraries in the Netherlands. A small number of scholars have examined seventeenth-century advertisements as evidence about paintings, atlases, other household furnishings and decorations, as well as clothing, materials, jewelry, and accessories. I draw below on M.G.A. (Bix) Schipper-van Lottum, *Advertenties en Berichten in de Amsterdamse Courant uitgetrokken op Kleding, Stoffen, Sieraden en Accessoires tussen de jaren 1672-1765*. Amsterdam: Gopher Publishers, 1993. Notices about stolen goods and missing persons often give a brief description of the appearance and clothing of the person involved. In some instances, mention is made of language, although that is not their main concern.

63   These three examples come, respectively, from Ibid., Aflevering 3 A-B, number 806, and Aflevering 2, numbers 467 and 479. The mentions of language in the advertisements represent an historical "trace," and are examples of unintentional evidence. That is to say, language was not mentioned with the intention of revealing its centrality in people's lives but was mentioned in terms of other concerns. For a distinction between traces and sources in modern historical scholarship, see Allan Megill, *Historical Knowledge, Historical Error: A Contemporary Guide to Practice*. Chicago: University of Chicago Press, 2007, 25-26.

64   See, for example, Richard Alba and Victor Nee, *Remaking the American Mainstream: Assimilation and Contemporary Immigration*. Cambridge, Mass.: Harvard University Press, 2003.

65   Exceptions are Kuijpers, *Migrantenstad*; and Lex Heerma van Vos, "North Sea Culture, 1550-1800" in Juliette Roding and Lex Heerma van Vos, eds., *The North Sea and Culture (1550-1800*. Hilversum: Verloren, 1996, 25-28.

66   Erika Kuijpers, "Lezen en schrijven: Onderzoek naar het alfabetiseringsniveau in zeventiende-eeuws Amsterdam," *Tijdschrift voor Sociale Geschiedenis* 23 (1997):507.

67   Cressy notes that "It is probable that the level of literacy measured by counting signatures and marks overestimates the number able to write with ease, underestimates the number able to read with hesitation, and indicates with some accuracy the number who were functionally literate by the standards of the seventeenth century." D. Cressy, *Literacy and Social Order: Reading and Writing in Tudor and Stuart England*. Cambridge: Cambridge University Press, 1980, 54-55.

68   Kuijpers, "Lezen en schrijven," 514-517. She concludes her analysis of literacy in seventeenth-century Amsterdam with the observation that little is known about the function and practice of writing (and reading) in the Dutch Republic.

69   "See, for example, Leo Noordegraaf and Jan Luiten van Zanden, "Early modern economic growth and the standard of living: did labour benefit from Holland's Golden Age?" in Davids and Lucassen, *A Mirror Mirrored*, 410-437.

70   Van Zanden, "What Happened to the Standard of Living?, 183-185.

71 Kuijpers, *Migrantenstad*, 344-354.
72 Ibid., 285.

CHAPTER 2

1 Johan E. Elias, *De vroedschap van Amsterdam*. Amsterdam: Israel, 1903-05, vol. 2, 617.
2 Maarten Hell, "Een 'profitabel' ambt: Het inkomen van de schouten tijdens de Republiek," *Amstelodamum* 84 (1997):137-148.
3 Elias, *Vroedschap*, 617.
4 Elias, *Vroedschap*.
5 Soltow and van Zanden, *Income and Wealth Inequality*, 38.
6 Ibid., 39.
7 Ibid., 41.
8 W.F.H. Oldewelt, *Kohier van de personeele quotisatie te Amsterdam, 1742*. Amsterdam: Genootschap Amstelodamum, 1945. A second source of tax data for the time is the *Liberaale Gifte* from 1747. See Tirtsah Levie and Henk Zantkuijl, *Wonen in Amsterdam in de 17de en 18de eeuw*. Amsterdam: Amsterdams Historisch Museum, 1980, 28-34.
9 Lee Soltow, "Annual Inequality through Four Centuries: Conjectures for Amsterdam." Unpublished manuscript, no date.
10 De Vries and van der Woude, *The First Modern Economy*, 565.
11 I originally calculated these figures in Muizelaar and Phillips, *Picturing Men and Women*, 22-25. I draw on that earlier discussion in what follows.
12 See the discussion in A.Th. van Deursen, *Plain Lives in a Golden Age: Popular Culture, Religion and Society in Seventeenth-Century Holland*. Cambridge: Cambridge University Press, 1991, 161-170.
13 A rare exception among the city's burgomasters was Cornelis Pietersz Hooft who complained about his colleagues' use of inside knowledge to line their pockets. Paul Spies, Koen Kleijn, Jos Smit, and Ernest Kurpershoek, eds., *The Canals of Amsterdam*. The Hague: SDU Uitgeverij Koninginnegracht, 1993, 102.
14 Julia Adams, "The familial state: Elite family practices and state-making in the early modern Netherlands." *Theory and Society* 23 (1994):505-539.
15 Porta, *Joan en Gerrit Corver*, 35-36.
16 Price, *Holland and the Dutch Republic*, 95.
17 Soltow and van Zanden, *Income and Wealth Inequality*. 50.
18 The wealth of the regents clearly involved social and cultural capital as well as that of an economic nature.
19 De Vries and van der Woude, *First Modern Economy*, 595.
20 Oldewelt, *Kohier*, 15-16.
21 Henk van Nierop, "Politics and the People of Amsterdam." In Peter van Kessel and Elisja Schulte, eds., *Rome*Amsterdam: Two Growing Cities in Seventeenth-Century Europe*. Amsterdam: Amsterdam University Press, 1997, 162.
22 Soltow and van Zanden, *Income and Wealth Inequality*, 46.
23 A.Th. van Deursen, "Rembrandt and his Age: The Life of an Amsterdam Burgher." In Christopher Brown, Jan Kelch, and Pieter van Thiel, eds., *Rembrandt: The Master and His Workshop*. New Haven and London: Yale University Press, 1991, 41.

24 Although the number of seamstresses is unknown, for women this was the most common type of paid work after domestic service. Seamstresses in Amsterdam, who had organized their own guild in 1579, were subordinate to the authority of the tailors' guild. Herald Deceulaer and Bibi Panhuysen, "Dressed to work: a gendered comparison of the tailoring trades in the Northern and Southern Netherlands, 16th to 18th centuries." In Prak et al, *Craft Guilds*, 147.

25 P. Lourens and J. Lucassen, "Ambachtsgilden binnen een handelskapitalistische stad: aanzetten voor een analyse van Amsterdam rond 1700." *NEHA-Jaarboek voor economische, bedrijfs-en techniekgesciedenis* 61 (1998):121-159. For early modern Europe more generally, see James R. Farr, *Artisans in Europe, 1300-1914*. Cambridge: Cambridge University Press, 2000.

26 Bos, "*Uyt Liefde*, 111-134.

27 I draw on Maarten Prak, "Corporate politics in the Low Countries: guilds as institutions, 14th to 18th Centuries." In Prak et al, *Craft Guilds*, 100-104.

28 For a comparison with monarchical England, see W. Speck, "Britain and the Dutch Republic." In Davids and Lucassen, *A Miracle Mirrored*, 173-195.

29 See Milja van Tielhof, "Stedelijke Regulering van Drensten op de stapelmarkt: De Amsterdamse Korengilden." In Clé Lesger and Leo Noordegraaf, eds., *Ondernemers & Bestuurders: Economie en politiek in de Noordelijke Nederlanden in de late Middeleeuwen en vroegmoderne tijd*. Amsterdam: NEHA, 1999, 491-523.

30 Ronald de Jager, "Meester, leerjongen, leertijd: Een analyse van zeventiende-eeuwse Noord-Nederlandse leerlingcontracten van kunstschilders, goud- en zilversmeden," *Oud Holland*, 104 (1990):79.

31 Sharpe suggests that apprenticeships, as a method of raising and educating young males, had a social control function as well. Apprenticeships, he writes, took young males "into a context where they were subjected to the discipline, potentially backed by physical punishment, of a master's control." There they were socialized for adult life. Although Sharpe is speaking of the situation in early modern England, more generally, apprenticeships had a similar social control function in the Dutch Republic. James A. Sharpe, "Social Control in Early Modern England: The Need for a Broad Perspective." In Herman Roodenburg and Pieter Spierenburg, eds., *Social Control in Europe, 1500-1800*. Colombus: Ohio State University Press, 2004, 44.

32 Nusteling, *Welvaart en werkgelegenheid*, 151-152.

33 For a critical view, see Willem Frijhoff, "Medical education and early modern Dutch medical practitioners: towards a critical approach." In Hilary Marland and Margaret Pelling, eds., *The Task of Healing: Medicine, religion and gender in England and the Netherlands, 1450-1800*. Rotterdam: Erasmus, 1996, 205-220.

34 Bos, *Uyt Liefde*, 55-85.

35 Marieke Doornick and Erika Kuijpers, *De geschoolde stad: Onderwijs in Amsterdam in de Gouden Eeuw*. Amsterdam: Historisch Seminarium van de Universiteit van Amsterdam, 1993, 47.

36 Bos, *Uyt Liefde*, 63.

37 Ernst van de Wetering, "De Schilder." In Beliën, Van Deursen, and Van Setten, *Gestalten*, 223-229.

38 De Jager, "Meester, leerjongen," No. 13 in Appendix, 99.

39 Maarten Prak, "Guilds and the development of the art market during the Dutch Golden Age," *Simiolus* 30 (2003):243. Nor did the painters' guild require a masterpiece. Ibid, 244.

40 This conforms with the estimate of Ad van der Woude, "The Volume and Value of Paintings in Holland at the Time of the Dutch Republic." In David Freedberg and

Jan de Vries, eds., *Art in History/History in Art*. Santa Monica: Getty Center for the History of Art and the Humanities, 1991.

41 Oldewelt, *Kohier*, indicates a lack of exact information about guild membership for 1742, but argues that the number listed in guilds for 1688 would have remained about the same at the latter date. This enables him to chart the earnings of men in different guilds. His figures are used here.

42 Ibid., 12-16.

43 With membership in the English Reformed Church, for example, the trade of each new member was given. Alice Clare Carter, *The English Reformed Church in Amsterdam in the Seventeenth Century*. Amsterdam: Municipal Archives, 1964, 116-117.

44 De Vries and van der Woude, *First Modern Economy*, 563.

45 Lourens and Lucassen, "Ambachtsgilden."

46 Kuijpers, *Migrantenstad*, 236-244, 260-270, 283-285.

47 Ibid., 406, Table 6-1.

48 Ibid., 213-214.

49 Ibid.

50 Leo Noordegraaf, "Dutch Industry in the Golden Age." In Karl Davids and Leo Noordegraaf, eds., *The Dutch Economy in the Golden Age*. Amsterdam: The Netherlands Economic History Archives, 1995, 146.

51 Catharina Lis and Hugo Soly, "Craft guilds in comparative perspective: the Northern and Southern Netherlands, a Survey." In Prak et al, *Craft Guilds*, 19. At the same time, the city fathers in Amsterdam often set a limit on the number of journeymen that a master could employ.

52 Maarten Prak, "Moral Order in the World of Work: Social Control and the Guilds in Europe" in Roodenburg and Spierenburg, *Social Control*, 186. This is a useful discussion of guilds in early modern Europe more generally.

53 Van Nierop, "Private Interests, Public Policies" in Wheelock and Seeff, *The Public and Private*, 33-39.

54 Noordegraaf, "Dutch Industry," 149.

55 Rudolf Dekker, "Handwerkslieden en arbeiders in Holland van de zestiende tot de achttiende eeuw: Identiteit, cultuur en protest" in Peter te Boekhorst, Peter Burke, and Willem Frijhoff, eds., *Cultuur en maatschappij in Nederland, 1500-1850: Een historisch-anthropologisch perspectief*. Boon: Open Universiteit, 1992, 128.

56 De Vries and van der Woude, *First Modern Economy*, 646. For discussions of the development of labor market segmentation in the seventeenth century, see Jan Lucassen, *Jan, Jan Salie en diens kinderen: Vergelijkend onderzoek naar continuiteit en discontinuiteit in de ontwikkeling van arbeidsverhoudingen*. Amsterdam: Stichting beheer IIGS, 1991; and Jan de Vries, "The Labour Market" in Davids and Noordegraaf, *The Dutch Economy*, 55-78.

57 Leo Noordegraaf, *Daglonen in Alkmaar, 1500-1800*. Amsterdam: Historisch Seminarium van de Universiteit van Amsterdam, 1984. 72-73. There were (partial) exceptions. When males and females received the same piece rates for the spinning work they did, for example, females were underrepresented in the best-paid segments of the industry and thus earned less. Elise van Nederveen Meerkerk, *De draad in eigen handen*, Chapter 8.

58 De Vries and van der Woude, *First Modern Economy*, 616; See also the informative article by Huibert Schijf and Bernadette van Woerkom, "Boekhouders en Peperwerkers: Werknemers van de Verenigde Oostindische Compagnie in Amsterdam tussen 1602 en 1689" in *De Verenigde Oostindisch Compagnie in Amsterdam*, verslag van een werkgroep, Amsterdam, 1982, 148.

59 De Vries and van der Woude, *First Modern Economy*, 562.
60 Nusteling, *Welvaart*, estimates that most earned between 180 and 200 guilders per annum, 171.
61 Schijf and van Woerkom, "Boekhouders and Peperwerkers," 116-118.
62 See my discussion of relevant studies in Phillips, *Just Social Order*, 386-392.
63 For a powerful argument about the importance of autonomy for individual well-being, see Amartya Sen, *Inequality Reexamined*. Oxford: Oxford University Press, 1992.
64 For a detailed study of credit in the early modern period, see Craig Muldrew, *The Economy of Obligation: The Culture of Credit and Social Relations in Early Modern England*. Basingstoke: Macmillan Press, 1998. See also, Anne E.C. McCants, "Inequality among the poor of eighteenth century Amsterdam," *Explorations in Economic History* 44 (2007):1-21.
65 Probate Inventory NAA 6240, folio 49-91.
66 Even though the guild for wine merchants was one of the city's most exclusive guilds, Kramer was unusually rich by their standards.
67 I am indebted to Bengtsson for the idea of a social ladder of responses to economic stress, although my rank order of options differs markedly from his. Tommy Bengtsson, "Living Standards and Economic Stress" in Bengtsson et al, *Life Under Pressure*, 35-36. In another study in which Bengtsson is involved, the ability to overcome short-term economic stress is used as an indicator of the standard of living and well-being. See Allen, Bengtsson, and Dribe, *Living Standards in the Past*, 427-460.
68 Bos, "A tradition of giving and receiving" in Prak et al, *Craft Guilds*, 184.
69 Leo Noordegraaf, "De arme" in Beliën et al, *Gestalten*, 319.
70 Nusteling, *Welvaart*, 115.
71 Ibid., 344-347.
72 See, for example, H. Diederiks, "Arm en rijk in Amsterdam: Wonen naar welstand in de 16e-18e eeuw" in W.F. Heinemeijer and others, eds., *Amsterdam in Kaarten*. Ede: Zomer & Keuning, 1987, 48-51; and Levie and Zantkuijl, *Wonen in Amsterdam*.
73 Noordegraaf, "De arme," 345.
74 Ibid.

CHAPTER 3

1 Sir William Temple, *Observations upon the United Provinces of the Netherlands*. Edited by Sir George Clark. Oxford: Clarendon Press, 1972. Originally published in 1673, 75-80.
2 Ibid., 80.
3 Ibid., 95.
4 De Vries and van der Woude, *The First Modern Economy*, 183.
5 See, for example, E.A. Wrigley, *Poverty, Progress, and Population*. Cambridge: Cambridge University Press, 2004, 355.
6 De Vries and van der Woude, *First Modern Economy*, 73.
7 For a comparison of the Dutch Republic with France and England during the seventeenth century, see de Vries, *European Urbanization*, 45-46.
8 This lack of knowledge about mortality is evidenced in the limited listings under "mortality" in de Vries and van der Woude, *First Modern Economy*, as well as elsewhere in the literature concerning the Dutch seventeenth century.

9   Philip T. Hoffman, David S. Jacks, Patricia A. Levin, and Peter H. Lindert, "Sketching the Rise of Real Inequality in Early Modern Europe." In Allen, Bengtsson, and Dribe, *Living Standards*, 133-138.

10 Leiden, with a population of 60,000 inhabitants, was the second largest city at the time. These population estimates for the year 1672 come from Israel, *The Dutch Republic*, 621.

11 Caspar Commelin, *Beschrijving van Amsterdam*. Amsterdam, 1693, 235.

12 Marco H.D. van Leeuwen and James E. Oeppen, "Reconstructing the Demographic Regime of Amsterdam 1681-1920," *Economic and Social History in the Netherlands* 5 (1993):61-102.

13 For a useful overview, see Mark Jenner, "Environment, Health and Population" in Peter Elmer, ed., *The Healing Arts: Health, Disease and Society in Europe 1500-1800*. Manchester: Manchester University Press, 2004, 284-314.

14 Mary J. Dobson, "Contours of death: disease, mortality, and the environment in early modern England," *Health Transition Review* 2 (1992), 79.

15 Ibid.

16 Cippola describes a mistaken theoretical paradigm in this regard. "The paradigm of medical science consisted not of microbes and their vectors but of humours and miasmas...People spoke of an ill-defined but universally recognized 'corruption and infection of the air', which degenerated into highly poisonous 'sticky' miasmas that killed the person they infected, either by inhalation or by contact." Carlo M. Cipolla, *Miasmas and Disease: Public Health and the Environment in the pre-industrial Age*. Trans. by Elizabeth Potter. New Haven and London: Yale University Press, 1992, 4.

17 James C. Riley, *Rising Life Expectancy : A Global History*. Cambridge: Cambridge University Press, 2001.

18 Within-city comparisons for cities today are also scarce. One such study is Colin McCord and Harold Freeman, "Excess Mortality in Harlem," *New England Journal of Medicine* 322 (1990):173-177.

19 The exceptions are mainly for early modern England. An exploration of the relationship between disease, social structure, and the built environment in seventeenth-century London is found in Justin Champion, "Epidemics and the built environment in 1665." In J.A.I. Champion, ed., *Epidemic Disease in London*. Centre for Metropolitan History Working Papers Series, No. 1, 1993, 35-52. Even more wide-ranging is John Landers, *Death and the Metropolis: studies in the demographic history of London 1670-1830*. Cambridge: Cambridge University Press, 1993. Also informative is Mary J. Dobson, *Contours of death and disease in early modern England*. Cambridge: Cambridge University Press, 1997.

20 Cited in de Vries, *European Urbanization*, 184.

21 Landers, *Death and the Metropolis*, 158.

22 Van Leeuwen and Oeppen, "Reconstructing the Demographic Regime," 61-102. They use life annuities from the time as the best available evidence for life expectancy in Amsterdam. See p.80, Table 7. Life annuities were purchased mainly by the wealthy: people who could look forward to a longer life than the majority of those in the city. In any case, evidence is scarce and van Leeuwen and Oeppen offer a "reconstruction."

23 Characteristics of the physical environment have an effect on mortality independent of the characteristics of the people living there. See, for example, S. MacIntyre and A. Ellaway, "Ecological approaches: Rediscovering the role of physical and social environment" in L.F. Berkman and I. Kawachi, eds., *Social Epidemiology*. New York: Oxford University Press, 2000, 332-348.

24 Riley presents an excellent discussion, *Rising Life Expectancy*, 162.

25 Ibid., 21.

26 Marzio Barbagli and David I. Kertzer, "Introduction" in David I. Kertzer and Marzio Barbagli, eds., *Family Life in Early Modern Times, 1500-1789*. New Haven and London: Yale University Press, 2001, xiii. For Amsterdam, the earliest evidence available is from 1795 when the percentage was 27.4%. Herman Diederiks, *Een Stad in Verval: Amsterdam Omstreeks 1800, demografisch, economisch, ruimtelijk*. Amsterdam: Meppel, 1982, 32.

27 Michael W. Finn, *The European Demographic System, 1500-1820*. Suffolk, The Harvester Press, 1981, 17. For Amsterdam in the period 1777-1811, the figure was 44%. Diederiks, *Een Stad in Verval*, 33.

28 Ibid., 130-131, Table 9.

29 Calculated from van Leeuwen and Oeppen, "Reconstructing the Demographic Regime."

30 Alfred W. Crosby, *Ecological Imperialism: The Biological Expansion of Europe, 900-1900*. Cambridge: Cambridge University Press, 1986, 201.

31 For useful overviews of present-day knowledge about the influence of residential and housing environments on health, see R. Burridge and D. Ormandy, eds., *Unhealthy housing: Research, remedies, and reform*. London: E. and F.N. Spon, 1993; J.R. Dunn, "Housing and health inequalities: Review and prospects for research," *Housing Studies* 15 (2000):341-366; World Health Organization, "Healthy environments for children." 25 April 2003; and Roderick J. Lawrence, "Housing and health: beyond disciplinary confinement," *Journal of Urban Health* 83 (May 2006):540-549.

32 In constructing this illustration, I draw on Diederiks, *Een Stad in Verval*; and C. Lesger, "Migranten in Amsterdam tijdens de 18e eeuw: residentiele spreiding en positie in de samenleving," *Jaarboek Amstelodamum* 89 (1997):43-68.

33 Ed Taverne, *In 't land van belofte: in de nieue stadt ideaal en werkelijkheid van de stads-uitleg in de Republiek 1580-1680*. Maarssen: Gary Schwartz, 1978, 546-547. An accessible English language discussion of the phases of development of the canal zone is Jannes de Haan, "The greatness and difficulty of the work: The growth of Amsterdam and the construction of the canal zone." In *The Canals of Amsterdam*. Edited by Paul Spies, Koen Kleijn, Jos Smit, and Ernest Kurpershoek. The Hague: SDU Uitgeverij Koninginnegracht, 1993, 28-45.

34 Taverne, *In 't land*, 166.

35 Land along this canal was more expensive than along the other two canals, with some plots selling for 7,000 guilders each. Land on all three canals was auctioned off for the building of large mansions, sometimes constructed on double building lots. Not unexpectedly, the men purchasing the newly created building lots in this prestigious area were the very same men responsible for regulations concerning purchase of the lots. Land speculation by the regent elite was, in fact, widespread. The 200 planned allotments were sold almost immediately. De Haan, "The greatness and difficulty," 40.

36 Ibid., 41.

37 Ibid., 42-43.

38 No one knows the exact percentages. I base my estimates of the percentages residing in the various residential areas mainly on Diederiks, *Stad in Verval*; Lesger, "Migranten in Amsterdam;" and Kuijpers, *Migrantenstad*, 389, Table 4.6. Whatever the exact percentages may have been, the distinctions among the various areas are not in dispute.

39 De Haan, "The greatness and difficulty," 41.

40 B. Speet, "Wonen in de 16ᵉ eeuw: Primitief, vuil en benauwd." In Heinemeijer et al, *Amsterdam in Kaarten*, 25.

41 Renée Kistemaker, "Amsterdam 1399-1700: van 'geringhe visschers' naar een 'kleyne wereldt'" in Ed Taverne and Irmin Visser, eds., *Stedebouw: De geschiedenis van de stad in de Nederlanden van 1500 tot heden*. Nijmegen: Uitgeverij SUN, 1993, 82; Taverne, *In 't land*, 547; and A. Knotter, "De 17ᵉ-eeuwse uitbreidingen" in Heinemeijer et al., *Amsterdam in Kaarten*, 44.

42 R. van Gelder, "De VOC en de WIC" In *Amsterdam in Kaarten*, 73.

43 Another 5-15 percent of the city's population was scattered elsewhere.

44 Families of a middling level also lived on the side streets of the main canals or in areas adjacent to where the rich resided. Some lived on the better streets and canals in the Jordaan, the Eastern and Western Islands, and the Noordse Bosch. But more lived in Amsterdam's old center than anywhere else.

45 Levie and Zantkuyl, *Wonen in Amsterdam*, 17.

46 Even the city's bridges were built to reflect the status of the different residential areas: attractive brick bridges with high arches over the canals where the rich resided, wooden drawbridges elsewhere in Amsterdam. R.E. Kistemaker, "The Public and the Private: Public Space in Sixteenth- and Seventeenth-Century Amsterdam." In Wheelock and Seeff, *The Public and Private*, 21.

47 Just as today, the rich and the rest sometimes mixed on the streets.

48 Little is known about how often people moved from one Amsterdam neighborhood to another. But it probably did not occur very frequently. Most of people's relationships seem to have been with others from the same residential area. In an earlier period in London, marriage partners often came from the same neighborhood. Ian W. Archer, *The Pursuit of Stability: Social Relations in Elizabethan London*. Cambridge: Cambridge University Press, 1991, 75. And in Amsterdam in the early nineteenth century, more than 30 percent of marital partners came from the same neighborhood and another 20 percent had the same address. Diederiks, *Stad in Verval*, 103-104.

49 H. Noordkerk, *Handvesten ofte Privilegien ende Octroyen; Mitsgaders Willekeuren, Constuimen, Ordonnantien en Handleidingen Der Stad Amsterdam*. Amsterdam: Hendrik van Waesberge en Salomon en Petrus Schouten, Boekverkoopers, MDCCXLVIII. Volume 2, 458. The ordinance also specified that people must show the *buurtmeester* the proper respect. Instructions from the city governors indicated that anyone appointed to the position of *buurtmeester* was not given the choice of refusing it. His duties included a number of other responsibilities, including keeping track of the deaths of foundlings placed by the city fathers in private homes in his neighborhood. Volume 2, 463.

50 Kuijpers, *Migrantenstad*, 303.

51 Within neighborhoods, there was always a degree of informal social control over the behavior of others through surveillance, gossip, denouncing people to the authorities, and the like. This was the case everywhere in early modern Europe. Carl A. Hoffman, "Social Control and the Neighborhood in European Cities" in Roodenburg and Spierenburg, *Social Control in Europe*, 309-327.

52 John Walsh, "Skies and Reality in Dutch Landscapes" in Freedberg and de Vries, *Art in history/History in art*, 95.

53 H. J. Zantkuijl, *Bouwen in Amsterdam: Het Woonhuis in de stad*. Amsterdam: Architectura & Natura, 1993, 8-11.

54 J.W. de Zeeuw, "Peat and the Dutch Golden Age: The Historical Meaning of Energy-Attainability," *A.A.G. Bijdragen*, 21. Wageningen, 1978:3-31.

55 Ad van der Woude, Akira Hayami, and Jan de Vries, eds., "Introduction" in *Urban-*

ization in History: A Process of Dynamic Interactions. Oxford: Clarendon Press, 1990, 8-11.

56 Thousands of laborers toiled in the peat bogs to dig and cut the enormous amount of peat necessary to supply the fuel needs of Amsterdam's 200,000 inhabitants and for the city's brewing, distilling, and other energy-intensive industries. The availability of water transport made the supply of fuel easier than if it had been necessary to bring peat and wood into the city on carts. The winters were much more severe than they are now. De Vries and van der Woude, *First Modern Economy*, 21-23. In cold, hard winters, there were periods when water transport was impossible. This is well-documented in Buisman's monumental study of the history of the weather in the Low Countries. J. Buisman, *Duizend Jaar Weer, Wind en Water in De Lage Landen*, Deel 5, 1675-1750. Franeker: Uitgeverij van Wijnen, 2006. William Temple speaks of the harbors being shut up for two or three months with ice, claiming that those in England were open and free. Temple, *Observations*, 79.

57 Zantkuijl, *Bouwen in Amsterdam*, 362-363.

58 For a discussion of sources of heat in Delft households around 1700, see Thera Wijsenbeek-Olthuis, *Achter de gevels van Delft*. Hilversum: Verloren, 1987, 235-237.

59 Koen Ottenheym, "From Architectura Moderna to Modern Architecture: Architecture on the Canals in the seventeenth and eighteenth centuries." In Spies et al., *Canals of Amsterdam*, 45-55.

60 Temple, *Observations*, 126.

61 For a more extended discussion of Amsterdam dwellings in the late seventeenth century, see Muizelaar and Phillips, *Picturing Men and Women*, 25-35.

62 I draw below on Juliette Roding, *Schoon en net: Hygiene in woning en stad*. 's-Gravenhage: Staatsuitgeverij, 1986, 24-33.

63 The inventories that Klaske Muizelaar and I examined for wealthy families in seventeenth-century Amsterdam usually listed these sanitary conveniences under the designations of a chamberpot (*waterpot*) or bedpan (*bedtpan*). Some houses contained a large number of such conveniences.

64 See Muizelaar and Phillips, *Picturing Men and Women*, 37-54.

65 Levie and Zantkuijl, *Wonen in Amsterdam*, chapter 4; and Willem van den Berg, Marco H.D. van Leeuwen, and Clé Lesger, "Residentiële segregatie in Hollandse steden: Theoriën, methodologie en empirische bevindingen voor Alkmaar en Amsterdam, 16ᵉ-19ᵉ eeuw," *Tijdschrift voor Sociale Geschiedenis* 24 (1998):402-436.

66 Zantkuijl, *Bouwen*, 431.

67 Ibid., 256-257.

68 The drawing, by Jan van der Heyden, is titled "Een uitgebrand huis aan de Bloedstraat." Amsterdams Historisch Museum. Information about the date and location of the house comes from R. Meischke, H.J. Zantkuijl, W. Raue, and P.T.E.E. Rosenberg, *Huizen in Nederland: Amsterdam*. Zwolle: Waanders, no date, 47. Information about the families in the building is from the brochure for the exhibition, *Fire! Jan van der Heyden schilder en uitvinder*. Rijksmuseum, Amsterdam, February 2007. The measurements are mine.

69 Hubert Nusteling, "The Population of Amsterdam and the Golden Age." In van Kessel and Schulte, *Rome*Amsterdam*, 74-75.

70 Levie and Zantkuijl, *Wonen in Amsterdam*, 66.

71 Van den Berg, van Leeuwen, and Lesger, "Residentiële Segregatie."

72 The best description of the physical characteristics of these areas is provided by Diederiks, *Een Stad in Verval*, 268-299.

73 Robert Jütte, *Poverty and Deviance in Early Modern Europe*. Cambridge: Cambridge University Press, 1994, 68.

74 I have been unable to find any exact numbers for seventeenth-century Amsterdam. My estimates here are based on figures for 1706-30 from Wijsenbeek's fine study of households in eighteenth-century Delft. Wijsenbeek-Olthuis, *Achter de gevels*, Appendix 2, page 456.

75 This was also true in early modern England. In Japan and China, by contrast, people bathed regularly and washed their hands after urinating and defecating. They used soap as well. Ann Bowman Jannetta, *Epidemics and Mortality in Early Modern Japan*. Princeton: Princeton University Press, 1987; James Z. Lee and Wong Feng, *One Quarter of Humanity: Malthusian Mythology and Chinese Realities, 1700-2000*. Cambridge: Harvard University Press, 1999.

76 Wijsenbeek indicates a greater frequency of various sorts of perfumes, pomades, and the like, than of soap – even in wealthy households. Ibid.

77 Riley, *Rising Life Expectancy*, 181.

78 Roding, *Schoon en net*, 33.

79 Judging by household inventories, most homes contained neither a comb nor a hair brush. In any case, they were not listed. Wigs, to pull on over people's (unwashed) hair, were far more common. Wijsenbeek, *Achter de gevels*, Appendix 2, page 456.

80 Sheldon Watts, *Epidemics and History: Disease, Power, and Imperialism*. New Haven and London: Yale University Press, 1997, 5-6.

81 Nusteling, *Welvaart en werkgelegenheid*, 39.

82 Human waste had no market value in early modern Europe. It was apparently thought unacceptable to use it for fertilizer for gardens or on farms. Otherwise, it would have been removed more frequently.

83 R. van Gelder, "De schone schijn van het water: De strijd tegen stank en vervuiling." In Heinemeijer et al. *Amsterdam in Kaarten*, 64-65.

84 Riley, *Rising Life Expectancy*, 179.

85 Mary Lindemann, *Medicine and Society in Early Modern Europe*. Cambridge: Cambridge University Press, 1999, 28.

86 Crosby writes of the "immunologically innocent" in this regard. Crosby, *Ecological Imperialism*, 31.

87 See Landers, *Death and the metropolis*, for the lack of immunological defenses against many "metropolitan" infections, 125.

88 This was the case in other European cities at the time and there is no reason to expect it to have been otherwise in Amsterdam. Pier Paolo Viazzo, "Mortality, Fertility, and Family." In Kertzer and Barbagli, *Family Life*, 182.

CHAPTER 4

1 Norbert Middelkoop et al., *Amsterdammers geportretteerd: Kopstukken 1600-1800*. Amsterdam: Uitgever THOTH, 2002, 11.

2 For discussions of the painting, see Eddy de Jongh, *Portretten van echt en trouw: Huwelijk en gezin in de Nederlandse kunst van de zeventiende eeuw*. Zwolle: Uitgeverij Waanders, 1986, 248-249; and Adolph Staring, *De Hollanders thuis: gezelschapstukken uit drie eeuwen*. The Hague: Nijhof, 1956, 90.

3 My examination of seventeenth-century family portraits at the Iconographic Bureau in

The Hague failed to uncover a single one in which a servant's identity was specified. Nor was anyone at the Bureau aware of any such portrait.

4   Lotte C. van de Pol, "The lure of the big city. Female migration to Amsterdam" in Kloek, Teeuwen, and Huisman, *Women of the Golden Age*, 80; and S. Sogner, "Young in Europe around 1700: Norwegian sailors and servant-girls seeking employment in Amsterdam" in *Mesurer et comprendre*. Paris, 1991, 515-532.

5   Soltow, "Income and Wealth Inequality in Amsterdam, 76-77; Donald Haks, *Huwelijk en gezin in Holland in de 17de en 18de eeuw*. Utrecht: Hes Uitgever, 1985, 19; Marybeth Carlson, *Domestic service in a changing city economy: Rotterdam, 1680-1780*. Unpublished dissertation, University of Wisconsin, 1993, 67; and Marybeth Carlson, "A Trojan horse of worldliness? Maidservants in the burgher household in Rotterdam at the end of the seventeenth century" in Kloek, Teeuwen, and Huisman, *Women of the Golden Age*, 87-96.

6   Soltow, "Income and Wealth Inequality." Table 3, p.77.

7   Few people at the time left written testimony about their feelings, experiences or observations; servants were not among those who did. Noting that women from the coastal area of Scandinavia often found work as servants in seventeenth-century Amsterdam, Kuijpers found that only one in 21 Scandinavian brides in 1650 and one in 15 in 1700 could write their names. Kuijpers, "Lezen en schrijven," 510. Few letters, diaries, or other autobiographical writings by servants have been located anywhere in early modern Europe. See Amelang, *The Flight of Icarus*, 27, 361.

8   Carlson cites various sources showing that it was the mistress of the house who controlled the household personnel. Carlson, "A Trojan horse," 89.

9   In many other ways, however, relationships between servants and different household members were the same everywhere in early modern Europe. Particularly useful for understanding the situation of servants in earlier centuries are Jean Hecht, *The Domestic Service Class in Eighteenth-Century England*. London: Routlege & Kegan Paul, 1956; Cissie Fairchilds, *Domestic Enemies: Servants and Their Masters in Old Regime France*. Baltimore: The Johns Hopkins University Press, 1984; Sarah C. Maza, *Servants and Masters in Eighteenth-Century France: The Uses of Loyalty*. Princeton: Princeton University Press, 1983; Christine Klapisch-Zuber, "Women Servants in Florence during the Fourteenth and Fifteenth Centuries" in Barbara A. Hanawalt, ed., *Women and Work in Preindustrial Europe*. Bloomington: Indiana University Press, 1986; Bridget Hill, *Servants, English Domestics in the Eighteenth Century*. Oxford: Clarendon Press, 1996; Leonore Davidoff, *Worlds Between: Historical Perspectives on Gender and Class*. New York: Routledge, 1995; Dennis Romano, *Housecraft and Statecraft: Domestic Service in Renaissance Venice, 1400-1600*. Baltimore and London: The Johns Hopkins University Press, 1996; Leonore Davidoff, Megan Doolittle, Janet Fink, and Katherine Holden, *The Family Story: Blood, Contract and Intimacy, 1830-1960*. London and New York: Longman, 1999; Timothy Meldrum, *Domestic Service and Gender: Life and Work in the London Household*. London: Longman, 2000; and Giovanna Benadusi, "Investing the Riches of the Poor: Servant Women and Their Last Wills," *American Historical Review* 109 (June 2004):805-826.

10 Haks, *Huwelijk en gezin*, 167-174; Carlson, "A Trojan Horse," 89.

11 Davidoff, *Worlds Between*, 37.

12 In legal documents a servant was rarely referred to by the courteous title of Miss (*Juffrouw*) as were other unmarried young women. Instead, she was usually described as "the maid" (*mejuffer*). Carlson, *Domestic Service*, 150-151.

13 For an excellent discussion of the difficulties involved in lighting and maintaining a fire in a damp climate such as that in the Netherlands, see William T. O'Dea,

The Social History of Lighting. London: Routledge and Kegan Paul, 1958, 233-242. Although it deals with New England rather than Amsterdam, Ulrich gives a wonderfully detailed description of the daily demands of cooking and other aspects of a wife's housekeeping chores in the seventeenth century. Laurel Thatcher Ulrich, *Image and Reality in the Lives of Women in Northern New England, 1650-1750*. New York: Alfred A. Knopf, 1982, 13-34.

14 It is difficult to find any reliable evidence concerning the time off that servants had, but Carlson cites a household manual mentioning Wednesday afternoons and Saturday evenings. *Domestic Service*, 144. Although concerned mainly with Rotterdam, Carlson's unpublished dissertation is the richest single source of information about servants in seventeenth- and eighteenth-century Holland. In her excellent study, she draws on notary archives, domestic management manuals, and a variety of other materials of the period.

15 "Servants," writes Judith Flanders, "were the consumer durables of their age. They were a symbol of status, signalling to the world the riches of the family who employed them." She notes this in a review of an exhibition at the National Portrait Gallery (2003-2004) called "Below Stairs: Four hundred years of servant's portraits." She then goes on to add: "The exhibition shies away from this notion, and tries to claim an affection for and attachment to the servants represented that it is sometimes hard to see." Judith Flanders, "Service with a smile." *Times Literary Supplement*, October 31, 2003:20.

16 Raffaella Sarti, "The Material Conditions of Family Life" in Kertzer and Barbali, *Family Life in Early Modern Times*, 9.

17 Or perhaps it was so that the master and mistress could keep a close eye on what the servant actually consumed. There were surely some households where the family was quite willing to have her join them at the table. But given the many tasks they had to perform, it seems unlikely that servants would have regularly sat at the table with the family that employed them.

18 The figure for wages is based on figures in the household inventories of sixty-two wealthy Amsterdam families, discussed in Muizelaar and Phillips, *Picturing Men and Women*; and on Carlson, *Domestic Service*, while information on times of payment comes from Haks, *Huwelijk en gezin*, 171.

19 Carlson, *Domestic Service*, 109.

20 There was, however, great variation in the amounts left in wills by the families mentioned in Muizelaar and Phillips, *Picturing Men and Women*. To some extent, this may reflect the number of years that a servant had been in service as well as the nature of the relationship between the servant and the person leaving her a legacy.

21 Carlson, *Domestic Service*, 121.

22 Davidoff, *Worlds Between*, 25.

23 Instances are discussed in Kooijmans, *Vriendschap*.

24 This was the case throughout Europe. See Carlo Marco Belfanti and Fabio Giusberti, "Clothing and social inequality in early modern Europe: introductory remarks," *Continuity and Change* 15 (December 2000):359-365.

25 Bibi Panhuysen, *Maatwerk: Kleermakers, naaisters, oudkleerkopers en de gilden (1500-1800)*. No publisher's name, 2000, 239.

26 See the discussion in Muizelaar and Phillips, *Picturing Men and Women*, 30.

27 Ibid., 25-26.

28 Carlson, *Domestic Service*, 144.

29 Ibid.

30 For an interesting consideration of how clothing placed people recognizably in

a somewhat earlier period, see Ann Rosalind Jones and Peter Stallybrass, *Renaissance Clothing and the Materials of Memory*. Cambridge: Cambridge University Press, 2000.

31 Although he is speaking about Renaissance Venice, clothing had important symbolic functions in Amsterdam as well. Stanley Chojnacki, *Women and Men and Renaissance Venice: Twelve Essays on Patrician Society*. Baltimore and London: The Johns Hopkins University Press, 2000, 158-159.

32 Ibid., 139.

33 Muizelaar and Phillips, *Picturing Men and Women*, Chapter 3.

34 See, in this regard, a similar argument made by Spierenburg in accounting for the Amsterdam government's increase in the severity of punishment for criminal offenses in the last half of the seventeenth century. Pieter Spierenburg, *The Spectacle of Suffering*. Cambridge: Cambridge University Press, 1984, 175-182.

35 H. Noordkerk, *Handvesten*, Volume 2, 450. This same ordinance specified that domestic servants must not show disrespect to their masters or mistresses (*Dienstboden moeten haar Meesters of Vrouwen niet qualijk bejegenen*), 449.

36 The translation from the Dutch comes from Carlson, *Domestic Service*, 142-143.

37 Ibid.

38 Ibid., 189.

39 Ibid., 194. Judging by notices in the *Amsterdamse Courant*, however, thefts by Amsterdam servants were not unknown. During the period 1672-1696 (with a gap in 1678-1683, when numbers are missing) there were a dozen notices about thefts by domestic servants. All concerned rather large amounts of cash or other valuables. These notices would certainly have caught the eye of the reader and, if nothing else, given the impression that servants were widely involved in stealing from their employers. Schipper-van Lottum, *Advertenties en Berichten*.

40 See the extended discussion in Anthony Fletcher, *Gender, Sex & Subordination in England, 1500-1800*. New Haven and London: Yale University Press, 1995.

41 Haks, *Huwelijk en gezin*, 76; and Carlson, *Domestic Service*, 201-202.

42 Hill, *Servants*, has an especially good discussion and analysis of the sexual vulnerability of female servants.

43 These autobiographical writings by Cats are cited and discussed in Domien ten Berge, *De Hooggeleerde en Zoetvlooiende Dichter Jacob Cats*. 's-Gravenhage: Martinus Nijhoff, 1979.

44 Ibid., 19-20. But Cats need not have been particularly worried since the legal authorities in Leiden had a contemptuous attitude toward women from the lower orders and would have tried to protect him against an unwelcome marriage. See the discussion in Muizelaar and Phillips, *Picturing Men and Women*, 156.

45 I wonder whether the many readers of Cats' autobiography shared his views about servants as sexual objects for the pleasure of wealthy young men. For given Cats' popularity in the seventeenth century, notes Bostoen, his autobiography must have had a large readership when it appeared in 1700. Karel Bostoen, "De autobiografie van Jacob Cats" in Mineke Schipper and Peter Schmitz, eds., *Ik is Anders: Autobiografie in verschillende culturen*. Barn: Ambo, 1991, 92.

46 In fact, men saw women more generally as having an insatiable sexual appetite that derived from their physiology. These men thus believed it to be their duty to protect their wives, sisters, and daughters against these female's own sexuality. See the discussions in Muizelaar and Phillips, *Picturing Men and Women*.

47 Carlson, *Domestic Service*, 198-199. See also, Inger Leemans, *De Woord is aan de onderkant: Radicale ideeën in Nederlandse pornografische romans 1670-1700*. Nijmegen: Uitgever Vantilt, 2002.

48 Hill, *Servants*, 47.
49 Ibid., 48.
50 Manon van der Heijden, *Huwelijk in Holland: Stedelijke rechtspraak en kerkelijke tucht, 1550-1700.* Amsterdam: Uitgeverij Bert Bakker, 1998, 124.
51 In plays, songs, conduct manuals, and even proverbs, servants were described in the most negative of terms, with a particular emphasis on their being sexually indecent. See the discussion in Gisela van Oostveen, "It takes all sorts to make a world: Sex and gender in Bredero's Farce of the Miller" in Kloek et al, *Women*, 60.
52 Haks, *Huwelijk en gezin*, 75-76.
53 Ibid., 93.
54 Ibid., 88-89.
55 Cited in Herman Roodenburg, *Onder Censuur*. Hilversum: Verloren, 1990, 260.
56 The same situation exists for young foreign girls employed as au pairs in wealthy households all over the world today.
57 Haks, *Huwelijk en gezin*; Peter Earle, *A City Full of People: Men and Women of London, 1650-1750*. London: Methuen, 1994, 129, Table 4.7
58 Carlson, *Domestic Service*, 165-168.
59 This was at least the case among those who were Christians. Little is known about domestic service among Jewish adolescents and young women. But because of the Jewish dietary laws, most would have been employed by Jewish households. Sephardic Jews in Amsterdam are known to have employed Ashkenazi girls as servants. Jona Schellekens, "Determinants of Age at First Marriage Among Jews in Amsterdam, 1625-1724," *Journal of Family History* 24 (April 1999):150.

CHAPTER 5

1 Unless indicated otherwise, all information about specifically-named individuals was collected by Klaske Muizelaar in connection with Muizelaar and Phillips, *Picturing Men and Women*.
2 The two servants shared a bed behind the kitchen in the basement. Information from Probate Inventory NA 7604, drawn up upon the death of Cornelia Bierens.
3 Ibid.
4 Muizelaar and Phillips, *Picturing Men and Women*, 2-5, 54-55, 67-68, 110-117.
5 Haks presents a somewhat lower figure, but excludes both married couples without children and orphans. Haks, *Huwelijk en gezin*, 147. He notes in a more recent publication that forty percent of households consisted of a widow, widower, or unmarried person living alone. Moreover, he says, some forty percent of households contained no children at all. Donald Haks, "Family Structure and Relationship Patterns in Amsterdam" in van Kessel and Schulte, *Rome*Amsterdam*, 93. Hence my estimate that only half of all households consisted of husband, wife, and children.
6 John Hajnal, "European Marriage Patterns in Perspective." In D.V. Glass and D.E.C. Eversley, eds., *Population in History: Essays in Historical Demography*. London: Edward Arnold, 1965, 101-143; and John Hajnal, "Two kinds of preindustrial household formation system," *Population and Development Review* 8 (1982):449-494. These articles have given rise to a large body of literature concerning the so-called "Hajnal hypothesis." For a recent overview, see Theo Engelen and Arthur P. Wolf, eds., *Marriage and the family in Eurasia: Perspectives on the Hajnal hypothesis*. Amsterdam: Aksant, 2005.

7   Hajnal, "European Marriage Patterns," 101.
8   Amy M. Froide, *Never Married: Singlewomen in Early Modern England*. Oxford: Oxford University Press, 2005, 3.
9   Hajnal, "European Marriage Patterns," 133-134.
10 Froide, *Never Married*, 2.
11 Kuijpers, *Migrantenstad*, 362, Table 2-4. Ashkenazi Jews married earlier than either Sephardic Jews or Christians in seventeenth-century Amsterdam. The reason, suggests Schellekens, was the greater willingness of their parents to take in and support married sons and their wives. Schellekens, "Determinants of Age at First Marriage."
12 Van Zanden, "What Happened to the Standard of Living?" In Allen, Bengtsson, and Dribe, *Living Standards*, 173-194.
13 Further evidence about late marriage comes from De Vries and van der Woude. They calculated the ages of brides at first marriage in Amsterdam for 1676/1677 and found that 33.3 percent were between twenty-five and twenty-nine, and 22.3 percent cent were thirty or older. De Vries and van der Woude, *The First Modern Economy*, 101.
14 Kuijpers, *Migrantenstad*, 96.
15 Ibid., 362, Table 2-4.
16 My estimate is based on the reconstruction of the age structure of the Amsterdam population as calculated by van Leeuwen and Oeppen, "Reconstructing the Demographic Regime." Table 10.
17 Hilde van Wijngaarden, *Zorg voor de kost: Armenzorg, arbeid en onderlinge hulp in Zwolle, 1650-1700*. Amsterdam: Uitgeverijen Prometheus/Bert Bakker, 2000, 210-217; Paul M.M. Klep, "Introduction to special issues: contradictory interests of offspring and parents, 1500-2000," *The History of the Family* 9 (2004):349-354; and Manon van der Heijden, "Contradictory interests: Work, parents, and offspring in early modern Holland," *The History of the Family* 9 (2004):355-370.
18 I draw here on Ariadne Schmidt, "Vrouwen en het recht. De juridische status van vrouwen in Holland in de vroegmoderne tijd," *Jaarboek van het Centraal Bureau voor Genealogie* (Den Haag, 2004):26-44.
19 Van de Pol and Kuijpers, "Poor Women's Migration," 49.
20 Reneé Kistemaker, Michiel Wagenaar, and Jos van Assendelft, *Amsterdam Marktstad*. Amsterdam: Dienst van het Marktwezen, 1984.
21 Ariadne Schmidt, "Vrouwenarbeid in de Vroegmoderne Tijd in Nederland," *Tijdschrift voor Sociale en Economische Geschiedenis* 2 (2005):8.
22 No figures exist for the female work force of seventeenth-century Amsterdam. Most studies of single working women focus on one city, one occupational group, or on poor women. Among studies which consider single women in the Dutch Republic are Carlson, *Domestic Service*; Gabrielle Maria Elisabeth Dorren, *Eenheid en verscheidenheid: De burgers van Haarlem in de Gouden Eeuw*. Amsterdam: Prometheus/Bert Bakker, 2001; Els Kloek, "*Wie hij zij, man of wijf*" *Vrouwengeschiedenis en de vroegmoderne tijd*. Hilversum: Verloren, 1990; Panhuysen, *Maatwerk*; van de Pol, *Het Amsterdams hoerdom*; Ingrid van der Vlis, *Leven in armoede. Delftse bedeelden in de zeventiende eeuw*. Amsterdam: Prometheus/Bert Bakker, 2001; van Wijngaarden, *Zorg voor de kost*; Elise van Nederveen Meerkerk, *De draad in eigen handen*; and a special journal number on women's labor in the early modern Netherlands. "Themanummer Vrouwenarbeid in de vroegmoderne tijd in Nederland," *Tijdschrift voor Sociale en Economisch Geschiedenis* 3 (2005).
23 Van de Pol, *Amsterdams Hoerdom*, 102.
24 Van de Pol and Kuijpers, "Poor Women's Migration," 49.

25 Mary E. Wiesner, *Women and Gender in Early Modern Europe*. New York: Cambridge University Press, 1993, 99.

26 Amy M. Froide, "Marital Status as a Category of Difference: Singlewomen and Widows in Early Modern England." In Judith Bennett and Amy M. Froide, eds., *Singlewomen in the European Past, 1250-1800*. Philadelphia: University of Pennsylvania Press, 1999, 249-250.

27 Van de Pol, *Amsterdams Hoerdom*, 102.

28 As I have mentioned several times, quantitative evidence for seventeenth-century Amsterdam is in short supply. It is clear, in any case, that there were far fewer ways for females than for males to earn a living.

29 Van de Pol and Kuijpers, "Poor women's migration," 49.

30 Among women arrested for prostitution in the period 1660-1720, 36 percent gave their occupation as seamstress, 30 percent reported work in the textile industry, 15 percent said they were servants, and smaller percentages claimed other kinds of work. A disproportionate number were immigrants. Van de Pol, *Amsterdams Hoerdom*, 103.

31 Kuijpers, *Migrantenstad*, 291-292.

32 I compare and contrast desert and entitlement in Phillips, *Just Social Order*, 356-357.

33 In Zwolle during the 1650-1700 period 27.2 percent of the households receiving charity consisted of a single woman and 5.5 percent of a single man. This differential was surely similar in Amsterdam, although I am aware of no exact figures. Van Wijngaarden, *Zorg voor de kost*, 88.

34 The pattern was the same elsewhere in Western Europe, even in the nineteenth century, and for the same reasons. A study of East London in 1848 found that the earnings of unmarried men were almost four times as much as those of unmarried women. Not surprisingly, 27 percent of those receiving poor relief were single women compared to just 2 percent who were single men. Richard Wall, "Some implications of the earnings, income and expenditure patterns of married women and populations in the past" in John Henderson and Richard Wall, eds., *Poor Women and Children in the European Past*. London and New York: Routledge, 1994, 313.

35 See, especially, Bennett and Froide, *Singlewomen*; and Froide, *Never Married*.

36 Froide, *Never Married*, 17.

37 I am paraphrasing Hufton's observation about women here. Olwen Hufton, *The Prospect Before Her: A History of Women in Western Europe, Volume One, 1500-1800*. London: HarperCollins, 1995, 251.

38 Leendert F. Groenendijk and Benjamin B. Roberts, eds., *Losbandige jeugd: Jongeren en moraal in de Nederlanden tijdens de late Middeleeuwen en de Vroegmoderne Tijd*. Hilversum: Verloren, 2004.

39 Benjamin Roberts, "Drinking Like a Man: The Paradox of Excessive Drinking for Seventeenth-Century Dutch Youths," *Journal of Family History* 29 (2004):253-273.

40 See, for example, Benjamin Roberts, "Rokende Soldaten: Mannelijke rolmodellen voor de jeugd in de vroege zeventiende eeuw?" in Groenendijk and Roberts, *Losbandige jeugd*, 53-71.

41 Despite the large numbers of young women employed as servants and doing other kinds of jobs, the work of single women was not acknowledged as essential in the same way as that of single men.

42 Mac Wingens, "Jeugdige lichtzinnigheid en losbandigheid, seksueel gedrag en seksuele beleving van studenten ten tijde van de Nederlandse Republiek" in Gert Hekma, Dorelies Kraakman, and Willem Melching, eds. *Balans & perspectief van de*

Nederlandse cultuurgeschiedenis: Grensgeschillen in de seks. Amsterdam: Rodofi, 1990.

43 In seventeenth-century England, Pepys's diary is full of instances of his kissing, fondling, and initiating sexual relations with servants, barmaids, the wives of friends, and just about any woman he found attractive. They seemed to differ in their response. See Samuel Pepys, *The Diary of Samuel Pepys*, eds. Robert Latham and William Matthews. London: G. Bell and Sons Ltd., 1970-1983, vol. 5.

44 Van der Heijden, *Huwelijk in Holland*, 134-141.

45 Froide, *Never Married*, 21-22.

46 See, for example, Jan Kok, "The Moral Nation: Illegitimacy and Bridal Pregnancy in the Netherlands from 1600 to the Present," *Economic and Social History of the Netherlands* 2 (1991):7-36. The sexual behavior of the seventeenth-century Dutch is discussed in Muizelaar and Phillips, *Picturing Men and Women*, 148-159.

47 Paintings, sitters, and portraits are discussed in Ibid., 66-72.

48 Schipper-van Lottum, *Advertenties en Berichten*, aflevering 3 A-B, 659 and 1094.

49 Notice published on May 25, 1690. Ibid., aflevering 2, 452.

50 Notice published on November 13, 1696, aflevering 3 A-B, 1328.

51 See the discussion in Muizelaar and Phillips, *Picturing Men and Women*, 124, 167-168. I know of no seventeenth-century Dutch novels in which plain or unattractive women are featured. They are, however, a recurring theme in the novels of nineteenth-century English novelists like Jane Austen and Charlotte Brontë. See, for example, Chapter X, "Old Maids" in Charlotte Brontë, *Shirley*. London: Penguin, 1994, originally published in 1849.

52 E.M. Kloek, "De Vrouw" in Bëlien, Van Deursen, and Van Setten, *Gestalten van de Gouden Eeuw*, 260.

53 See Kuijpers, *Migrantenstad*, Table 2-6.

54 Lotte C. van de Pol, "Hoeveel soorten volk? Een reactie op Maarten Prak," *Jaarboek Amstelodamum* 91 (1999):59

55 Applying the three to two ratio of women to men in Amsterdam to the year 1680, I have estimated the "excess" of women over men in the 15-19, 20-24, and 25-29 age groups. The number of women exceeded the number of men by 3,556, 3,774, and 3,652 in the three categories. This means that among young people 15-29 years of age, there were 10,882 more women than men competing in the Amsterdam marriage market. I again use figures from van Leeuwen and Oeppen. They estimate the number of people in the 15-19 age group, for example, at 18,953. Applying the three to two sex ratio, there were 11,137 women and 7,581 men, an excess of 3,556 women. I have no way of estimating the differences by neighborhood.

56 Van de Pol, "The Lure of the Big City, 77-80.

57 A reminder by Jane Austen writing to her young niece in the early nineteenth century. Cited in Josephine Ross, *Jane Austen: A Companion*. New Brunswick, N.J.: Rutgers University Press, 2003, 131. Women's opportunities were limited then, just as they had been in earlier periods.

58 In an annotated bibliography of roughly fifty historical publications concerning single men and women in earlier centuries, most of them journal articles, fewer than a third focus on women in the early modern period and none on men. Bella M. DePaulo, "The Scientific Study of People Who are Single: An Annotated Bibliography." American Association for Single People (AASP), January 2, 2004. It is only within the last few years that there have been books devoted entirely to the subject of single women in the early modern period. Particularly noteworthy are Bennett and Froide, *Singlewomen*; and Froide, *Never Married*. Similar studies of single men have yet to appear.

59 See Antoinette Fauve-Chamoux, "Marriage, Widowhood, and Divorce" in Kertzer and Barbagli, *Family Life*, 225-227; Judith Bennett and Amy M. Froide, "A Singular Past" in Bennett and Froide, *Singlewomen*, 2; and Maryanne Kowaleski, "Singlewomen in Medieval and Early Modern Europe: The Demographic Perspective." In Ibid., 50-51.

60 From her analysis of various studies, Froide concludes that at least one-fifth of both men *and* women in early modern England never married, and goes on to add that "we know virtually nothing about this group." Froide, *Never Married*, 2. Her book is aimed at correcting this lack of knowledge. She is quite successful with regard to women, but says little about men.

61 Van de Pol and Kuijpers estimate that perhaps a quarter of the women in Amsterdam remained single. But the figure must have been higher. Van de Pol and Kuijpers, "Poor Women's Migration," 48.

62 Kuijpers, *Migrantenstad*, 101-104.

63 The same was true for women elsewhere in the early modern period. See, for example, Margaret R. Hunt, *The Middling Sort: Commerce, Gender, and the Family in England, 1689-1780*. Berkeley: University of California Press, 1996, 76. Even today, little is known about single women in this regard. E. Kay Trimberger, *The New Single Woman*. Boston, MA: Beacon Press, 2005.

64 Paul M.M. Klep, "An adult life before marriage: Children and the Hajnal hypothesis" in Engelen and Wolf, *Marriage and the Family*, 249-251.

65 Married women in Amsterdam must have made a point of not hiring an especially attractive young woman as a servant. Some of these young women would have ended up working for unmarried men and others for widowers.

CHAPTER 6

1 Sherrin Marshall, *The Dutch Gentry, 1500-1650: Family, Faith, and Fortune*. New York: Greenwood Press, 1987; and Julia Adam, *The Familial State: Ruling Families and Merchant Capitalism in Early Modern Europe*. Ithaca and London: Cornell University Press, 2005, 77-78. For an extended argument about kinship orientation based on blood relations at a later period in England, see Ruth Perry, *Novel Relations: The Transformation of Kinship in English Literature and Culture, 1748-1818*. Cambridge: Cambridge University Press, 2004.

2 Similarly, the members of such families were bound by unquestioned ties to earlier generations. With their quasi-aristocratic pretensions, notes Price, regents "believed that their privileged position was justified not just by personal merit, but by the status and history of their family." J.L. Price, *Dutch Society, 1588-1713*. Essex: Longman, 2000, 176. Genealogies were produced by the higher orders to document their (real and imagined) backgrounds and accomplishments.

3 Judith Hokke, "'Mijn alderliefste Jantielief.' Vrouw en gezin in de Republiek: regentenvrouwen en hun relaties," *Jaarboek voor vrouwengeschiedenis* 8 (1987):50-53.

4 Elias, *De Vroedschap van Amsterdam*. Because of their primary orientation to the family of birth, husband and wife in wealthy families had more frequent and intense contact with relatives than did most married couples. See, for example, Kooijmans, *Vriendschap*.

5 Haks, *Huwelijk en Gezin*, 114-119.

6 Given life expectancy at the time, there would indeed have been many instances where both parents were dead. In the case of young men and women coming from distant countries, it would have been virtually impossible for the Dutch authorities to check on such claims. It would also have been difficult to establish that an individual was not already married in the place of origin.

7 Kuijpers, *Migrantenstad*, 401, Tables 5-5 and 5.6.

8 Ibid.

9 Ibid., 188. These figures cast doubt upon the suggestion that late marriage in the early modern period was a consequence of parental power and constraints. See, for example, Paul M.M. Klep, "An adult life before marriage: Children and the Hajnal hypothesis." In Engelen and Wolf, *Marriage and the Family*.

10 Haks, *Huwelijk en Gezin*, 219-222.

11 Hokke, "'Mijn alderliefste,'" 53-58.

12 As Hartman notes, this was a consequence of the late marriage pattern in north-western Europe more generally. Mary S. Hartman, *The Household and the Making of History: A Subversive View of the Western Past*. Cambridge: Cambridge University Press, 2004, 32. Because of the high proportion of single women, I believe that this was even more common in Amsterdam than elsewhere.

13 Van Nederveen Meerkerk, *De draad in eigen handen*, 209-218.

14 Ariadne Schmidt, "Zelfstandig en bevoogd: de speelruimte van vrouwen rond 1650," *Tijdschrift voor Sociale Geschiedenis* 29 (2003):28-34.

15 Hartman, *The Household*. For a contrary view, at least for early modern England, see Hunt, *The Middling Sort*, 135-136.

16 See, for example, instances related in Lotte van de Pol, *Het Amsterdams hoerdom*, 113, 416.

17 Hokke, "'Mijn alderliefste.'" For seventeenth-century England, see Laura Gowing, *Common Bodies: Women, Touch, and Power in Seventeenth-Century England*. New Haven and London: Yale University Press, 2003.

18 Jan de Vries, "Between Purchasing Power and the World of Goods: Understanding the Household Economy in Early Modern Europe" in John Brewer and Roy Porter, eds., *Consumption and the World of Goods*. London and New York: Routledge, 1993, 117.

19 De Vries and van der Woude, *The First Modern Economy*, 512.

20 Erotic depictions of Susannah, Bathsheba, Venus, and other attractive women in paintings, on marriage chests, and on birth trays in the conjugal chamber may have been intended to encourage sexuality and help husband and wife achieve the sexual excitement and mutual orgasms thought necessary for conception. See the discussion in Muizelaar and Phillips, *Picturing Men and Women*, 143-146.

21 Wrigley presents an excellent short discussion of sterility. Wrigley, *Poverty, Progress*, 410-411.

22 Ibid., 351-352.

23 In wealthy families births were often attended by a large number of relatives, but no neighbors. See, for example, Kooijmans, *Vriendschap*, 186.

24 Benjamin Roberts, *Through the keyhole: Dutch child-rearing practices in the 17th and 18th century*. Hilversum: Verloren, 1998, 72-74. At least some fathers were present at the birth of their children in fifteenth-century Germany as well. See Steven Ozment, *When Fathers Ruled: Family Life in Reformation Europe*. Cambridge, Mass.: Harvard University Press, 1983, 115-116.

25 Smith, *The Gender of History*, 60.

26 An overview of the situation in the seventeenth-century Dutch Republic is presented

in Helena Adelheid van der Borg, *Vroedvrouwen: beeld en beroep*. Wageningen: Wageningen Academic Press, 1992. For the eighteenth century, see Hilary Marland, "'Stately and dignified, kindly and God-fearing': midwives, age and status in the Netherlands in the eighteenth century" in Hilary Marland and Margaret Pelling, eds., *The Task of Healing: Medicine, religion and gender in England and the Netherlands, 1450-1800*. Rotterdam: Erasmus Publishing, 1996, 271-305. For a useful discussion of seventeenth-century England, see Adrian Wilson, "Participant or patient: Seventeenth century childbirth from the mother's point of view" in Roy Porter, ed., *Patients and practitioners: Lay perceptions of medicine in pre-industrial society*. Cambridge: Cambridge University Press, 1985, 129-144.

27 Van der Heijden, *Huwelijk in Holland*, 122-127; and Manon van der Heijden, "Secular and Ecclesiastical Marriage Control: Rotterdam, 1550-1770" in Anton Schuurman and Pieter Spierenburg, eds., *Private domain, public inquiry: Families and life-styles in the Netherlands and Europe, 1550 to the present*. Hilversum: Verloren, 1996, 47.

28 Jonathan I. Israel, "Dutch influence on urban planning, health care and poor relief: The North Sea and Baltic regions of Europe, 1567-1720" in Ole Peter Grell and Andrew Cunningham, eds., *Health Care and Poor Relief in Protestant Europe 1500-1700*. London and New York: Routledge. 1997, 78.

29 Fransje W. van der Waals, "Doorbraken in de verloskunde" in H.M. Dupuis, et al., *Een Kind Onder Het Hart*. Amsterdam: Meulenhoff, 1987, 22-23.

30 The figures are for the late seventeenth and the early eighteenth century. Van der Borg, *Vroedvrouwen*, 118-119. Surprisingly, an encyclopedic overview of the early modern period in the Netherlands provides no figures regarding the earnings of midwives. But the authors are clear about women receiving low pay compared to men, even when doing similar kinds of work. De Vries and van der Woude, *The First Modern Economy*, 689-695.

31 In early modern Europe more generally, men in positions of authority made and justified policies that assured the maintenance of the gender hierarchy. See Ogilvie, "How Does Social Capital Affect Women?"

32 A detailed consideration of early modern England is found in Roy Porter and Dorothy Porter, *In sickness and in health: The British experience 1650-1850*. London: Fourth Estate, 1988.

33 A good discussion is found in Richard Lalou, "Endogenous Mortality in New France: At the Crossroads of Natural and Social Selection" in Alain Bideau, Bertrand Desjardins, and Hector Perez Brignoli, eds., *Infant and Child Mortality in the Past*. Oxford: Clarendon Press, 1997, 203-215.

34 George Alter, Matteo Manfredini, Paul Nystedt, et al., "Gender Differences in Mortality." In Bengtsson et al., *Life Under Pressure*, 350-351.

35 Malcolm Potts and Roger Short, *Ever Since Adam and Eve: The evolution of human sexuality*. Cambridge: Cambridge University Press, 1999, 146-155.

36 For the seventeenth-century Netherlands, see Dekker, *Uit de schaduw*, 51, 142-155. Two general studies are Valerie Fides, *Wet nursing: A History from antiquity to the present*. Oxford: Basil Blackwell, 1988; and Sara F. Matthews Grieco and Carlo A. Corsini, *Historical perspectives on breastfeeding*. Florence: Unicef International Child Development Center, 1991.

37 Dekker, *Uit de schaduw*, 154.

38 Norton reports the same for wet-nurses in early America. Mary Beth Norton, "'Either Married or To Bee Married': Women's Legal Inequality in Early America" in Carla Gardina Pestana and Sharon V. Slaughter, eds., *Inequality in Early America*. Hanover and London: University Press of New England, 1999, 30.

39 Hermanus Verbeeck, *Memoriaal Ofte Mijn Levensraijsinghe*. Uitgave verzorgd door Jeroen Blaak. Hilversum: Verloren, 1999. Orig. 1621-1657. Such an autobiography was quite unusual, as is the fact that it survives to this day.

40 There is little support for the claim advanced by some historians about an emotional indifference toward children before the eighteenth century. For the reactions of (wealthy) parents in seventeenth-century Amsterdam to the death of a child, see Roberts, *Through the Keyhole*. For early modern England, see Paul Griffith, *Youth and Authority: formative experiences in England 1560-1640*. Oxford: Clarendon Press, 1996; and Margaret Pelling, *The Common Lot: sickness, medical occupations and the urban poor in early modern England*. London: Longman, 1998.

41 Dekker, *Uit de schaduw*, 51-52.

42 S. Blankaart, *Verhandelinge van der opvoedinge en ziekte der kinderen*. Amsterdam, 1684; and Jacob Cats, *Huwelijk*. Middelburgh, 1625.

43 Lawrence Stone, *The Family, Sex and Marriage in England 1500-1800*. London: Weidenfeld and Nicolson, 1977:422.

44 The mechanism responsible is described as follows: "When the baby suckles on the nipple, nervous impulses pass from the breast to the brain, to inhibit the release from the pituitary gland to the hormones responsible for ovulation." Potts and Short, *Ever Since Adam and Eve*, 152.

45 Dickens gives examples of women knowing this in the ancient world and in the Middle Ages. Emma Dickens, *The Extraordinary Story of Birth Control – from the First Fumblings to the Present Day*. London: Robsen Books, 2000, 26, 38. In fourteenth-century Italy a writer on medical subjects reminded women that breastfeeding would help them live longer since they would not get pregnant again so soon. Cited in an excellent discussion of breastfeeding and wet-nursing in Rudolph M. Bell, *How to Do It: Guides to Good Living for Renaissance Italians*. Chicago: University of Chicago Press, 1999, 124-137.

46 Etienne van de Walle, "Birth prevention before the era of modern contraception," *Population and Societies*, 418 (December 2005):1.

47 Roberts, *Through the keyhole*, 84.

48 The hiring of a wet-nurse is mentioned in a handful of diaries and autobiographies written by wealthy men. These are discussed by Dekker, *Uit de schaduw*, 142-155. Unfortunately, there seem to be no such reports in writings by women at the time.

49 Bertrand Desjardins, "Family Formation and Infant Mortality in New France" in Bideau et al., *Infant and Child Mortality*, 182.

50 The information was originally gathered for a study of paintings in the domestic and imaginative lives of sixty-two wealthy Amsterdam families in the seventeenth century. See Muizelaar and Phillips, *Picturing Men and Women*. Among the families were several regents, including four burgomasters, directors of the East India Company, wealthy merchants, and other members of the political or economic elite. Most were among the richest 2-3 percent of Amsterdam families, and all among the richest 10 percent. We were able to obtain information about exact birth dates of children for only thirty of the families.

51 For an example of an expectant mother being urged by her husband to engage a wet-nurse while receiving contrary advice from her parents, see Ibid., 84.

52 Willem Noltenius was a highly successful businessman until he went bankrupt. At that time, it was not unusual for merchants to gain, lose, and then regain wealth. This was the case for Willem Noltenius. Probate inventory GAA, 5072, no. 410, fol. 158-194.

53 The burial tax paid at the time of Catharina de Wit's death indicates that she was assessed as belonging to the wealthiest category of Amsterdam residents.

54 I have been unable to find a burial date or assessment for the death of Willem Noltenius.
55 If a woman is breast-feeding her child and menstruation has not returned, she has
only a two percent chance of conceiving in the first six months after giving birth.
Potts and Short, *Ever Since Adam and Eve*, 153.
56 An infant breast-fed by a wet-nurse would have regarded her as its natural mother
and experienced the bonding associated with suckling. Experts today emphasize the
trauma experienced by children wet-nursed in early-modern Europe. For example,
"When the child was returned to its biological mother, it was subject to a triple
emotional trauma: separation from the wet-nurse whom it would regard as its natural
mother; its initial resentment on being returned to its real mother who was virtually
a complete stranger; and the mother's own difficulty in accepting the unwilling child
back into her family, having had one or two more children since its birth." Potts and
Short, *Ever Since Adam and Eve*, 155. I have no evidence about the existence of such
traumas among children wet-nursed in the Netherlands in the seventeenth century.
57 The couple owned several history paintings with an obvious erotic component, including a painting of naked women by Daniel Vertangen whose work had a strong
erotic quality. Perhaps the couple believed that the paintings encouraged sexuality
and the birth of a child.
58 Lalou, "Endogenous Mortality," 206.
59 Michel Oris, Renzo Derosas, Marco Breschti et al., "Infant and Child Mortality" in
Bengtsson et al., *Life Under Pressure*, 372.
60 Gregory Clark and Gillian Hamilton, "Survival of the Richest: The Malthusian
Mechanism in Pre-Industrial England," *The Journal of Economic History* 66 (September 2006):707-736.
61 Ibid., 391. Landers is especially informative with regard to the determinants of expo-
sure to, and resistance against, infectious agents. Landers, *Death and the metropolis*.
62 I draw in the following on Muizelaar and Phillips, *Picturing Men and Women*, 39-41,
115-117.
63 Research on the bones of skeletons from early modern England indicate that many
men had suffered from illness in childhood and had been exposed to everyday knocks
and stresses while engaged in heavy manual labor from an early age. Alex Warner,
London Bodies: The changing shape of Londoners from Prehistoric times to the present day.
London: Museum of London, 1988, 64.
64 Hoffman, et al. "Sketching the Rise of Real Inequality", especially 138-145.
65 See, for example, G. Doblhammer, *The Late Life Legacy of Very Early Life*. Berlin:
Springer, 2004.
66 Bengtsson, "Living Standards," 41-45; and Robert I. Rotberg and Theodore K.
Rabb, eds., *Hunger and History: The Impact of Changing Food Production and Consumption Patterns of Society*. Cambridge: Cambridge University Press, 1985, 308.
67 There is a general absence of information about infectious diseases and mortality
rates in seventeenth-century Amsterdam. For a useful summary of the situation in
the period 1776-1805, see Diederiks, *Stad in Verval*, 43-47.
68 Dekker, *Uit de schaduw*, 200.
69 The painting is in the Rijksmuseum in Amsterdam.
70 Given the presence of water virtually everywhere in Amsterdam, it is likely that some
children were the victims of drowning. For early modern England, see Elizabeth
Towner and John Towner, "Developing the history of unintentional injury: the use
of coroners' records in early modern England," *Injury Prevention* 6 (2000):102-105.

CHAPTER 7

1   Cited in Saskia Kuus, "Children's Costume in the Sixteenth and Seventeenth Centuries" in Jan Baptist Bedaux and Rudi Ekkart, eds., *Pride and Joy: Children's Portraits in the Netherlands 1500-1700*. Ghent/Amsterdam: Ludion Press, 2000, 75.

2   Ibid.

3   As in other times and places, mothers and fathers preferred male offspring. This preference has the status of a universal, existing in all societies. See, for example, Marion J. Levy, *Our Mother-Tempers*. Berkeley: University of California Press, 1989, xiii. But, as Conley reports is the case today, many parents probably desired at least one child of each sex. Dalton Conley, *The Pecking Order: Which Siblings Succeed and Why*. New York: Pantheon, 2004, 67.

4   Liam Hudson and Bernadine Jacot, *The Way Men Think: Intellect, Intimacy and the Erotic Imagination*. New Haven and London: Yale University Press, 1991, 25.

5   Mothers are, and always have been, asymmetrically influential in shaping children during their formative years. This is most cogently argued in Levy, *Our Mother-Tempers*.

6   Ralph Greenson, a psychoanalyst, seems to have been the first author to emphasize a little boy's need to separate himself imaginatively from his mother and identify instead with his father. Ralph R. Greenson, "Dis-identifying from mother: its special importance for the boy," *International Journal of Psychoanalysis*, 49 (1968),370. This has been elaborated upon by Dorothy Dinnerstein, *The Mermaid and the Minotaur*. New York: Harper and Row, 1976; Nancy Chodorow, *The Reproduction of Mothering*. Berkeley: University of California Press, 1978. Updated edition with new preface by the author, 1999; and other writers since the time.

7   See, for example, Alison Earle and S. Jody Heymann, "Work, Family, and Social Class." In Brim, Ryff, and Kessler, eds., *How Healthy Are We?* 485-513.

8   There is little documentary evidence about the relationships of parents and children in the Dutch seventeenth century and virtually nothing about the relationship between fathers and young children. Autobiographies and other writings, mostly by wealthy men, do make clear that fathers were concerned about the health and well-being of newborn children and were often grief-stricken when children died prematurely. But nothing is known about wealthy men handling infants and young children, caring for them in their wife's absence, or playing with them. Dekker, *Uit de schaduw*; and Dekker, "Children on their Own, Changing Relations in the Family: The Experience of Dutch Autobiographers, Seventeenth to Nineteenth Centuries" in Schuurman and Spierenburg, *Private Domain, Public Inquiry*, 61-71.

9   Joop de Jong, *Een Deftige Bestaan*. Utrecht/Antwerp: Uitgeverij Kosmos, 1987, 144.

10 I draw here on the excellent study by Schijf and van Woerkom, "Boekhouders en Peperwerkers."

11 Although they cannot be taken as accurate representations of the way things really were, surviving paintings from the time show a father spoon-feeding a child and walking a baby at night while his wife sleeps. See the discussion in Simon Schama, *The Embarrassment of Riches: An Interpretation of Dutch Culture in the Golden Age*. New York: Knopf, 1987, 541-544.

12 Kuus, "Children's Costume," 82.

13 No such portraits were made of children in the families of ordinary people. It is entirely possible that the children of immigrants were dressed in accordance with the customs of wherever they came from. Whatever the fashion at a particular period, says Kuus, children were always dressed in a manner thought appropriate for their gender, age, and social standing. Ibid.

14 For a useful overview of schooling in seventeenth-century Amsterdam, see Doorninck and Kuijpers, *De geschoolde stad*.

15 Although there were laws against the misuse of laboring children, boys and girls of just six or eight years of age sometimes labored 10 or more hours a day. J.C. Vleggert, *Kinderarbeid in Nederland, 1500-1874: Van Berusting tot Beperking*. Assen: Van Gorcum, 1964, 9-15.

16 E.P. de Booy, "Naar School: Schoolgaande kinderen in de Noordelijke Nederlanden in de zeventiende en achttiende eeuw," *Tijdschrift voor Geschiedenis* 94 (1981):427-441.

17 The source here is a study by Fortgens of the Latin School in the seventeenth century. H.W. Fortgens, *Schola Latina*. Zwolle: N.V. Uitgevers-Mij, 1958, 43-44, 56-60.

18 For a consideration of similar views in other times and places, see Phillips, *Looking Backward*.

19 Such conflicts are almost a dominant theme in Kooijmans.

20 There are, however, exceptions. Important recent publications regarding siblings are Davidoff, *Worlds Between*; Juliet Mitchell, *Siblings*. Cambridge: Polity Press, 2003; and Conley, *Pecking Order*. See also, Naomi J. Miller and Naomi Yavneh, eds., *Sibling Relations and Gender in the Early Modern World*. Aldershot: Ashgate, 2006.

21 Davidoff, *Worlds Between*, 209.

22 See, for example, Sula Wolff, *Childhood & Human Nature: The Development of Personality*. London and New York: Routledge, 1989, 86-88.

23 Probate inventory NAA 7234. Acte 151.

24 A.R. Pebley, A.I. Hermalin, and J. Knodel, "Birth spacing and infant mortality: evidence for eighteenth and nineteenth century German villages," *Journal of Biosocial Science* 23 (October 1991):445-459; Frank Falkner, ed., *Infant and Child Nutrition Worldwide: Issues and Perspectives*. Boca Raton: CRC Press, 1991; and Ladzo Ruzicka, Guillaume Wunsch, and Penny Kane, *Differential Mortality: Methodological Issues and Biosocial Factors*. Oxford: Oxford University Press, 1993, are informative in this regard.

25 Pebley, Hermalin, and Knodel, "Birth spacing," 2.

26 In several of the wealthy families whom Klaske Muizelaar and I studied, the birth intervals were as short as 10 or 11 months. As in the case of Johanna Timmers, the intervals were shorter with earlier-born than later-born children.

27 Viazzo, "Mortality, Fertility, and Family," 174.

28 Finn, *The European Demographic System*, 88-91.

29 Bedaux and Ekkart, *Pride and Joy*, 152.

30 Johanna Timmers outlived her husband and most of their children. In the inventory made at the time of her death, two family portraits are listed. NAA 7234, Acte 151. One wonders which children were portrayed, since it was not unheard of for a portrait of the family to include dead children (or a dead husband or wife).

31 For the seventeenth-century Netherlands, see Dekker, *Uit de schaduw*, 200-222. For early modern England, see Linda Pollock, *Forgotten Children: Parent-Child Relations from 1500 to 1900*. Cambridge: Cambridge University Press, 1983.

32 Grief-like responses are universal. But manifestations of grief vary from one time and place to another. Margaret S. Stroebe, Robert O. Hansson, and Wolfgang Stroebe, "Contemporary themes and controversies in bereavement research" in Margaret S. Stroebe, Wolfgang Stroebe, and Robert O. Hansson, eds., *Handbook of bereavement: Theory, research, and intervention*. Cambridge: Cambridge University Press, 1993, 457-475.

33 Mothers everywhere have more intense reactions than fathers to the death of a child.

See, for example, Linda Edelstein, *Maternal Bereavement: Coping With the Unexpected Death of a Child*. New York: Praeger Publishers, 1984; Simon Shimshon Rubin, "The Death of a child is forever: The life course impact of child loss" in Stroebe, Stroebe, and Hansson, *Handbook*, 285-295; and Catherine M. Sanders, "Risk factors in bereavement outcomes," in ibid., 255-267.

34 Jeroen Dekker, Leendert Groenendijk, and Johan Verberckmoes, "Proudly Raising Vulnerable Youngsters" in Bedaux and Ekkert, *Pride and Joy*, 51.

35 Two of the children were buried in the Noorderkerk, the third in the Ouderkerk. Only the relatively well-to-do could afford burials inside a church. Three-quarters of the people who died in Amsterdam were buried in the city's six cemeteries. Diederiks, *Een Stad in Verval*, 18.

36 Nevertheless, fathers can also be devastated by the death of a child. Dekker reports two dramatic instances, *Uit de schaduw*, 213.

37 The extinguisher torch, it is argued, is a metaphor for death. Bedaux and Ekkart, *Pride and Joy*, 192.

38 For a good discussion of the psychological impact of household objects, see Leora Auslander, "Beyond Words," *American Historical Review* 110 (October 2005):1015-1045.

39 Hokke, "'Mijn alderliefste Jantielief,'" 69-72; and Thera Wijsenbeek-Olthuis, "Ziekte en tegenslag" in Marijke Gijswijt-Hofstra and Florike Egmond, eds., *Of Bidden Helpt? Tegenslag en cultuur in Europa, circa 1500-2000*. Amsterdam: Amsterdam University Press, 1997:71-86.

40 In plague years, however, all families were vulnerable.

41 The importance to a child of a room of its own, with a place to display its most cherished possessions, is discussed at length in Eugene Rochberg-Halton, *Social Theory in the Pragmatic Attitude*. Chicago: University of Chicago Press, 1986, 147-184.

42 Parents were aware of the danger of brother-sister incest, since it was a topic in literature, history, mythology, and the Bible. Social and biblical prohibitions were taken quite seriously, and parents must have tried to take precautions in this regard. They must have recognized that having a brother and sister share a room, let alone a bed, was to invite sex play. Where they could, parents probably tried to see that sleeping arrangements ensured the separation of the sexes, but it was not always possible.

43 Mitchell, *Siblings*, 76.

44 Haks, *Huwelijk en gezin*, 35-48.

45 An example is found in Kooijmans, *Vriendschap*, 121.

46 Van der Heijden, *Huwelijk in Holland*, 165-169.

47 Ibid., 14.

48 Mitchell, *Siblings*. Dunn's research on sibling relationships reveals that even in old age people vividly recall crucial incidents that occurred between themselves and their siblings. Judy Dunn, "Sibling Studies and the Developmental Impact of Critical Incidents" in P.B. Baltes and O.G. Brim, eds., *Life-Span Development and Behavior*. New York and London: Academic Press, 1983, 335-353. See also Judy Dunn and Carol Kendrici, *Siblings: Love, Envy, and Understanding*. Cambridge, Mass.: Harvard University Press, 1982.

49 A notable exception is the indication of a warm and loving relationship between the two brothers David and Hendrik Beck. David Beck, *Spiegel van mijn leven. Een Haags dagboek uit 1624*. Hilversum: Verloren, 1993.

50 I will mention two examples. One is Hermanus Verbeek, the man who with his wife, Clara Molenaers, employed a wet-nurse for their infant son who later died. His brothers and sisters regarded him as a failure at everything he tried, yet they helped

him financially to avoid having the family name brought into discredit. Hermanus Verbeek, *Memoriaal Ofte Mijn Levens-Raijsinghe*. Editie Jeroen Blaak. Egodocument-en deel 16. Hilversum: Verloren, 1999, 22. A second example is Cornelia Bierens, who we saw in a family portrait (Illustration 3.1) and who left money to her two servants. She left her most valuable painting – valued at an extraordinary 1,000 guilders – to her younger brother, Anthony Bierens. This was, she wrote in her last will and testament, in gratitude for his many-sided friendship, as evidenced by what she describes as his courtesy towards her and the trouble he had taken on her behalf. Sister and brother must have had a deep affection and respect for each other. NAA 7604. For a recent discussion of relationships between brothers (David and Hendrik Beck, and Hermanus and Pieter Verbeeck), see Irma Thorn, *Strategic Affection: Gift Exchange in Seventeenth-Century Holland*. Amsterdam: Amsterdam University Press, 2007, 151-164.

51 Some girls and women attempted to pass as men as a way of experiencing an independent existence for at least a short period. Lotte C. van de Pol and Rudolf M. Dekker, *The Tradition of Female Transvestism in Early Modern Europe*. Basingstoke: Macmillan, 1989.

52 Three well-known seventeenth-century examples are Anna Maria van Schurman, Maria Tesselschade, and Maria Sibylla Merian, all three of whom challenged contemporary views about the capabilities and roles of women. Some of Van Schurman's writings are available in English in Anna Maria van Schurman, *Whether a Christian Woman Should Be Educated and Other Writings from her Intellectual Circle*, edited and translated by Joyce L. Irwin. Chicago: University of Chicago Press, 1998. For a discussion of Maria Tesselschade, see Mieke B. Smits-Veldt, *Maria Tesselschade: Leven met talent en vriendschap*. Zutphen: Walburg Pers, 1994. For Merian, see Kurt Wettengl, ed., *Maria Sibylla Merian, 1647-1717: Artist and Naturalist*. Verlag Gerd Hatje, no date; and Natalie Zemon Davis, *Women on the Margins. Three Seventeenth-Century Lives*. Cambridge, Mass.: Harvard University Press, 1995. Merian was born in Germany, but lived in Holland for many years.

53 Not only is there an absence of evidence about women's awareness of their lack of power and consequent vulnerability in the surviving diaries and other personal writings by women at the time, but female novelists dealing with feelings and emotions were generally unknown in the seventeenth-century Dutch Republic. See Riet Schenkeveld-van de Dussen et al., eds., *Met en zonder lauwerkrans: schrijvende vrouwen uit de vroegmoderne tijd 1550-1850: van Anna Bijns tot Elise van Calcar*. Amsterdam: Amsterdam University Press, 1997; and Riet Schenkeveld-van de Dussen, *De geheimen van het vrouwelijk hart*. Amsterdam: Koninklijke Nederlandse Academie van Wetenschappen, 2001. In England, by contrast, fiction by women dealt at length with the experiences, needs, hopes, and fears of women. Women's sexuality was a common theme, as was anger about their disadvantaged position. See, for example, Paula R. Backscheider and John J. Richetti, eds., *Popular Fiction by Women 1660-1730*. Oxford: Oxford University Press, 1996. Some Dutch women were, however, aware of novels by English, French, and other women writers. See Suzan van Dijk et al., eds., *"I have heard about you." Foreign woman's writing crossing the Dutch border: from Sappho to Selma Lagerlöf*. Trans. Jo Nesbitt. Hilversum: Verloren, 2004.

54 Arguing against those who claim that people in certain times and places were *unable* to question the fairness of dominant social arrangements, Moody-Adams specifies two conditions that make such questioning possible: (1) that there is at least one class of people who suffer hardships as a result of the practice in question, while receiving comparatively few of its benefits; and (2) that there is good reason to assume that

those reaping the benefits of the practice would not choose to be members of the group suffering most of the burdens. Michele M. Moody-Adams, *Fieldwork in Familiar Places: Morality, Culture, & Philosophy*. Cambridge: Harvard University Press, 1997, 85-103. These conditions certainly existed in seventeenth-century Amsterdam. As she notes, "every human being has the capacity to question existing practices, and to imagine that one's social world might be better than it is." Ibid., 100.

CHAPTER 8

1   Sara F. Matthews Grieco, "The Body, Appearance, and Sexuality" in Natalie Zemon Davis and Arlette Farge, eds., *A History of Women in the West. III. Renaissance and Enlightenment Paradoxes*. Cambridge: Harvard University Press, 1993, 79.

2   Little is known about the frequency of sexual relations between married couples. But in a diary kept by the wealthy regent, Joan Huydecoper, he recorded the number of times he had sexual intercourse with his wife. During the year 1659, after three years of marriage, he indicates that they had intercourse seventy-five times-up to just two weeks before she gave birth. See Kooijmans, *Vriendschap*, 152-153.

3   Andrejs Plakans and Charles Wetherell, "Households and kinship networks: the costs and benefits of contextualization," *Continuity and Change* 18 (2003):65. Italics in original.

4   For individuals registering to marry in 1650, only one-third of the women and one-fifth of the men had relatives living in Amsterdam. Kuijpers, *Migrantenstad*, 189.

5   For a particularly insightful discussion, see Bartky's "Unplanned Obsolescence: Some Reflections on Aging" in Sandra Lee Bartky, *Sympathy and Solidarity*. Lanham: Rowman & Littlefield, 2002, 91-111.

6   Ibid., 102-104; and Joan Didion, *The Year of Magical Thinking*. London: Fourth Estate, 2005, 197.

7   To the extent that an individual's self-image and sense of esteem are dependent on relationships with his or her spouse, the spouse's death may be either highly destructive or enormously liberating. That is to say, widowhood also sets people free.

8   See Phyllis S. Silverman and J. William Worden, "Children's reactions to the death of a parent" in Stroebe, Stroebe, and Hansson, *Handbook*, 457-475.

9   This was the figure in Western Europe and would have been similar in Amsterdam. Viazzo, "Mortality, Fertility, and Family" in Kerzer and Barbagli, *Family Life*, 185.

10 Schipper-van Lottum, *Advertenties en Berichten*, aflevering 1, 24, item from a April 14, 1674.

11 In examining the inventories of household possessions drawn up after the death of a spouse, Klaske Muizelaar and I found that every woman whose husband had died was identified as the widow of so-and-so. Women who had lost two husbands were identified as the widows of both men. Not one man whose wife had died was identified as a widower.

12 Dineke Hempenius-van Dijk, "Widows and the Law: The legal position of widows in the Dutch Republic during the seventeenth and eighteenth centuries" in Jan Bremmer and Lourens van den Bosch, eds., *Between Poverty and the Pyre*. London and New York: Routledge, 1995, 93-94; and Marshall, *The Dutch Gentry*, 53.

13 Olwen Hufton, "Women, Work, and Family" in Davis and Farge, *History of Women*, 45.

14 For a sample of what she refers to as poor to middling households in Amsterdam a century later, McCants calculates the cost of the average "burial package" at 28 guilders. Given the same income distributions as in the seventeenth century, this is a sizeable sum and would have been beyond the means of many families. Burial costs were, she notes, a major source of unpaid debts. McCants, "Inequality among the poor," 10-11. Klaske Muizelaar and I found that in rich families the burial costs often exceeded 600 guilders.

15 Hempenius-van Dijk, ""Widows and the Law, 97; and van der Heijden, *Huwelijk in Holland*, 53.

16 Such a male-female difference was quite standard in Western Europe. See Hufton, *The Prospect Before Her*, 220-221.

17 Stroebe, Hansson, and Stroebe, "Contemporary themes," 465. Another study concludes that it takes the average widow several years after her spouse's death to regain her former level of life satisfaction. Cited in Didion, *Year of Magical Thinking*, 170.

18 For mourning clothes in the Dutch Republic, see J.C. Dekker and K.P.C. de Leeuw, *Levensloop, cultuur en mentaliteit. Een geschiedenis van het alledaagse bestaan*. Tilburg: Tilburg University Press, 1990; and K.P.C. de Leeuw, *Kleding in Nederland*. Hilversum: Verloren, 1992. For the early modern Europe more generally, see Phyllis Cunnington and Catherine Lucas, *Costumes for Births, Marriages and Deaths*. London: A.& C. Black, 1972; and Lou Taylor, *Mourning Dress: A Costume and Social History*. London: George Allen & Unwin, 1983.

19 Wayne E. Franits, *Paragons of Virtue: Women and Domesticity in Seventeenth-Century Dutch Art*. Cambridge: Cambridge University Press, 1993, 189.

20 For a somewhat later period, McCants found that each additional child decreased a widow's chance of remarrying by 12 percent, while the number of children a widower had made little difference for his chances of remarrying. Anne E.C. McCants, "The Not-So-Merry Widows of Amsterdam," *Journal of Family History* 24 (2999):441-467.

21 Matthews Grieco, "The Body, Appearance, and Sexuality" 46-84.

22 Sandra Cavallo and Lyndan Warner, "Introduction" in Sandra Cavallo and Lyndan Warner, eds., *Widowhood in Medieval and Early Modern Europe*. Essex: Longman, 1999, 10.

23 Elias, *De vroedschap*.

24 This was true in preindustrial Europe more generally. For a penetrating discussion, see Bell, *How to Do It*, 258-278.

25 This information comes from the household inventory made at the time of Clara Valkenier's death. Inventory Number NAA 4664 (filmnr. 6120), Fol.6-51.

26 In some instances, however, moderately-wealthy husbands purchased life annuities that provided an income for their widows. See J.C. Riley, "That Your Widow May Be Rich" Providing for Widowhood in Old Regime Europe," *Economisch- en Sociaal-Historisch Jaarboek* 45 (1982):58-76.

27 A similar situation existed in Germany at the time. See Dagmar Friest, "Religious difference at the experience of widowhood in seventeenth- and eighteenth-century Germany" in Cavallo and Warner, *Widowhood*, 168.

28 Gorski, *The Disciplinary Revolution*, 62.

29 Sheila D. Muller, *Charity in the Dutch Republic: Pictures of Rich and Poor for Charitable Institutions*. Ann Arbor, Mich.: UMI Research Press, 122.

30 M.H.D. van Leeuwen, "Amsterdam en de armenzorg tijdens de Republiek," *NEHA-Jaarboek* 50 (1996):132-161. This possibility is implicit in Carter, *The English Reformed Church*, 143, 151. The same was true in early modern England where widows

who had been better-off before the death of their husbands received higher levels of assistance. Paul Slack, *Poverty and Policy in Tudor and Stuart England*. London: Longman, 1988, 179. See also Keith Wrightson, *Earthly Necessities: Economic Lives in Early Modern Britain*. New Haven and London: Yale University Press, 2000, 218.

31 This is suggested by Kuijpers, *Migrantenstad*, 308. Hindle argues that receipt of poor relief in early modern England was always the final state in a process of negotiation between applicants and parish officials. Steve Hindle, *On the Parish: The micro-politics of poor relief in rural England, c.1550-1750*. Oxford: Clarendon, 2004.

32 Bos, *"Uyt Liefde*, 343.

33 Ibid.

34 The above discussion of the consequences of a woman's being widowed is indebted to Schmidt's study of the implications of widowhood for the legal, social, and economic status of women in seventeenth-century Leiden. Ariadne Schmidt, *Overleven na de dood: Weduwen in Leiden in de Gouden Eeuw*. Amsterdam: Prometheus/Bert Bakker, 2001. Also useful is Ariadne Schmidt, "The Winter of Her Life? Widowhood and the Lives of Dutch Women in the Early Modern Era" in Anneke B. Mulder-Bakker and Renée Nip, eds., *The Prime of Their Lives: Wise Old Women in Pre-Industrial Europe*. Leuven-Paris-Dudley,Ms.: Peeters, 2004, 138-148.

35 Noordegraaf, "De Arme." In Beliën, van Deursen, and van Setten, eds., *Gestalten*, 331. The situation was similar elsewhere in the Dutch Republic. See, for example, van der Vlis, *Leven in armoede*.

36 Kuijpers, *Migrantenstad*, 289.

37 Ibid.,304.

38 In Zwolle, notes van Wijngaarden, this resulted in "an enormous variation in the levels and kinds of assistance for each poor family." van Wijngaarden, *Zorg voor de kost*, 391-392 (English summary).

39 Carter, *English Reformed Church*, 143-145.

40 See, for example, Elise van Nederveen Meerkerk, *De draad in eigen handen: Vrouwen en loonarbeid in de Nederlandse textielnijverheid, 1581-1810*. Amsterdam: Aksant, 2007, 226.

41 Carter, *English Reformed Church*, 144; Van Wijngaarden, *Zorg voor de kost*, 138-143.

42 For England, see Pamela Sharpe, "Survival strategies and stories: poor widows and widowers in early industrial England" in Cavallo and Warner, *Widowhood*, 228.

43 Kuijpers, *Migrantenstad*, 168, 198.

44 Van Nederveen Meerkerk, *De Draad in eigen handen*, 230.

45 Schmidt, "Winter of Her Life?," 146.

46 Van Wijngaarden, *Zorg voor de Kost*, 330.

47 Ibid.,166. As already noted, women were paid considerably less even when they did exactly the same work as men.

48 Simon Groenveld, "'For the Benefit of the Poor': Social Assistance in Amsterdam" in van Kessel and Schulte, *Rome/ Amsterdam*, 204-207.

49 Kuijpers, *Migrantenstad*, 320-324; and Erika Kuijpers, "Poor, Illiterate and Superstitious? Social and Cultural Characteristics of the 'Noordse Natie' in the Amsterdam Lutheran Church in the Seventeenth Century." In Louis Sticking, Harry de Bles, and Erlend des Bouvrie, eds., *Dutch Light in the Norwegian Night: Maritime Relations and Migration Across the North Sea in Early Modern Times*. Hilversum: Verloren, 2004, 66.

50 Similarly in early modern Britain where, notes Wrightson, officials had to balance the benefits of a steady supply of labor against the potential expenses involved in poor relief. Wrightson, *Earthly Necessities*, 219-220.

51 Muller, *Charity in the Dutch Republic*, 87. In seventeenth-century Zeist more than a third of the households receiving poor relief consisted of a widow with children, while only 1.5 percent consisted of a widower and children. See van Wijngaarden, *Zorg voor de kost*, 88. I am unaware of any figures for Amsterdam.

52 Cavallo and Warner, "Introduction" to *Widowhood*, 23.

53 Acts 6:1, Mark 12:40-44; 1 Timothy 5.

54 Margaret Pelling, "Finding widowers: men without women in English towns before 1700." In Ibid., 46; Lyndan Warner, "Widows, widowers and the problem of 'second marriages' in sixteenth-century France" in Ibid., 87; Friest, "Religious Differences" in Ibid., 166.

55 Pelling, "Finding widowers," 48.

56 Michael R. Cunningham, Perri B. Druen, and Anita P. Barbee, "Angels, Mentors, and Friends: Trade-Offs among Evolutionary, Social, and Individual Variables in Physical Appearance." In Jeffrey A. Simpson and Douglas T. Tenrik, *Evolutionary Social Psychology*. Mahwah: Erlbaum, 1997, 109-140.

57 Pelling, "Finding Widowers," 51.

58 My estimate is based on the various studies cited in Cavallo and Warner, *Widowhood*; Antoinette Fauve-Chamoux, "Marriage, Widowhood, and Divorce" in Kertzer and Barbagli, *Family Life*, 241-255; E.M. Kloek, "De Vrouw", 259-262, and Kuijpers, *Migrantenstad*.

59 In some instances, however, a widow's second husband was both younger than her first and younger than she was. This was especially the case among young men attracted to widows who had Amsterdam citizenship.

60 Van der Heijden, *Huwelijk in Holland*, 175, 231-235.

61 For the Dutch Republic, see Ibid. For preindustrial Europe, see Viazzo, "Mortality, Fertility, and Family;" and Linda A. Pollock, "Parent-Child Relations" in Kertzer and Barbagli, *Family Life*, 214-215.

CHAPTER 9

1 Hugh Cunningham, *Children and Childhood in Western Society since 1500*. London and New York: Longman, 1995, 97; and Viazzo, "Mortality, Fertility, and Family" in Kertzer and Barbagli, *Family Life*, 184-187.

2 My estimates are based on van Leeuwen and Oeppen, "Reconstructing the Demographic Regime," Table 10.

3 Kuijpers, *Migrantenstad*, 209.

4 Ibid., 203.

5 I draw here on Silverman and Worden, "Children's reactions to the death of a parent," 457-475.

6 See the extended discussion of household inventories in Muizelaar and Phillips, *Picturing Men and Women*, 175-183.

7 On notaries in seventeenth-century England, see C.W. Brooks, B.H. Hemholz, and P.G. Stein, *Notaries Public in England Since the Reformation*. Norwich: Erskine Press, 1991.

8 De Vries and van der Woude, *The First Modern Economy*, 139.

9 A. Pitlo, "Iets over de geschiedenis van het notariaat in Nederland," *Weekblad voor Privaatrecht, Notaris-ambt en Registratie*," of November 1 and 8, 1941, Nos. 3749 and 3750.

10 Probate Inventory NAA 5503, Akte. No. 4.

11 See the discussion in Marshall, *The Dutch Gentry*, xvii, 41-59.

12 In the case of children admitted to the municipal orphanage, the Burgerweeshuis, McCants estimates that only 6 percent did not have close relatives in Amsterdam. Anne E.C. McCants, *Civic Charity in a Golden Age: Orphan Care in Early Modern Amsterdam*. Urbana and Chicago: University of Illinois Press, 1997, 33.

13 Van Wijngaarden, *Zorg voor de kost*, 210-216.

14 Simon Groenveld, "'For the Benefit of the Poor," 192-208. Some half orphans were also admitted to the orphanages, as in cases where the father was out of the country with the VOC at the time a child's mother died. S. Groenveld, J.J.H. Dekker, and T.R.M. Willemse, *Wezen en boefjes: Zes eeuwen zorg in wees- en kinderhuizen*. Hilversum: Verloren, 1997, 130-133.

15 J.T. Engels, *Kinderen van Amsterdam*. Amsterdam: De Walburg Pers, 1989, 14.

16 McCants, *Civic Charity*, 82.

17 McCants speaks of the "middling classes." While she suggests that the group consisted of around one-third of Amsterdam households, I estimate that they made up one-quarter at most. McCants, *Civic Charity*, 27, 240.

18 McCants indicates an absence of information about inventories for the seventeenth century. Her analysis of a sample of 912 inventories for the period 1740-1782, however, reveals that the majority of estates had very limited assets. McCants, "Inequality," 1-21. In fact, most estates were too small to cover the expenditure of the Burgerweeshuis for more than six months of care for a child, 10.

19 McCants, *Civic Charity*, 152; Groenveld et al., *Wezen en boefjes*, 119.

20 Jo Spans, "Early Modern Orphanages between Civic Pride and Social Discipline: Francke's Use of Dutch Models" in Udo Sträter, and Josef N. Neumann, *Waisenhäuser in der Frühen Neuzeit*. Tübingen: Halliesche Forschungen, 2003, 6.

21 Ibid., 61.

22 Elsewhere in the Dutch Republic, there were the same clear qualitative differences between orphanages for the children from middling and disadvantaged backgrounds. Groenveld, et al., *Wezen en boefjes*.

23 Groenveld et al., *Wezen en boefjes*, 97.

24 Spans, "Early Modern Orphanages," 9.

25 For an analysis of elite women today seeking power through similar kinds of volunteer activities, see Diana Kendall, *The Power of Good Deeds: Privileged Women and the Social Reproduction of the Upper Class*. Lanham, MD: Rowman and Littlefield, 2002.

26 She would, in any case, have had to approve the portrait as at least a likeness of her actual appearance.

27 Michiel Jonker, "Public or Private Portraits: Group Portraits of Amsterdam Regents and Regentesses" in Wheelock and Seeff, *The Public and Private*, 214.

28 Ibid., 208.

29 The rule was that a man could serve only two out of every three years as Burgomaster. Johannes Hudde did so. See Elias, *De Vroedschap*, 528-529.

30 Adriaen Backer's portrait "De Regentessen van het Burgerweeshuis" is described in Middlekoop et al., *Kopstukken*, 191.

31 Jonker, "Public or Private Portraits."

32 For discussions of the portrayals of orphans in seventeenth-century Dutch art, see Muller, *Charity in the Dutch Republic*; and Linda Stone-Ferrier, "Metsu's Justice Protecting Widows and Orphans: Patron and Painter Relationships and Their Involvement in the Social and Economic Plight of Widows and Orphans in Leiden" in Wheelock and Seeff, *The Public and Private*, 227-265.

33 Groenveld et al., *Wezen en boefjes*, 101.
34 Ibid., 151-154.
35 McCants, *Civic Charity*, 147-150.
36 It is quite extraordinary that in an orphanage in Woerden Evert Willemsz. was encouraged by officials to apply to the Latin school and that he was later awarded a scholarship to attend the State College for theology in Leiden. As Frijhoff notes, it was generally taken for granted that children would learn a trade similar to that of their fathers or others from their social background. Willem Frijhoff, *Wegen van Evert Willemsz.: Een Hollands Weeskind op zoek naar zichzelf, 1607-1647*. Nijmegen: SUN, 1995, 269. He makes it clear that Evert Willemsz. was a highly unusual individual.
37 Cited in Bontemantel, *De Regeering van Amsterdam*, vol 2, 519. Resolution from the Burgomasters January 8; 1652.
38 McCants, *Civic Charity*, 71.
39 Contract presented in de Jager, "Meester, leerjongen," 98-99.
40 I have been unable to find any trace of Erick van den Weerelt as a seventeenth-century Dutch painter.
41 Groenveld et al., *Wezen en boefjes*, 61.
42 Diederiks, *Een Stad in Verval*, 53.
43 McCants, *Civic Charity*, 54.
44 Kuijpers, *Migrantenstad*, 203-205.
45 Groenveld et al., *Wezen en boefjes*, 148-149. In his excellent study of the life of an orphan in Woerden, Frijhoff reports that in 1622 the 15-year-old boy shared a bed with his two younger half-brothers. It was the rule, Frijhoff found, that several children should share the limited number of beds in the orphanage. Frijhoff, *Wegen*, 250-251.
46 Engels, *Kinderen*, 42.
47 McCants, *Civic Charity*, 76.
48 Ibid.
49 De Vries and van der Woude, *The First Modern Economy*, 606.
50 McCants, *Civil Charity*, 28.
51 Ibid., 75.
52 Ibid., 70-76.
53 Ibid., 26-27.
54 Ibid., especially 6-10, 28, 202-202. For an argument about how the regents obtained the tacit consent of other citizens in the latter's exclusion from political participation, see van Nierop, "Private Interests, Public Policies" in Wheelock and Seeff, *The Public and Private*, 33-39.
55 Groenveld et al., *Wezen en boefjes*, 59-69.
56 My estimate is based on Groenveld et al., *Wezen en boefjes*; Engels, *Kinderen*; and Gorski, *The Disciplinary Revolution*.
57 Kuijpers, *Migrantenstad*, 205.
58 Schipper-van Lottum, *Advertensies en Berichten*, issue 3 A-B, 1260.
59 Groenveld et al., *Wezen en boefjes*, 149-151.
60 Ibid., 149. Frijhoff provides a particularly informative picture of life inside a small orphanage (about 30 children). Frijhoff, *Wegen*, 244-258, 275-285. For orphanages in the Netherlands more generally, see Ingrid van der Vlis, *Weeshuizen in Nederland: De wisselende gestalten van een weldadig instituut*. Zutphen: Walburg Pers, 2002.
61 Mary McCarthy, *Memories of a Catholic Childhood*. New York: Penguin Books, 1957, 35. When both parents died in an influenza epidemic, she and her three younger

brothers were raised by their paternal grandparents. Like children in orphanages, they were treated, writes McCarthy, like "pieces of furniture." Little has been written about growing up behind orphanage walls, and nothing about early modern Amsterdam. As with much else regarding love, loss, and the emotions, autobiographies and the masterpieces of imaginative writing extend our knowledge of the orphan experience. Orphans are everywhere in Charles Dickens, with *David Copperfield* and *Oliver Twist* perhaps the best known. Charlotte Bronte's *Jane Eyre* is an orphan, as are the two boys in Mark Twain's *Adventures of Tom Sawyer* and *Adventures of Huckleberry Finn*.

62 Eileen Simpson, *Orphans: Real and Imaginary*. London: Weidenfeld and Nicolson, 1987, 135. This sensitive book illuminates the orphan experience. Also useful is Baruch Hochman and Ilja Wachs, *Dickens: The Orphan Condition*. Madison and Teaneck: Fairleigh Dickinson University Press, 1999.

BIBLIOGRAPHY

Adams, Fran. *Below the Breadline: Living on the Minimum Wage.* London: Profile Books, 2002.

Adams, Julia. "The familial state: Elite family practices and State-making in the early modern Netherlands." *Theory and Society* 23 (1994):505-539.

—. *The Familial State: Ruling Families and Merchant Capitalism in Early Modern Europe.* Ithaca and London: Cornell University Press, 2005.

Alba, Richard, and Victor Nee. *Remaking the American Mainstream: Assimilation and Contemporary Immigration.* Cambridge: Harvard University Press, 2003.

Allen, Robert C., Tommy Bengtsson, and Martin Dribe, eds. *Living Standards in the Past: New Perspectives on Well-Being in Asia and Europe.* Oxford: Oxford University Press, 2005.

Alphen, Marc A. van. "The Female Side of Dutch Shipping: Financial Bonds of Seamen Ashore in the 17th and 18th Centuries" in *Anglo-Dutch Mercantile Marine Relations, 1700-1850,* edited by J.R. Bruijn and W.F.J. Mörzen Bruyns. Amsterdam: Rijksmuseum, 1991, 125-133.

Alter, George, Matteo Manfredini, Paul Nystedt, et al. "Gender Differences in Mortality" in *Life Under Pressure: Mortality and Living Standards in Europe and Asia, 1700-1900,* edited by Tommy Bengtsson, Cameron Campbell, James Z. Lee, et al. Cambridge and London: MIT Press, 2004.

Amelang, James S. *The Flight of Icarus: Artisan Autobiography In Early Modern Europe.* Stanford: Stanford University Press, 1998.

Anand, Sudhir, and Amartya Sen, "The Income Component of the Human Development Index." *Journal of Human Development* 1 (2000):83-106.

Annas, Julia. "Women and the Quality of Life: Two Norms or One?" in *The Quality of Life,* edited by Martha Nussbaum and Amartya Sen. Oxford: Clarendon Press, 1993, 287-291.

Archer, Ian W. *The Pursuit of Stability: Social Relations in Elizabethan London.* Cambridge: Cambridge University Press, 1991.

Armbrust, Annemarie, Marguérite Corporaal, & Marjolein van Dekken, eds. *'Dat gy mij niet vergeet.' Correspondentie Van vrouwen in de zeventiende en achttiende eeuw.* Amsterdam: Aksant Academic Publishers, 2006.

Auslander, Leora. "Beyond Words." *American Historical Review* 110 (October 2005):1015-1045.

Backscheider, Paula R., and John J. Richetti, eds. *Popular Fiction by Women, 1660-1730.* Oxford: Oxford University Press, 1996.

Baggerman, Arianne, and Rudolf Dekker. "'De Gevaarlijkste van Alle Bronnen: Ego-documenten, nieuwe wegen en Perspectieven." *Tijdschrift voor Sociale en Economische Geschiedenis* 1 (2004):3-22.

Bandura, Albert. *Self-efficacy: The exercise of control.* New York: Freeman, 1997.

Barbagli, Marzio and David I. Kertzer. "Introduction" in *Family Life in Early Modern Times, 1500-1789,* edited by David I. Kertzer and Marzio Barbagli. New Haven and London: Yale University Press, 2001.

Barbalet, J.M. *Emotion, Social Theory, and Social Structure.* Cambridge: Cambridge University Press, 2001.

Bartky, Sandra Lee. *Femininity and Domination.* New York and London: Routledge, 1990.

—. *Sympathy and Solidarity.* Lanham: Rowman & Littlefield, 2002.

Bay, Mia. *The White Image in the Black Mind: African-American Ideas about White People, 1830-1925.* New York: Oxford University Press, 2000.

Beck, David. *Spiegel van mijn leven. Een Haags dagboek uit 1624.* Hilversum: Verloren, 1993.

Bedaux, Jan Baptist, and Rudi Ekkart. *Pride and Joy: Children's Portraits in the Netherlands 1500-1700.* Ghent/Amsterdam: Ludion Press, 2000.

Belfanti, Carlo Marco, and Fabio Giusberti. "Clothing and Social inequality in early modern Europe: introductory remarks." *Continuity and Change* 15 (December 2000):359-365.

Bell, Rudolph M. *How to Do It: Guides to Good Living for Renaissance Italians.* Chicago: University of Chicago Press, 1999.

Benadusi, Giovanna. "Investing the Riches of the Poor: Servant Women and Their Last Wills." *American Historical Review* 109 (June 2004):805-826.

Bengtsson, Tommy. "Living Standards and Economic Stress." In *Life Under Pressure: Mortality and Living Standards in Europe and Asia, 1700-1900,* edited by Tommy Bengtsson, Cameron Campbell, James Z. Lee et al. Cambridge and London: MIT Press, 2004.

Bengtsson, Tommy, Cameron Campbell, and James Z. Lee, eds, *Mortality and Living Standards in Europe and Asia.* Cambridge, Ma.: MIT Press, 2004.

Bennett, Judith, and Amy M. Froide. "A Singular Past" in *Singlewomen in the European Past, 1250-1800.* Philadelphia: University of Pennsylvania Press, 1999.

Berg, Willem van den, Marco H.D. van Leeuwen, and Clé Lesger. "Residentiële segregatie in Hollandse steden: Theorien, methodologie en empirische bevindingen voor Alkmaar en Amsterdam, 16ᵉ-19ᵉ eeuw." *Tijdschrift voor Sociale Geschiedenis* 24 (1998):402-436.

Berge, Domien ten. *De Hooggeleerde en Zoetvlooiende Dichter Jacob Cats.* 's-Gravenhage: Martinus Nijhoff, 1979.

Blankaart, S. *Verhandelinge van der opvoedinge en ziekte der Kinderen.* Amsterdam, 1684.

Bontemantel, Hans. *De Regeeringe van Amsterdam, Soo in 't Civiel als Crimineel en Militaire (1653-1672).* Uitgegeven door G.W. Kernkamp. 's-Gravenhage, 1897. Two volumes.

Boone, Marc and Maarten Prak, eds. *Individual, corporate, and judicial status in European Cities (late middle ages and early modern period).* Leuven/Apeldoorn: Garant Publishers, 1996.

Booy, E.P. de. "Naar School: Schoolgaande kinderen in de Noordelijke Nederlanden in de zeventiende en achttiende eeuw." *Tijdschrift voor Geschiedenis* 94 (1981):427-441.

Borg, Helena Adelheid van der. *Vroedvrouwen: beeld en beroep.* Wageningen: Wageningen Academic Press, 1982.

Bos, Sandra. *"Uyt liefde tot malcander. Onderlinge Hulpverlening binnen de Noord-Nederlandse gilden in Internationaal perspectief 1570-1820."* IISG: Studies & Essays 27. Amsterdam: Internationaal Instituut voor Sociale Geschiedenis, 1998.

—. "A tradition of giving and receiving: Mutual aid within the guild system." In *Craft*

Guilds in the Early Modern Low Countries: Work, Power, and Representation, edited by Maarten Prak, Catherine Lis, Jan Lucassen, and Hugo Soly. Aldershot and Burlington: Ashgate, 2002, 174-193.

Bostoen, Karel. "De autobiografie van Jacob Cats." In *Ik is Anders: Autobiografie in verschillende culturen*, edited By Mineke Schipper and Peter Schmitz. Baarn: Ambo, 1991.

Brim, Orville Gilbert, Carol D. Ryff, and Ronald C. Kessler, eds. *How Healthy Are We? A National Study of Well-Being at Midlife*. Chicago: University of Chicago Press, 2004.

Bronte, Charlotte. *Shirley*. London: Penguin, 1994, originally published in 1849.

Brooks, C.W., B.H. Hemholz, and P.G. Stein. In *Notaries Public in England Since the Reformation*. Norwich: Erskine Press, 1991.

Bruijn, Jaap R. *The Dutch Navy of the Seventeenth and Eighteenth Centuries*. Columbia: University of South Carolina Press, 1993.

Buisman, J. *Duizend Jaar Weer, Wind en Water in De Lage Landen*. Volume 5, 1675-1750. Franeker: Uitgeverij van Wijnen, 2006.

Burridge, R., and D. Ormandy. *Unhealthy housing: Research, Remedies, and reform*. London: E. and F.N. Spon, 1993.

Carlson, Marybeth. *Domestic Service in a changing city economy: Rotterdam, 1680-1780*. Unpublished dissertation, University of Wisconsin, 1993.

—. "A Trojan horse of worldliness? Maidservants in the burgher household in Rotterdam at the end of the seventeenth century" in *Women of the Golden Age: An international debate on women in seventeenth- century Holland, England and Italy*, edited by Els Kloek, Nicole Teeuwen, and Marijke Huisman. Hilversum: Verloren, 1994.

Carter, Alice Clare. *The English Reformed Church in Amsterdam in the Seventeenth Century*. Amsterdam: Municipal Archives, 1964.

Cats, Jacob. *Huwelijk*. Middelburgh, 1625.

Cavallo, Sandra, and Lyndan Warner. "Introduction" in *Widowhood in Medieval and Early Modern Europe*, edited by Sandra Cavallo and Lyndan Warner. Essex: Longman, 1999.

Champion, Justin. "Epidemics and the built environment in 1665." In *Epidemic Disease in London*, edited by Justin Champion. Centre for Metropolitan History Working Papers Series, No. 1, 1993.

Chiappero Martinetti, Enrica. "A Multidimensional Assessment of Well-Being Based on Sen's Functioning Approach." *Revista Internazionale di Scienze* 108 (2000):207-239.

Chodorow, Nancy. *The Reproduction of Mothering*. Berkeley: University of California Press, 1978. Updated edition, 1999.

Chojnacki, Stanley. *Women and Men and Renaissance Venice: Twelve Essays on Patrician Society*. Johns Hopkins University Press, 2000.

Cippola, Carlo M. *Miasmas and Disease : Public Health and the Environment in the pre-industrial Age*. Translated by Elizabeth Potter. New Haven and London: Yale University Press, 1992.

Clark, Gregory, and Gillian Hamilton, "Survival of the Richest: The Malthusian Mechanism in Pre-Industrial England." *The Journal of Economic History* 66 (September 2006):707-736.

Clark, Peter. "Migration in England during the late-seventeenth and early-eighteenth centuries." *Past and Present* 83 (1979):57-90.

Commelin, Caspar. *Beschrijvinge van Amsterdam*: Amsterdam, 1693.

Conley, Dalton. *The Pecking Order: Which Siblings Succeed and Why*. New York: Pantheon, 2004.

Cressy, D. *Literacy and social order: reading and writing in Tudor and Stuart England*. Cambridge: Cambridge University Press, 1980.

Crosby, Alfred W., *Ecological Imperialism: The Biological Expansion of Europe, 900-1900*. Cambridge: Cambridge University Press, 1986.

Cruson, Cees. "De vluchtelingenpolitiek van de Amsterdamse Magistraat in de periode 1681-1685." In *De Stad: Beheersing van de stedelelijke ruimte*, edited by C.I. Cruson and J. Dronkers. Bohn Staflue Van Loghum, 1990, 89-109.

Cunningham, Hugh. *Children and Childhood in Western Society Since 1500*. London and New York: Longman, 1955.

Cunningham, Michael R., Perri B. Druen, and Anita P. Barbee. "Angels, Mentors, and Friends: Trade-Offs among Evolutionary, Social, and Individual Variables in Physical Appearance." In *Evolutionary Social Psychology*, edited by Jeffrey A. Simpson and Douglas T. Tenrik. Mahwah: Erlbaum, 1997, 109-140.

Cunningham, Phyllis, and Catherine Lucas. *Costumes for Births, Marriages and Deaths*. London: A & C. Black, 1972.

David, C.A. "De Zeeman." In *Gestalten van de Gouden Eeuw*, edited by H.M. Beliën, A. Th. Van Deursen, and G.J. Van Setten. Amsterdam: Bert Bakker, 1995.

Davidoff, Leonore. *Worlds Between: Historical Perspectives on Gender and Class*. New York: Routledge, 1995.

—. Megan Doolittle, Janet Fink, and Katherine Holden, eds. *The Family Story: Blood, Contract, and Intimacy, 1830-1960*. London and New York: Longman, 1999.

Davids, Karel, and Jan Lucassen, eds. *A Miracle Mirrored: The Dutch Republic in European Perspective*. Cambridge: Cambridge University Press, 1995.

Davis, Natalie Zemon. *Women on the Margins. Three Seventeenth-Century Lives*. Cambridge, Mass.: Harvard University Press, 1995.

Dekker, J.C., and K.P.C. de Leeuw. *Levensloop, cultuur en Mentality. Een geschiedenis van het alledaagse bestaan*. Tilburg: Tilburg University Press, 1990.

Dekker, Jeroen, Leendert Groenendijk, and Johan Verberckmoes. "Proudly Raising Vulnerable Youngsters" in *Pride and Joy: Children's Portraits in the Netherlands 1500-1700*, edited by Jan Baptist Bedaux and Rudi Ekkart. Ghent/ Antwerp: Ludion Press, 2000.

Dekker, Rudolf. "Labour Conflicts and Working-Class Culture in Early Modern Holland." *International Review of Social History* 35 (1990).

—. "Handwerkslieden en arbeiders in Holland van de zestiende tot de achttiende eeuw: Identiteit, cultuur en protest" in *Cultuur en maatschappij in Nederland, 1500-1850: Een historisch-anthropologisch perspectief*, edited by Peter te Boekhorst, Peter Burke, and Willem Frijhoff. Boon: Open Universiteit, 1992.

—. *Uit de schaduw in 't grote licht: Kinderen in ego-documenten van de Gouden Eeuw tot de Romantiek*. Amsterdam: Wereldbibliotheek, 1995.

—. "Children on their Own, Changing Relations in the Family: The Experience of Dutch Autobiographies, Seventeenth to Nineteenth Centuries" in *Private Domain, Public Inquiry, Families and Life-Styles in the Netherlands and Europe*, edited by Anton Schuurman and Pieter Spierenburg. Hilversum: Verloren, 1996.

—. "Egodocuments in the Netherlands from the Sixteenth to the Nineteenth Century." In *Envisioning Self and Status: Self-Representation in the Low Countries, 1499-1700*, edited by Erin Griffey. Hull: Association for Low Countries Studies in Great Britain and Ireland, 1999.

DePaulo, Bella M. "The Scientific Study of People Who are Single: An Annotated Bibliography." American Association For Single People (AASP), January 2, 2004.

Deploige, Jeroen. "Studying Emotions: The Medievalist as Human Scientist.: In *Emotions in the Heart of the City (14th-16th century)*, edited by Elodie Lecuppre-Desjardin and Anne-Laure Van Bruaene. Turnhout: Brepole, 2005, 3-24.

Desjardins, Bertrand. "Family Formation and Infant Mortality In New France" in *Infant and Child Mortality in the Past*, edited by Alain Bideau, Bertrand Desjardins, and Hector Perez Brignoli. Oxford: Clarendon Press, 1997.

Deursen, A.Th. van. *Plain Lives in a Golden Age: Popular Culture, Religion and Society in Seventeenth-Century Holland*. Cambridge: Cambridge University Press, 1991.

—. "Rembrandt and his Age: The Life of an Amsterdam Burgher" in *Rembrandt: The Master and His Workshop*, edited by Christopher Brown, Jan Kelch, and Pieter van Thiel. New Haven and London: Yale University Press, 1991.

Dickens, Emma. *The Extraordinary Story of Birth Control – from the First Fumblings to the Present Day*. London: Robsen Books, 2000.

Didion, Joan. *The Year of Magical Thinking*. London: Fourth Estate, 2005.

Diederiks, Herman. *Een Stad in Verval: Amsterdam Omstreeks 1800, demografisch, economisch, ruimtelijk*. Amsterdam: Meppel, 1982.

—. "Arm en rijk in Amsterdam: Wonen naar welstand in de 16ᵉ-18ᵉ eeuw." In *Amsterdam in Kaarten*, edited by W.F. Heinmeijer et al. Ede: Zomer & Keuning, 1987.

Dijk, Suzan van, et al. *"I have heard about you." Foreign Women's writing crossing the Dutch border: from Sappho to Selma Lagerlof*, translated by Jo Nesbitt. Hilversum: Verloren, 2004.

Dinnerstein, Dorothy. *The Mermaid and the Minotaur*. New York: Harper and Row, 1976.

Doblhammer, G. *The Late Life Legacy of Very Early Life*. Berlin: Springer, 2004.

Dobson, Mary J. "Contours of death: disease, mortality, and the environment in early modern England." *Health Transition Review* 2 (1992).

—. *Contours of death and disease in early modern England*. Cambridge: Cambridge University Press, 1997.

Dooren, Gabrielle Maria Elisabeth. *Eenheid en verscheidenheid: De burgers van Haarlem in de Gouden Eeuw*. Amsterdam: Prometheus/Bert Bakker, 2001.

Doornick, Marieke and Erika Kuijpers. *De geschoolde stad: Onderwijs in Amsterdam in de Gouden Eeuw*. Amsterdam: Historisch Seminarium van de Universiteit van Amsterdam, 1993.

Dowrick, Steve. "Income-Based Measures of Average Well-Being." In *Human Well-Being: Concept and Measurement*, edited by Mark McGillivray. Basingstoke: Palgrave McMillan, 2007.

Dunn, J.R. "Housing and health inequalities: Review and prospects for research." *Housing Studies* 15 (2000):341-366.

Dunn, Judy. "Sibling Studies and the Developmental Impact of Critical Incidents" in *Life-Span Development and Behavior*, edited by P.B. Baltes and O.G. Brim. New York and London: Academic Press, 1983, 335-353.

—. and Carol Kendrici. *Siblings: Love, Envy, and Understanding*. Cambridge: Harvard University Press, 1982.

Earle, Alison, and S. Jody Heymann. "Work, Family, and Social Class." In *How Healthy Are We? A National Study of Well-Being at Midlife*, edited by Orville Gilbert Brim, Carol D. Ryff, and Ronald C. Kessler. Chicago: University of Chicago Press, 2004, 485-513.

Earle, Peter, "The Female Labour Market in London in the Late Seventeenth and Early Eighteenth Centuries." *Economic History Review* (2d ser.) 42 (1989):328-353.

—. *A City Full of People: Men and Women of London, 1650- 1750*. London: Methuen, 1994.

Edelstein, Linda. *Maternal Bereavement: Coping with the Unexpected Death of a Child*. New York: Praeger Publishers, 1984.

Edwards, Elizabeth. "Roles, Status and Power: Amsterdam Regents in the Later Part of the Seventeenth Century" in *Envisioning Self and Status: Self-Preservation in the Low Countries, 1400-1700*, edited by Erin Griffey. Hull: Association for Low Countries Studies in Great Britain and Ireland, 1999.

Ehrenreich, Barbara. *Nickel and Dimed: On (Not) Getting By in America*. New York: Henry Holt and Company, 2001.

Elias, Johan E. *De vroedschap van Amsterdam*. Amsterdam: Israel, 1903-05, vol. 2.

Engelen, Theo, and Arthur P. Wolf, eds. *Marriage and the Family in Eurasia: Perspectives on the Hajnal hypothesis*. Amsterdam: Aksant, 2005.

Engels, J.Th. *Kinderen van Amsterdam*. Amsterdam: De Walburg Pers, 1989.

Faber, Sjoerd, Jacobine Huisken, and Friso Lammertse. *Van heeren, die hunn' stoel en kussen niet beschaerman: het stadsbestuur van Amsterdam in de 17ᵉ en 18ᵉ eeuw*. Translated by Michael Hoyle as *Lords, who seat, nor cushion do ashame: the governance of Amsterdam in the 17ᵗʰ and 18ᵗʰ Centuries*. Amsterdam: Stichting Koninklijk Paleis, 1987.

Fairchilds, Cissie. *Domestic Enemies: Servants and Their Masters in Old Regime France*. Baltimore: Johns Hopkins University Press, 1984.

Falker, Frank, ed. *Infant and Child Nutrition Worldwide: Issues and Perspectives*. Boca Raton: CRC Press, 1991.

Farr, James. *Artisans in Europe, 1300-1914*. Cambridge: Cambridge University Press, 2000.

Fauve-Chamoux, Antoinette. "Marriage, Widowhood, and Divorce" in *Family Life in Early Modern Times*, edited by David I. Kertzer and Marzio Barbagli. New Haven and London: Yale University Press, 2001.

Fides, Valerie. *Wet nursing: A History from antiquity to the Present*. Oxford: Basil Blackwell, 1988.

Finn, Michael W. *The European Demographic System, 1500-1820*. Suffolk: The Harvester Press, 1981.

Flanders, Judith. "Service with a smile." *Times Literary Supplement* October 31, 2003:20.

Fletcher, Anthony. *Gender, Sex & Subordination in England, 1500-1800*. New Haven and London: Yale University Press, 1995.

Fortgans, H.W. *Schola Latina*. Zwolle: Uitgevers-Mij, 1958.

Franits, Wayne E. *Paragons of Virtue: Women and Domesticity In Seventeenth-Century Dutch Art*. Cambridge: Cambridge University Press, 1993.

Freemantle, Katherine. *The Baroque Town Hall of Amsterdam*. Utrecht: Haentjens Dekker & Gumbert, 1959.

Friest, Dagmar. "Religious difference at the experience of widowhood in seventeenth- and eighteenth-century Germany" in *Widowhood in Medieval and Early Modern Europe*, edited by Sandra Cavallo and Lyndan Warner. Essex: Longman, 1999.

Frijhoff, Willem. *Wegen van Evert Willemsz.: Een Hollands Weeskind op zoek naar zichzelf, 1607-1647*. Nijmegen: SUN, 1995.

—. "Medical education and early modern Dutch medical practitioners: towards a critical approach" in *The Task of Healing: Medicine, religion and gender in England and the Netherlands, 1450-1800*, edited by Hilary Marland and Margaret Pelling. Rotterdam: Erasmus, 1996, 205-220.

Froide, Amy M. "Marital Status as a Category of Difference: Singlewomen and Widows in Early Modern England" in *Singlewomen in the European Past, 1250-1800*, edited by Judith Bennett and Amy M. Froide. Philadelphia: University of Pennsylvania Press, 1999.

—. *Never Married: Singlewomen in Early Modern England*. Oxford: Oxford University Press, 2005.

Gelder, Roelof van. "De VOC en de WIC: De invloed van de Wereldhandel, 19ᵉ-18ᵉ eeuw." In *Amsterdam in Kaarten: Verandering van de stad in vier eeuwen cartografie*, edited by W.F. Heinemeijer et al. Ede/Antwerp: Zomer & Keuning, 1987.

—. "De schone schijn van het water: De strijd tegen stank en vervuiling" in *Amsterdam in Kaarten: Verandering van de stad in vier eeuwen cartografie*, edited by W.F. Heinemeijer et al. Ede/Antwerp: Zomer & Keuning, 1987.

—. *Het Oost-Indisch avontuur: Duitsers in Dienst van de VOC (1600-1800)*. Nijmegen: Uitgeverij SUN, 1997.

Gewirth, Alan, *Self-Fulfillment*. Princeton: Princeton University Press, 1998.

Glick, Peter, and Susan T. Fiske, "The Ambivalent Sexism Inventory: Differentiating hostile and benevolent sexism." *Journal of Personality and Social Psychology* 70 (1996):491-512.

Gorski, Philip S. *The Disciplinary Revolution: Calvinism and the Rise of the State in Early Modern Europe*. Chicago: University of Chicago Press, 2003.

Gowing, Laura. *Common Bodies: Women, Touch, and Power in Seventeenth-Century England*. New Haven and London: Yale University Press, 2003.

Greenson, Ralph R. "Dis-identifying from mother: its special importance for the boy." *International Journal of Psychoanalysis*. 49 (1968).

Griffith, James. *Well-Being*. Oxford: Clarendon Press, 1986.

Griffith, Paul. *Youth and Authority: formative experiences in England 1560-1640*. Oxford: Clarendon Press, 1966.

Groenendijk, Leendert, and Benjamin B. Roberts, eds. *Losbandige jeud: Jongeren en moraal in de Nederlanden Tijdens de late Middeleeuwen en de Vroegmoderne Tijd*. Hilversum: Verloren, 2004.

Groenveld, Simon. "'For the Benefit of the Poor': Social Assistance in Amsterdam" in *Rome*Amsterdam: Two Growing Cities in Seventeenth-Century Europe*, edited by Peter van Kessel and Elisja Schulte. Amsterdam: University of Amsterdam Press, 1997.

—. J.J.J.H. Dekker, and Th.R.M. Willemse. *Wezen en boefjes: Zes eeuwen zorg in wees- en kinderhuizen*. Hilversum: Verloren, 1997.

Grusky, David B., and Jesper B. Sorensen, "Can Class Analysis Be Salvaged?" *American Journal of Sociology* 103 (March 1997).

Haan, Jannes de. "The greatness and difficulty of the work: The growth of Amsterdam and the construction of the canal zone" in *The Canals of Amsterdam*, edited by Paul Spies, Koen Kleijn, Jos Smit, and Ernest Kurpershoek. The Hague: SDU Uitgeverij Koninginnegracht, 1993.

Hacker, Andrew, "The Rich and Everyone Else." *The New York Review of Books*, May 25, 2006:16-19.

Hajnal, John. "European Marriage Patterns in Perspective" in *Population in History: Essays in Historical Demography*, edited by D.V. Glass and D.E.D. Eversley. London: Edward Arnold, 1965, 101-143.

—. "Two kinds of preindustrial household formation systems." *Population and Development Review* 7 (1882):449- 494.

Haks, Donald. *Huwelijk en gezin in Holland in de 16ᵉ en 17ᵉ eeuw*. Utrecht: Hes Uitgever, 1985.

—. "Family Structure and Relationship Patterns in Amsterdam." In *Rome*Amsterdam: Two Growing Cities in Seventeenth-Century Europe*, edited by Peter van Kessel and Elisja Schulte. Amsterdam: Amsterdam University Press, 1997.

Harkness, Susan. "Social and Political Indicators of Human Well-Being." In *Human Well-Being: Concept and Measurement*, edited by Mark McGillivray. Basingstoke: Palgrave McMillan, 2007.

Harline, Craig E. *Pamphlets, Printing, and Political Culture in the Early Dutch Republic.* Dordrecht: Martinus Nijhoff, 1987.

Hart, Simon. *Geschrift en Getal: Eeen keuze uit de demografisch,-economisch,-en sociaal-historische studiën op grond van Amsterdamse en Zaanse archivalia, 1699-1800.* Dordrecht: Hollandsche Studien, 1976.

Hartman, Mary S. *The Household and the Making of History: A Subversive View of the Western Past.* Cambridge: Cambridge University Press, 2004.

Hecht, Jean. *The Domestic Service Class in Eighteenth-Century England.* London: Routledge & Kegan Paul, 1956.

Heijden, Manon van der. "Secular and Ecclesiastical Marriage Control: Rotterdam, 1550-1770." In *Private domain, public inquiry: Families and life-styles in the Netherlands and Europe, 1550 to the present*, edited by Anton Schuurman and Pieter Spierenburg. Hilversum: Verloren, 1996.

—. *Huwelijk in Holland: Stedelijke Rechtspraak en kerkelijke tucht, 1550-1700.* Amsterdam: Bert Bakker, 1998.

—. "Contradictory interests: Work, parents, and offspring in early modern Holland." *The History of the Family* 9 (2004):355-370.

Hell, Maarten, "Een 'profitabel' ambt: Het inkomen van de Schouten tijdens de Republiek," *Amstelodamum 84 (1997): 137-148.*

Hempenius-van Dijk, Dineke. "Widows and the Law: The legal position of widows in the Dutch Republic during the seventeenth and eighteenth centuries" in *Between poverty and the pyre*, edited by Jan Bremmer and Lourens van den Bosch. London and New York: Routledge, 1995.

Henderson, John, and Richard Wall, eds. *Poor Women and Children in the European Past.* London and New York: Routledge, 1994.

Hendrix, Harald, and Marijke Meijer Drees, eds. *Beschaafde Burgers: Burgerlijkheid in de vroeg moderne tijd.* Amsterdam: Amsterdam University Press, 2001.

Hill, Bridget. *Servants, English Domestics in the Eighteenth Century.* Oxford: Clarendon Press, 1996.

Hindle, Steve. *On the Parish: The micro-politics of poor relief in rural England, c.1550-1750.* Oxford: Clarendon, 2004.

Hochman, Baruch, and Ilja Wachs. *Dickens: the Orphan Condition.* Madison and Teaneck: Fairleigh Dickinson University Press, 1999.

Hoffman, Carl A. "Social Control and the Neighborhood in European Cities" in *Social Control in Europe*, edited by Herman Roodenburg and Pieter Spierenburg. Columbus: Ohio State University Press, 2004, 309-327.

Hoffman, Philip T., David S. Jacks, Patricia A. Levin, and Peter H. Lindert. "Sketching the Rise of Real Inequality in Early Modern Europe" in *Living Standards in the Past: New Perspectives on Well-Being in Asia and Europe*, edited by Robert C. Allen, Tommy Bengtsson, and Martin Tribe. Oxford: Oxford University Press, 2005.

Hokke, Judith. "'Mijn alderliefste Jantielief.' Vrouw en gezin in de Republiek: regenten-vrouwen en hun relaties." *Jaarboek voor vrouwengeschiedenis* 8 (1987).

Hudson, Liam, and Bernadine Jacot. *The Way Men Think: Intellect, Intimacy and the Erotic Imagination.* New Haven and London: Yale University Press, 1991.

Hufton, Olwen. "Women, Work, and Family." In *A History of Women in the West. III. Renaissance and Enlightenment*, edited by Natalie Zemon Davis and Ariette Farge. Cambridge: Harvard University Press, 1993.

—. *The Prospect Before Her: A History of Women in Western Europe, Volume 1, 1500-1800.* London: HarperCollins, 1995.

Hunt, Margaret R. *The Middling Sort: Commerce, Gender, and the Family in England, 1689-1780.* Berkeley: University of California Press, 1996.

Israel, Jonathan. *The Dutch Republic: Its Rise, Greatness, And Fall, 1477-1806.* Oxford: Clarendon Press, 1995.
—. "Dutch influence on urban planning, health care and poor relief: The North Sea and Baltic regions of Europe, 1567-1920" in *Health Care and Poor Relief in Protestant Europe 1500-1700,* edited by Ole Peter Grell and Ander Cunningham. London and New York: Routledge, 1997.

Jackman, Mary R. "Gender, Violence, and Harassment" in *Handbook of the Sociology of Gender,* edited by Janet Chafetz Saltman. New York: Kluwer Academic/Plenum Publishers, 1999, 45-61.
—. "License to Kill: Violence and Legitimacy in Expropriative Social Relations" in *Psychology of Inequality,* edited by John T. Joost and Brena Major. Cambridge: Cambridge University Press, 2001, 437-467.
Jager, Ronald de. "Meester, leerjongen, leertijd: Een analyse van zeventiende-eeuwse Noord-Nederlandse leerlingcontracten van kunstschilders, goud- en zilversmeden." *Oud Holland* 104 (1990).
Jagger, Alison M. "Reasoning about Well-Being: Nussbaum's Methods of Justifying the Capabilities." *Journal of Political Philosophy* 14 (September 2006):301-322.
Jannetta, Ann Bowman. *Epidemics and Mortality in Early Modern Japan.* Princeton: Princeton University Press, 1987.
Jenner, Mark. "Environment, Health and Population" in *The Healing Arts: Health, Disease and Society in Europe 1500-1800,* edited by Peter Elmer. Manchester: Manchester University Press, 2004.
Jones, Ann, and Peter Stallybrass. *Renaissance Clothing and the Materials of Memory.* Cambridge: Cambridge University Press, 2000.
Jonker, Michiel. "Public or Private Portraits: Group Portraits Of Amsterdam Regents and Regentesses" in *The Public and Private in Dutch Culture of the Golden Age,* edited by Arthur W. Wheelock, Jr. and Adele Seeff. Newark: University of Delaware Press, 2000.
Jong, Joop de. *Een Deftige Bestaan.* Utrecht/Antwerp: Uitgeverij Kosmos, 1987.
Jongh, Eddy de. *Portretten van echt en trouw: Huwelijk en gezin in de Nederlandse kunst van de zeventiende eeuw.* Zwolle: Uitgeverij Waanders, 1986.
Jordanova, Ludmilla. *History in Practice.* London: Arnold, 2000.
Jutte, Robert. *Poverty and Deviance in Early Modern Europe.* Cambridge: Cambridge University Press, 1994.

Kendall, Diana. *Privileged Women and the Social Reproduction of the Upper Class.* Lanham: Rowman and Littlefield, 2002.
Kistenmaker, Renée. "Amsterdam 1399-1700: van 'geringhe Visschers' naar een 'kleyne wereldt" in *Stedebouw: De geschiedenis van de stad in de Nederlanden van 1500 tot Heden,* edited by Ed Taverne and Irmin Visser. Nijmegen: Uitgeverij SUN, 1993.
—. "The Public and the Private: Public Space in Sixteenth- and Seventeenth-Century Amsterdam. In *The Public and the Private in Dutch Culture of the Golden Age,* edited by Arthur K. Wheelock, Jr. and Adele Seeff. Newark: University of Delaware Press, 2000.
—. and Roelof van Gelder, *Amsterdam: The Golden Age: 1275-1795.* New York: Abbeville Press,
—. Michael Wagenaar, and Jos van Assendelft. *Amsterdam Markstad.* Amsterdam: Dienst van het Marktwezen, 1984.

Klapish-Zuber, Christine. "Women Servants in Florence during the Fourteenth and Fifteenth Centuries" in *Women and Work in Preindustrial Europe*, edited by Barbara A. Hanawalt. Bloomington: Indiana University Press, 1986.

Klep, Paul M.M. "Introduction to special issues: Contradictory interests of offspring and parents, 1500- 2000." *The History of the Family* 9 (2004):349-354.

—. "An adult life before marriage: Children and the Hajnal hypothesis" in *Marriage and the family in Eurasia: Perspectives on the Hajnal hypothesis*, edited by Theo Engelen and Arthur P. Wolf. Amsterdam: Aksant, 2005.

Kloek, Els. *"Wij hij zij, man of wijf", Vrouwengeschiedenis en de vroegmoderne tijd.* Hilversum: Verloren, 1990.

—. "De Vrouw" in *Gestalten van de Gouden Eeuw*, edited by H.M. Beliën, A.Th. van Deursen, and G.J. van Setten. Hilversum: Verloren, 1995.

—. Nicole Teeuwen, and Marijke Huisman, eds. *Women of the Dutch Golden Age: An international debate on women in seventeenth-century Holland, England and Italy*. Hilversum: Verloren, 1994.

Knotter, Ad. "De 17e-eeuwse uitbreidingen" in *Amsterdam in Kaarten, Verandering van de stad in vier eeuwen cartografie*, edited by W.F. Heinemeijer et al. Ede/Antwerp: Zomer & Keuning, 1987.

—. "Vreemdelingen in Amsterdam in de 17e eeuw: Groepsvorming, arbeid en ondernemerschap." *Historisch Tijdschrift Holland* 27 (februari 1995):219-235.

Kok, Jan. "The Moral Nation: Illegitimacy and Bridal Pregnancy in the Netherlands from 1600 to the Present." *Economic and Social History of the Netherlands* 2 (1991):7-36.

Kooijmans, Luuc. *Vriendschap en de Kunst van het Overleven in de Zeventiende en Achttiende Eeuw*. Amsterdam: Uitgeverij Bert Bakker, 1997.

Kowaleski, Maryanne. "Singlewomen in Medieval and Early Modern Europe: The Demographic Perspective." In *Singlewomen in the European Past, 1250-1800*, edited by Judith Bennett and Amy M. Froide. Philadelphia: University of Pennsylvania Press, 1999.

Kuijpers, Erika. "Lezen en schrijven: Onderzoek naar het Alfabetiseringsniveau in zeventiende-eeuw Amsterdam." *Tijdschrift voor Sociale Geschiedenis* 23 (1997).

—. "Poor, Illiterate and Superstitious? Social and Cultural Characteristics of the 'Noordse Natie' in the Amsterdam Lutheran Church in the Seventeenth Century" in *Dutch Light in the Norwegian Night: Maritime Relations and Migration Across the North Sea in Early Modern Times*, edited by Louis Sticking, Harry de Bles, and Erlend des Bouvries. Hilversum: Verloren, 2004.

—. *Migrantenstad: Immigratie en Sociale Verhoudingen in 17e-Eeuws Amsterdam*. Hilversum, Verloren, 2005.

—, and Maarten Prak. "Burger, ingezetene, vreemdeling: burgerschap in Amsterdam in de 17e en 18e eeuw" in *Burger*, edited by Joost Kloek and Karin Tilmans. Amsterdam: Amsterdam University Press, 2002, 113-132.

Kuus, Saskia. "Children's Costume in the Sixteenth and Seventeenth Centuries" in *Pride and Joy: Children's Portraits in the Netherlands 1500-1700*, edited by Jan Baptist Bedaux, and Rudi Ekkart. Ghent/Amsterdam: Ludion Press, 2000.

Lalou, Richard. "Endogenous Mortality in New France: At the Crossroads of Natural and Social Selection" in *Infant and Child Mortality in the Past*, edited by Alain Bideau, Bertrand Desjardins, and Hector Perez Brignoli. Oxford: Clarendon Press, 1997, 203-215.

Landers, John. *Death and the Metropolis: studies in the demographic history of London 1670-1830*. Cambridge: Cambridge University Press, 1993.

Lawrence, Roderick J. "Housing and health: beyond disciplinary confinement." *Journal of Urban Health* 83 (May 2006):540-549.

Layard, Richard. *Happiness: Lessons from a New Science*. London: Allen Lane, 2005.

Lee, James Z., and Wong Feng. *One Quarter of Humanity, Malthusuan Mythology and Chinese Realities, 1700-2000*. Cambridge: Harvard University Press, 1999.

Leemans, Inger. *De Woord is aan de onderkant: Radicale ideeën in Nederlandse pornografische romans 1670-1700*. Nijmegen: Uitgever Vertilt, 2002.

Leeuw, K.P.C. *Kleding in Nederland*. Hilversum: Verloren, 1992.

Leeuwen, Marco H.D, van. "Amsterdam en de armenzorg tijdens de Republiek." *NEHA Jaarboek* 50 (1996):132-161.

—. and James E. Oeppen. "Reconstructing The Demographic Regime of Amsterdam 1681-1920." *Economic and Social History in the Netherlands* 5 (1993): 61-102.

Lennenberg, E.H. *Biological Foundations of Language*. New York: Wiley, 1967.

Lesger, C. "Migranten in Amsterdam tijdens de 18e eeuw: Residentiele spreiding en positie in de samenleving." *Jaarboek Amstelodamum* 89 (1997):43-68.

Levie, Tirtsah, and Henk Zantkuijl. *Wonen in Amsterdam in de 17de en 18de eeuw*. Amsterdam: Amsterdams Historisch Museum, 1980.

Levy, Marion J., *Our Mother-Tempers*. Berkeley: University of California Press, 1989.

Lindeman, R., Y. Scherf, and R.M. Dekker. *Egodocumenten van Noord-Nederlanders uit de zestiende tot begin negentiende eeuw, Een chronologische lijst*. Haarlem: Stichting Egodocumenten, 1993.

Lindemann, Mary. *Medicine and Society in Early Modern Europe*. Cambridge: Cambridge University Press, 1999.

Lis, Catharina and Hugo Soly. "Craft guilds in comparative perspective: the Northern and Southern Netherlands, a survey" in *Craft Guilds in the Early Modern Low Countries*, edited by Maarten Prak, Catharina Lis, Jan Lucassen, and Hugo Soly. Aldershot and Burlington: Ashgate, 2006.

Loonen, P.L.M. *For to Learne to Buye and Sell: Learning English in the Low Dutch Areas Between 1500 and 1800, A Critical Survey*. Groningen: Universiteits-drukkerij, 1900. Proefschrift [dissertation], Universiteit van Nijmegen.

Lourens, P., and J. Lucassen. "Ambachtsgilden binnen een Handelskapitalistische stad: aanzetten voor een analyse van Amsterdam rond 1700." *NEHA-Jaarboek voor economische, bedrijfs-en techniekgeschiedenis* 61 (1998):121-159.

Lucassen, Jan. *Migrant Labour in Europe 1600-1900*, translated by Donald A. Bloch. London: Crown Helm, 1987.

—. *Jan, Jan Solie en diens kinderen: Vergelijkend onderzoek naar continuiteit en discontinuiteit in de ontwikkeling van arbeidsverhoudingen*. Amsterdam: Stichting beheer IIGS, 1991.

—. "The Netherlands, the Dutch, and long distance migration in the late sixteenth to early nineteenth centuries." In *Europeans on the Move: Studies on European Migration, 1500-1800*, edited by N. Canny. Oxford: Oxford University Press, 1994, 153-191.

—. "Labor and Early Economic Development" in *A Miracle Mirrored: The Dutch Republic in European Perspective*, edited by Karel Davids and Jan Lucassen. Cambridge: Cambridge University Press, 1995.

Marland, Hilary. "'Stately and dignified, kindly and God-fearing': midwives, age and status in the Netherlands in the eighteenth century." In *The Task of Healing: medicine, religion, and gender in England and the Netherlands, 1450-1800*, edited by Hilary Marland and Margaret Pelling. Rotterdam: Erasmus Publishing, 1996.

Marmot, Michael. *Status Syndrome*. London: Bloomsbury, 2004.

Marshall, Sherrin. *The Dutch Gentry, 1500-1650: Family, Faith, and Fortune*. New York: Greenwood Press, 1987.

Matthews, Sara F., and Carlo A. Corsini. *Historical perspectives on breastfeeding*. Florence: Unicef International Child Development Center, 1991.

Matthews Grieco, Sara F. "The Body, Appearance, and Sexuality" in *A History of Women in the West. III. Renaissance and Enlightenment Paradoxes*, edited by Natalie Zemon Davis. Cambridge: Harvard University Press, 1993.

Maza, Sarah C. *Servants and Masters in Eighteenth-Century France: The Uses of Loyalty*. Princeton: Princeton University Press, 1983.

McCants, Anne E.C. *Civic Charity in a Golden Age : Orphan Care in Early Modern Amsterdam*. Urbana and Chicago: University of Illinois Press, 1997.

—. "The Not-So-Merry Widows of Amsterdam." *Journal of Family History* 24 (1999):441-467.

—. "Inequality among the poor of eighteenth century Amsterdam." *Explorations in Economic History* 44 (2007):1-21.

McCarthy, Mary. *Memories of a Catholic Childhood*. New York: Penguin Books, 1957.

McCord, Colin, and Harold Freeman. "Excess Mortality in Harlem." *New England Journal of Medicine* 322 (1990): 173-177.

McGillivray, Mark, ed. *Human Well-Being: Concept and Measurement*. Basingstoke: Palgrave McMillan, 2007.

McIntyre, S., and A. Ellaway. "Ecological approaches: rediscovering the role of physical and social environment." In *Social Epidemiology*, edited by L.F. Berkman and I. Kawachi. New York: Oxford University Press, 2000, 332-348.

McLemee, Scott. "Getting Emotional." *The Chronicle of Higher Education* (February 21, 2003):1-12.

Megill, Allan. *Historical Knowledge, Historical Error: A Contemporary Guide to Practice*. Chicago: University of Chicago Press, 2007.

Meldrum, Timothy. *Domestic Service and Gender: Life and Work in the London Household*. London: Longman, 2000.

Meijer Drees, Marijke, "Zeventiende-eeuwse literatuur in de Republiek: burgerlijk?" in *Beschaafde Burgers: Burgerlijkheid in de vroeg moderne tijd*, edited by Harold Hendrix and Marijke Meijer Drees. Amsterdam: Amsterdam University Press, 2001.

Meischke, R., H.J. Zantkuijl, W. Raue, and P.T.E.E. Rosenberg. *Huizen in Nederland: Amsterdam*. Zwolle: Waanders, no date.

Meyers, Diana. "Personal Autonomy and the Paradox of Feminine Socialization." *Journal of Philosophy* 84 (1987):619-628.

Middelkoop, Norbert et al. *Amsterdammers geportretteerd: Kopstukken 1600-1800*. Amsterdam: Uitgever THOTH, 2002.

Miller, J., and Naomi Yavneh eds. *Sibling Relations and Gender in the Early Modern World*. Aldershot: Ashgate, 2006.

Miller, William Ian. *Humiliation*. Ithaca and London: Cornell University Press, 1993.

Mitchell, Juliet. *Siblings*. Cambridge: Polity Press, 2003.

Moody-Adams, Michele M. *Fieldwork in Familiar Places: Morality, Culture & Philosophy*. Cambridge, Mass.: Harvard University Press, 1997.

—. "The Virtue of Nussbaum's Essentialism." *Metaphilosophy* 29 (October 1998):263-272.

Muizelaar, Klaske, and Derek Phillips. *Picturing Men and Women in the Dutch Golden Age: Paintings and People in Historical Perspective*. New Haven and London: Yale University Press, 2003.

Muldrew, Craig. *The Economy of Obligation: The Culture of Credit and Social Relations in Early Modern England.* Basingstoke: MacMillan Press, 1998.

Muller, Sheila D. *Charity in the Dutch Republic: Pictures of Rich and Poor for Charitable Institutions.* Ann Arbor, Mich.: UMI Research Press, 1985.

Nederveen Meerkerk, Elise. *De draad in eigen handen: Vrouwen en Loonarbeid in de Nederlandse textielnijverheid, 1581- 1810.* Amsterdam: Aksant, 2007.

Nierop, Henk van. "Popular participation in politics in the Dutch Republic" in *Resistance, Representation, and Community,* edited by Peter Blickle. Oxford: Oxford University Press, 1997, 272-290.

—. "Politics and the People of Amsterdam" in *Rome* Amsterdam: Two Growing Cities in Seventeenth-Century Europe,* edited by Peter van Kessel and Elisja Schulte. Amsterdam: Amsterdam University Press, 1997.

—. "Private Interests, Public Policies: Petitions in the Dutch Republic." In *The Public and Private in Dutch Culture of the Golden Age,* edited by Arthur W. Wheelock, Jr. and Adele Seef. Newark: University of Delaware Press, 2000, 33-39.

Noordegraaf, Leo. *Daglonen in Alkmaar, 1500-1800.* Amsterdam: Historisch Seminarium, Universiteit van Amsterdam, 1984.

—. *Hollands welvaren? Levensstandaard in Holland 1450-1650.* Bergen: Octavo, 1985.

—. "Dutch Industry in the Golden Age" in *The Dutch Economy in the Golden Age,* edited by Karel Davids and Leo Noordegraaf. Amsterdam: The Nederlands Economic History Archives, 1995.

—. "De Arme" in *Gestalten van de Gouden Eeuw,* edited by H.M. Beliën, A.Th. van Deursen, and G.J. van Setten. Amsterdam: Bert Bakker, 1995.

—. and Jan Luiten van Zanden. "Early modern economic growth and the standard of living: did labour benefit from Holland's Golden Age?" in *A Miracle Mirrored: The Dutch Republic in European Perspective,* edited by Karl Davids and Jan Lucassen. Cambridge: Cambridge University Press, 1995, 410-437.

Noordkerk, H. *Handvesten ofte Privilegien ende Octroyen; Mitsgaders Willekeuren, Constuimen, Ordonnantien en Handleidingen Der Stad Amsterdam.* Amsterdam: Hendrik van Waesberge en Saloman en Petrus Schouten, Boekverkoopers, MDCCXLVIII, Volume 2.

Norton, Mary Beth. "'Either Married or to Bee Married': Women's Legal Inequality in Early America." In *Inequality In Early America,* edited by Carla Gardina Pestans and Sharon V. Slaughter. Hanover and London: University Press of New England, 1999.

Nussbaum, Martha. *Women and Human Development: The Capabilities Approach.* Cambridge: Cambridge University Press, 2000.

Nusteling, Hubert. *Welvaart en werkgelegenheid in Amsterdam, 1540-1860.* Amsterdam: De Bataafsche Leeuw, 1985.

—. "The Population of Amsterdam and the Golden Age" in *Rome*Amsterdam,* edited by Peter van Kessel and Elisja Schulte. Amsterdam: Amsterdam University Press, 1997.

O'Dea, William T. *The Social History of Lighting.* London: Routledge and Kegan Paul, 1958.

Ogilvie, Sheilagh, "How Does Social Capital Affect Women? Guilds and Communities in Early Modern Germany." *The American Historical Review* 109 (April 2004):325-359.

Okin, Susan Moller. "Poverty, Well-Being, and Gender: What Counts, Who is Heard?" *Philosophy and Public Affairs* 31 (2003):280-316.

Oldewelt, W.F.H. *Kohier van de personeele quotisatie te Amsterdam, 1742.* Amsterdam: Genootschap Amstelodamum, 1945.

O'Neill, Onora. "Justice, Gender, and International Boundaries" in *The Quality of Life*, edited by Martha Nussbaum and Amartya Sen. Oxford: Clarendon Press, 1993, 303-335.

Oostveen, Gisela. "It takes all sorts to make a world: Sex and Gender in Brodero's Farce of the Miller" in *Women of the Golden Age: An international debate on women in seventeenth-century Holland, England and Italy*, edited by Els Kloek, Nicole Teeuwen, and Marijke Huisman. Hilversum: Verloren, 1994.

Oris, Michel, Renzo Derosas, Marco Breschti et al., "Infant and Child Mortality." In *Life Under Pressure: Mortality and Living Standards in Europe and Asia, 1700-1900*, edited by Tommy Bengtsson, Cameron Campbell, James Z. Lee et al. Cambridge: the MIT Press, 2004.

Ottenheym, Koen. "From Architectura Moderna to Modern Architecture: Architecture on the Canals in the seventeenth and eighteenth centuries." In *The Canals of Amsterdam*, edited by Paul Spies, Koen Kleijn, Jos Smit, and Ernest Kurpershoek. The Hague: SDU Uitgeverij Koninginnegracht, 1993, 45-55.

Ovid, *Metamorphoses.* Translated with an introduction by Mary M. Innes. London: Penguin Classics, 1955.

Ozment, Steven. *When Fathers Ruled: Family Life in Reformation Europe.* Cambridge: Harvard University Press, 1983.

Panhuysen, Bibi. *Maatwerk: Kleermakers, naaisters, oudkleerkopers en de gilden (1500-1800).* No publisher's name, 2000.

—. "Dressed to Work" in *Craft Guilds in the Early Modern Low Countries: Work, Power, and Representation*, edited by Maarten Prak, Catherine Lis, Jan Lucassen, and Hugo Soly. Aldershot and Burlington: Ashgate, 2006.

Pebley, A.R., A.I. Hermalin, and J. Knodel. "Birth spacing and infant mortality: evidence for eighteenth and nineteenth century German villages." *Journal of Biosocial Science* 23 (October 1991).

Pelling, Margaret. *The Common Lot: sickness, medical occupations and the urban poor in early modern England.* London: Longman, 1998.

—. "Finding widowers: men without women in English towns before 1700" in *Widowhood in Medieval and Early Modern Europe*, edited by Sandra Cavallo and Lyndan Warner. Essex: Longman, 1999.

Pepys, Samuel. *The Diary of Samuel Pepys.* Edited by Robert Latham and William Matthews. London: G. Bell and Sons, Ltd., 1970-1983, vol. 5.

Perry, Ruth. *Novel Relations: The Transformation of Kinship In English Literature and Culture, 1748-1818.* Cambridge: Cambridge University Press, 2004.

Phillips, Derek L. *Knowledge from What: Theories and Methods In Social Research.* Chicago: Rand McNally, 1971.

—. *Toward a Just Social Order.* Princeton: Princeton University Press, 1986.

—. *Looking Backward: A Critical Appraisal of Communitarian Thought.* Princeton: Princeton University Press, 1993.

—. Work, Welfare, and Well-Being" in *Social and Secure? Politics and Culture of the Welfare State: A Comparative Inquiry*, edited by Hans Bak, Frits van Holthoon, and Hans Krabbendam. Amsterdam: VU Press, 1996, 19-46.

—. and Kevin J. Clancy. "Modeling Effects in Survey Research." *Public Opinion Quarterly* 36 (Summer 1971):246- 253.

—. "Some Effects of 'Social Desirability' in Survey Studies." *American Journal of Sociology* 77 (March 1972): 921-940.

Pitlo, A. "Iets over de geschiedenis van het notariaat in Nederland." *Weekblad voor Privaatrecht, Notaris-ambt en Registratie* November 1 and 8, 1941, Nos. 3749 and 3750.

Plakans, Andrejs, and Charles Wetherell, "Households and kinship networks: the costs and benefits of contextualization." *Continuity and Change* 18 (2003).

Pol, Lotte van de. *Amsterdams hoerdom: Prostitutie in de zeventiende en achttiende eeuw*. Amsterdam: Wereldbibliotheek, 1966.

—. "The Lure of the big city. Female migration to Amsterdam" in *Women of the Golden Age: An international debate on women in seventeenth-century Holland, England and Italy*, edited by Els Kloek, Nicole Teeuwen, and Marijke Huisman. Hilversum: Verloren, 1994.

—. "Hoeveel soorten volk? Een reactie op Maarten Prak." *Jaarboek Amstelodamum* 91 (1999).

—. and Rudolf M. Dekker. *The Tradition of Female Transvestism in Early Modern Europe*. Basingstoke: Macmillan, 1989.

—. and Erika Kuijpers, "Poor Women's Migration to the City: The Attraction of Amsterdam Health Care and Social Assistance in Early Modern Times." *Journal of Urban History* 32 (November 2005).

Pollock, Linda. *Forgotten Children: Parent-Child Relations from 1500 to 1900*. Cambridge: Cambridge University Press, 1983.

—. "Parent-Child Relations" in *Family Life in Early Modern Times*, edited by David I. Kerzer and Marzio Barbagli. New Haven and London: Yale University Press, 2001.

Porta, Antonio. *Joan en Gerrit Corver: De politieke macht van Amsterdam (1702-1748)*. Assen: Van Gorcum, 1975.

Porter, Roy, and Dorothy Porter. *In sickness and in health: the British experience 1650-1850*. London: Fourth Estate, 1988.

Potts, Malcolm, and Roger Short. *Ever Since Adam and Eve: The evolution of human sexuality*. Cambridge: Cambridge University Press, 1999.

Prak, Maarten. "Armenzorg 1500-1800." In *Studies over Zekerheidsarrangementen: Risicos, risicobestrijding en verzekeringen in Nederland vanaf de Middeleeuwen*, edited by Jacques van Gerwen and Marco H.D. van Leeuwen. Amsterdam/The Hague: Nederlandsch Economisch Historisch Archief Verbond van Verzekeraars, 1998.

—. *Republikeinse veelheid, democratische Enkelvoud: Sociale verandering in het Revolutietijdvak 's-Hertogenbosch 1770-1820*. Nijmegen: Uitgeverij SUN, 1999.

—. "Velerlei soort van volk: Sociale verhouding in Amsterdam in de zeventiende Eeuw." *Amstelodamum* (1999):29-54.

—. "Het oude recht der burgers: De betekenis van burgerschap in het Amsterdam van de zestiende en zeventiende eeuw." In *Beschaafde Burgers, Burgerlijkheid in de vroegmoderne tijd*, edited by Harald Hendrix and Marijke Meijer Drees. Amsterdam: Amsterdam University Press, 2001.

—. "The politics of intolerance: citizenship and religion in the Dutch Republic (seventeenth to eighteenth centuries)." In *Calvinism and Religious Toleration in the Dutch Golden Age*, edited by R. Po-Chia and Henk van Nierop. Cambridge: Cambridge University Press, 2002.

—. "Guilds and the development of the art market during the Dutch Golden Age." *Simiolus* 30 (2003).

—. "Moral Order in the World of Work: Social Control and the Guilds in Europe." In *Social Control in Europe, 1500-1800*, edited by Herman Roodenburg and Pieter Spierenburg. Columbus: Ohio State University Press, 2004.

—. "Towards an economic interpretation of citizenship: The Dutch Republic between Medieval Communes and Modern Nation States." Unpublished manuscript, 2004.

—. *The Dutch Republic in the Seventeenth Century*. Cambridge: Cambridge University Press, 2005.

—. "Corporate politics in the Low Countries: guilds as institutions, 14th to 18th centuries." In *Craft Guilds in the Early Modern Low Countries*, edited by Maarten Prak, Catharina Lis, Jan Lucassen, and Hugo Soly. Aldershot and Burlington: Ashgate, 2006.

Prevenier, Walter. "Methodological and Historiographical Footnotes on Emotions in the Middle Ages and the Early Modern Period" in *Emotions in the Heart of the City (14th-16th century)*, edited by Elodie Lecuppre-Desjardin and Anne-Laure Van Bruaene. Turnhout: Brepols, 2005, 273-293.

Price, J.L. *Holland and the Dutch Republic in the Seventeenth Century: The Politics of Particularism*. Oxford: Clarendon Press, 1994.

—. *Dutch Society, 1588-1713*. Essex: Longman, 2000.

Rapley, Mark. *Quality of Life Research: A Critical Introduction*. London: Sage Publications, 2003.

Richards, David. "Rights and Autonomy." *Ethics* 92 (1981):3-20.

Rijksmuseum. *Fire! Jan van der Heyden schilder en uitvinder*. Amsterdam: Rijksmuseum, 2007.

Riley, James C. "That Your Widow May Be Rich: Providing for Widowhood in Old Regime Europe." *Economisch-en-Sociaal-Historisch Jaarboek* 45 (1982):58-76.

—. *Rising Life Expectancy: A Global History*. Cambridge: Cambridge University Press, 2001.

Roberts, Benjamin. *Through the keyhole: Dutch child-rearing practices in the 17th and 18th century*. Hilversum: Verloren, 1998.

Robeyns, Ingrid. "Sen's Capability Approach and Gender Inequality: Selecting Relevant Capabilities." *Feminist Economics* 9 (2003).

—. "Rokende Soldaten: Mannelijke rolmodellen voor de jeugd in de vroege zeventiende eeuw?" in *Losbandige jeugd: Jongeren en moraal in de Nederlanden tijdens de late Middeleeuwen en de Vroegmoderne Tijd*, edited by Leendert F. Groenendijk and Benjamin B. Roberts. Hilversum: Verloren, 2004, 53-71.

—. "Drinking Like a Man: The Paradox of Excessive Drinking for Seventeenth-Century Dutch Youths." *Journal of Family History* 29 (2004):253-173.

Rochberg-Halton, Eugene. *Social Theory in the Pragmatic Attitude*. Chicago: University of Chicago Press, 1986.

Roding, Juliette. *Schoon en net: Hygiene in woning en stad*. The Hague: Stadsuitgeverij, 1986.

Romano, Dennis. *Housecraft and Statecraft: Domestic Service in Renaissance Venice, 1400-1600*. Baltimore and London: Johns Hopkins University Press, 1996.

Roodenburg, Herman. *Onder Censuur*. Hilversum: Verloren, 1990.

Rosenwein, Barbara H. "Worrying about Emotions in History." *American Historical Review* 3 (June 2002):821-845.

Ross, Josephine. *Jane Austen: A Companion*. New Brunswick: Rutgers University Press, 2003.

Rotberg, Robert I., and Theodore K. Rabb, eds. *Hunger and History: The Impact of Changing Food Production and Consumption Patterns of Society*. Cambridge: Cambridge University Press, 1985.

Rubin, Simon Shimshon. "The death of a child is forever: The life course impact of child loss" in *Handbook of bereavement: Theory, research, and intervention*, edited by Margaret S. Stroebe, Wolfgang Stroebe, and Robert O. Hansson. Cambridge: Cambridge University Press, 1993, 285-295.

Ruzicka, Guillaume Wunsch, and Penny Kane. *Differential Mortality: Methodological Issues and Biosocial Factors*. Oxford: Oxford University Press, 1993.

Ryan, Richard M., and Edward L. Deci. "On Happiness and Human Potentials: A Review of Research on Hedonic and Eudaimonic Well-Being." *Annual Review of Psychology* 52 (2001):141-166.

Sanders, M. "Risk factors in bereavement outcomes" in *Handbook of bereavement: Theory, research, and intervention*, edited by Margaret S. Stroebe, Wolfgang Stroebe, and Robert O. Hansson. Cambridge: Cambridge University Press, 1983, 255-267.

Sarti, Raffaella. "The Material Conditions of Family Life" in *Family Life in Modern Times, 1500-1789*, edited by David I. Kertzer and Marzio Barbali. New Haven and London: Yale University Press, 2001.

Scanlon, Thomas, "Value, Desire, and Quality of Life. in *The Quality of Life*, edited by Martha Nussbaum and Amartya Sen. Oxford: Clarendon Press, 1993, 185-200.

Schama, Simon. *The Embarrassment of Riches: An Interpretation of Dutch Culture in the Golden Age*. New York: Knopf, 1987.

Schellekens, Joan. "Determinant of Age at First Marriage Among Jews in Amsterdam, 1625-1724." *Journal of Family History* 24 (April 1999).

Schenkeveld, Maria A. *Dutch Literature in the Age of Rembrandt: Themes and Ideas*. Amsterdam and Philadelphia: John Benjamin Publishing Company, 1991.

Schenkeveld-van de Dussen, Riet. *De geheimen van het Vrouwelijk hart*. Amsterdam: Koninklijke Nederlandse Academie van Wetenschappen, 2001.

—. et al., eds. *Met en zonder Lauwerkrans: schrijvende vrouwen uit de vroegmoderne Tijd 1550-1850: van Anna Bijns tot Elise van Calcar*. Amsterdam: Amsterdam University Press, 1997.

Schijf, Huibert, and Bernadette van Woerkom. "Boekhouders en Peperwerkers: Werknemers van de Verenigde Oostindische Compagnie in Amsterdam tussen 1602 en 1689" in *De Verenigde Oostindische Compagnie in Amsterdam*. Verslag van een werkgroep, Amsterdam, 1982, 96-154.

Schipper-van Lottum, M.G.A. (Bix). *Advertenties en Berichten In de Amsterdamse Courant uitgetrokken op Kleding, Stoffen, Sieraden en Accessoires tussen de jaren 1672- 1765*. Amsterdam: Gopher Publishers, 1993.

Schmidt, Ariadne. *Overleven na de dood: Weduwen in Leiden in De Gouden Eeuw*. Amsterdam: Prometheus/Bert Bakker, 2001.

—. "Zelfstandig and bevoogd: de speelruimte van Vrouwen rond 1650." *Tijdschrift voor Sociale Geschiedenis* 29 (2003):28-34.

—. "Vrouwen en het recht. De juridische status van vrouwen in Holland in de vroegmoderne tijd." *Jaarboek Voor Geneaelogie*. Den Haag, 2004:26-44.

—. "The Winter of Her Life? Widowhood and the Lives of Dutch Women in the Early Modern Era" in *The Prime of Their Lives: Wise Old Women in Pre-Industrial Europe*, edited by Anneke B. Mulder-Bakker, and René Nip. Leuven-Paris-Dudley: Peeters, 2004, 138-148.

—. et al. "Themanummer Vrouwenarbeid in the Vroegmoderne tijd in Nederland." *Tijdschrift voor Sociale en Economische Geschiedenis* 3 (2005).

Schmidt, Adriadne. "Vrouwenarbeid in de Vroegmoderne Tijd in Nederland." *Tijdschrift voor Sociale en Economische Geschiedenis* 1 (2005).

Schneider, Maarten, and Jan Hemels. *De Nederlandse krant 1618- 1798*. Baarn: Wereldvenster, 1979.

Schurman, Anna Maria, van *Whether a Christian Woman Should Be Educated and Other Writings from her Intellectual Circle*. Edited and translated by Joyce L. Irwin. Chicago: University of Chicago Press, 1998.

Scott, James C. *Domination and the Arts of Resistance: Hidden Transcripts*. New York and London: Yale University Press, 1990.

Sen, Amartya. *Inequality Reexamined*. Oxford: Oxford University Press, 1992.

—. *On Economic Equality*. Expanded edition. Oxford: Clarendon Press, 1997.

Sennett, Richard, and Jonathan Cobb. *The Hidden Injuries of Class*. New York: Vintage Books, 1972.

Sewel, Wm. *A Compendious Guide to the Low-Dutch Language. The Second Edition, with Some Additions*. Amsterdam. Printed for the Widow of Stephen Swart, Bookseller, on the Westside of the Exchange, at the signe of the Crowned Bible, 1706.

Sharpe, James A. "Social Control in Early Modern England: The Need for a Broad Perspective" in *Social Control in Europe, 1500-1800*, edited by Herman Roodenburg and Pieter Spierenburg. Columbus: Ohio State University Press, 2004.

Sharpe, Pamela. "Survival strategies and stories: poor widows and widowers in early industrial England." In *Widowhood in Medieval and Early Modern Europe*, edited by Sandra Cavallo and Lyndan Warner. London: Longman, 1999.

Silverman, Phyllis S., and J. William Worden. "Children's reactions to the death of a parent" in *Handbook of bereavement: Theory, research, and intervention*, edited by Margaret S. Stroebe, Wolfgang Stroebe, and Robert O. Hansson. Cambridge: Cambridge University Press, 1993, 457-475.

Simpson, Eileen. *Orphans: Real and Imaginary*. London: Weidenfeld and Nicolson, 1987.

Slack, Paul. *Poverty and Policy in Tudor and Stuart England*. London: Longman, 1988.

Smith, Bonnie G. *The Gender of History: Men, Women, and Historical Practice*. Cambridge: Harvard University Press, 1998.

Smits-Veldt, Mieke B. *Maria Tesselschade: Leven met talent en vriendschap*. Zutphen: Walburg Pers, 1994.

—. "Images of Private Life in Some Early-Seventeenth- Century Ego-Documents" in *The Public and Private in Dutch Culture in the Golden Age*, edited by Arthur K. Wheelock, Jr., and Adele Seeff. Newark: University of Delaware Press, 2000, 164-177.

Sogner, S. "Young in Europe around 1700: Norwegian sailors and servant-girls seeking employment in Amsterdam." *Mesurer et comprendre*. Paris (1991):515-532.

Soltow, Lee, "Income and Wealth Inequality in Amsterdam, 1585- 1805." *Economisch En Sociaal Historisch Jaarboek* 52 (1989):72-95.

—. "Annual Inequality through Four Centuries: Conjectures for Amsterdam." Unpublished manuscript, no date.

—. and Jan Luiten van Zanden. *Income and Wealth Inequality in the Netherlands, 16th-20th Century*. Amsterdam: Spinhuis, 1998.

Spans, Jo. "Early Modern Orphanages between Civic Pride and Social Discipline: Francke's Use of Dutch Models." In *Waisenhäuser in der Frühen Neuzeit*, edited by Udo Sträter, and Josef N. Neumann. Tübingen: Halliesche Forschungen, 2003.

Speck, W. "Britain and the Dutch Republic" in *A Miracle Mirrored: The Dutch Republic in European Perspective*, edited by Karel Davids and Jan Lucassen. Cambridge: Cambridge University Press, 1995, 173-195.

Speet, B. "Wonen in de 16e eeuw: Primitief, vuil en benauwd" in *Amsterdam in Kaarten, Verandering van de stad in vier eeuwen cartografie*. Ede/Antwerp: Zomer & Keuning, 1987.

Spierenburg, Pieter. *The Spectacle of Suffering*. Cambridge: Cambridge University Press, 1984.

Spies, Paul, Koen Kleijn, Jos Smit, and Ernest Kurpershoek, eds. *The Canals of Amsterdam*. The Hague: SDU Uitgeverij Koninginnegracht, 1993.

Staring, Adolf. *De Hollanders thuis: gezelschapstukken uit drie eeuwen*. The Hague: Nijhof, 1956.

Stone, Lawrence. *The Family, Sex and Marriage in England, 1500-1800*. London: Weidenfeld and Nicolson, 1977.

Stone-Ferrier, Linda. "Metsu's Justice Protecting Widows and Orphans: Patron and Painter Relationships and Their Involvement in the Social and Economic Plight of Widows and Orphans in Leiden" in *The Public and Private in Dutch Culture of the Golden Age*, edited by Arthur W. Wheelock, Jr. and Adele Seeff. Newark: University of Delaware Press, 2000, 227-265.

Stroebe, Margaret S., Robert O. Hansson, and Wolfgang Stroebe. "Contemporary themes and controversies in bereavement research" in *Handbook of bereavement: theory, research, and intervention*, edited by Margaret S. Stroebe, Wolfgang Stroebe, and Robert O. Hansson. Cambridge: Cambridge University Press, 1993, 255-267.

Switzer, H.L. "De Soldaat" in *Gestalten van de Gouden Eeuw*, edited by H.M. Beliën,, A. T.h van Deursen, and G.J. van Setten. Amsterdam: Bert Bakker, 1995.

Taverne, Ed. *In 't land van belofte: in de nieue stadt ideaal en werkelijkheid van de stadsuitleg in de Republiek 1580-1680*. Maarssen: Gary Schwartz, 1978.

Taylor, Lou. *Mourning Dress: A Costume and Social History*. London: George Allen & Unwin, 1983.

Temple, Sir William. *Observations upon the United Provinces of the Netherlands*. Edited by Sir George Clark. Oxford: Clarendon Press, 1972. Originally published in 1673.

Thorn, Irma. *Strategic Affection? Gift Exchange in Seventeenth-Century Amsterdam*. Amsterdam: Amsterdam University Press, 2007.

Tielhof, Milja van. "Stedelijke Regulering van Drenten op de Stapelmarkt: De Amsterdamse Korengilden" in *Ondernemers & Bestuurders: Economie en politiek in de Noordelijke Nederlanden in de late Middeleeuwen en vroegmoderne tijd*, edited by Clé Lesger and Leo Noordegraaf. Amsterdam: NEHA, 1999, 491-523.

Tilly, Charles. *Coercion, Capital, and European States, AD 990-1990*. Cambridge: Basil Blackwell, 1990.

—. "Identity and Social History." *International Review of Social History* 40 (1995):1-17.

Towner, Elizabeth, and John Towner. "Developing the history of unintentional injury: the use of coroners' records in early modern England." *Injury Prevention* 6 (2000): 102-105.

Trimberger, E. Kay. *The New Single Woman*. Boston: Beacon Press, 2005.

Ulrich, Laurel Thatcher. *Image and Reality in the Lives of Women in Northern New England, 1650-1750*. New York: Alfred A. Knopf, 1982.

Verbeeck, Hermanus. *Memoriaal Ofte Mijn Levensraijsinghe*. Published by Jeroen Blaak. Hilversum: Verloren, 1999.

Viazzo, Pier Paolo. "Mortality, Fertility, and Family" in *Family Life in Early Modern Times, 1500-1789*, edited by David I. Kertzer and Marzio Barbagli. New Haven and London: Yale University Press, 2001.

Vleggert, J.C. *Kinderarbeid in Nederland, 1500-1874: Van Berusting tot Beperking*. Assen: Van Gorcum, 1964.

Vlis, Ingrid van der. *Leven in armoede. Delftse bedeelden in de zeventiende eeuw*. Amsterdam: Prometheus/Bert Bakker, 2001.

Vos, Lex Heerma van. "North Sea Culture" in *The North Sea And Culture (1550-1800)*, edited by Juliette Roding and Lex Heerma van Vos. Hilversum: Verloren, 1996.

Vries, Jan de. *European Urbanization, 1500-1800*. London: Methuen, 1984.

—. "Between Purchasing Power and the World of Goods: Understanding the Household Economy in Early Modern Europe" in *Consumption and the World of Goods*, edited by John Brewer and Roy Porter. London and New York: Routledge, 1993.

—. "The Labour Market" in *The Dutch Economy in the Golden Age*, edited by Karel Davids and Leo Noordegraaf. Amsterdam: the Netherlands Economic History Archives, 1995.

—. and Ad van der Woude. *The First Modern Economy: Success, Failure, and Perseverance of the Dutch Economy, 1500-1815*. Cambridge: Cambridge University Press, 1997.

Waals, Fransje W. van der. "Doorbraken in de verloskunde" in *Een Kind Onder Het Hart*, edited by H.M. Dupois et al. Amsterdam: Meulenhoff, 1987.

Walle, Etienne van de. "Birth prevention before the era of modern contraception." *Population and Societies* 418 (December 2005).

Walsh, John. "Skies and Reality in Dutch Landscapes" in *Art in history/History in Art*, edited by David Freedberg and Jan de Vries. Santa Monica: Getty Center for the History of Art and the Humanities, 1991.

Warner, Alex. *London Bodies: The changing shape of Londoners from Prehistoric times to the present day*. London: Museum of London, 1988.

Warner, Lyndan. "Widows, widowers and the problem of 'second marriages' in sixteenth-century France." In *Widowhood in Medieval and Early Modern Europe*, edited by Sandra Cavallo and Lyndan Warner. Essex: Longman, 1999.

Watts, Sheldon. *Epidemics and History: Disease, Power, and Imperialism*. New Haven and London: Yale University Press, 1997.

Wetering, Ernst van de. "De Schilder" in *Gestalten van de Gouden Eeuw*, edited by H.M. Beliën, A.Th. van Deursen, and G.J. van Setten. Amsterdam: Bert Bakker, 1996.

Wettengl, ed. *Maria Sibylla Merian, 1647-1717: Artist and Naturalist*. Verlag Gerd Hatje, no date.

Wiesner, Mary E. *Women and Gender in Early Modern Europe*. New York: Cambridge University Press, 1993.

Wijngaarden, Hilde van. *Zorg voor de kost: Armenzorg, arbeid en onderlinge hulp in Zwolle, 1650-1700*. Amsterdam: Uitgeverijen Prometheus/Bert Bakker, 2000.

Wijsenbeek-Olthuis, Thera. *Achter de gevels van Delft*. Hilversum: Verloren, 1987.

—. "Noblesse Oblige: Material Culture of the Nobility in Holland" in *Private Domain, Public Inquiry: Families and Life-Styles in the Netherlands and Europe, 1550 to the Present*, edited by Anton Schuurman and Pieter Spierenburg. Hilversum: Verloren, 1996.

—. "Ziekte en tegenslag" in *Of Bidden Helpt? Tegenslag en cultuur in Europa, circa 1500-2000*, edited by Marijke Gijswijt-Hofstra and Florike Egmond. Amsterdam: Amsterdam University Press, 1997, 71-86.

Wilson, Adrian. "Participant or patient: Seventeenth-century childbirth from the mother's point of view" in *Patients and Practitioners: Lay perceptions of medicine in preindustrial society*, edited by Roy Porter. Cambridge: Cambridge University Press, 1985, 129-144.

Wingens, Mac. "Jeugdige lichtzinnigheid en losbandigheid, seksueel gedrag van studenten ten tijde van de Nederlandse Republiek" in *Balans & perspectief van de Nederlandse cultuurgeschiedenis: Grensgeschillen in de Seks*, edited by Gert Hekma, Dorelies Kraakman, and Willem Melching. Amsterdam: Rodolfi, 1990.

Wolff, Sula. *Childhood & Human Nature: The Development of Personality*. London and New York: Routledge, 1989.

World Health Organization. "Healthy environments for children." April 25, 2003.

Woude, Ad van der. "The Volume and Value of Paintings in Holland at the Time of the Dutch Republic" in *Art in History/History in Art*, edited by David Freedberg and Jan de Vries. Santa Monica: Getty Center for the History of Art and the Humanities, 1991.

—. Akira Hayami, and Jan de Vries. "Introduction" in *Urbanization in History: A Process of Dynamic Interaction*, edited by Ad van der Woude, Akira Hayami, and Jan de Vries. Oxford: Clarendon Press, 1990.

Wrightson, Keith. *Earthly Necessities: Economic Lives in Early Modern Britain*. New Haven and London: Yale University Press, 2000.

Wrigley, E.A. *Poverty, Progress, and Population*. Cambridge: Cambridge University Press, 2004.

Zanden, J.L. van. *The Rise and Decline of Holland's Economy: Merchant Capitalism and the Labor Market*. Manchester and New York: Manchester University Press, 1993.

—. "What Happened to the Standards of Living Before the Industrial Revolution? New Evidence From the Western Part of the Netherlands." In *Living Standards of the Past: New Perspectives on Well-Being in Asia and Europe*, edited by Robert C. Allen, Tommy Bengtsson, and Martin Tribe. Oxford: Oxford University Press, 2005.

—. and Arthur van Riel. *The Strictures of Inheritance: The Dutch Economy in the Nineteenth Century*. Princeton: Princeton University Press, 2004.

Zantkuijl, H.J. *Bouwen in Amsterdam: Het Woonhuis in de stad*. Amsterdam: Architectura & Natura, 1993.

Zeeuw, J.W. de. "Peat and the Dutch Golden Age: The Historical Meaning of Energy-Attainability." *A.A.G. Bijdragen* 21. Wageningen, 1978, 3-31.

THE AUTHOR

Derek Phillips, emeritus professor at the University of Amsterdam, has lived and worked in Amsterdam since 1971. His books
include *Knowledge from What? Theories and Methods in Social
Research; Wittgenstein and Scientific Knowledge; Toward a Just Social Order;
Looking Backward: A Critical Appraisal of Communitarian Thought; and (with
Klaske Muizelaar) Picturing Men and Women in the Dutch Golden Age: Paintings and People in Historical Perspective.*

INDEX

Levie, Tirtsah, 43, 68, 71, 72
Levin, Patricia A., 62
Levy, Marion J., 134
Lievens, Jan, 177
life expectancy, 19-19, 63
Lindeman, R., 21
Lindemann, Mary, 75
Lindert, Peter H., 62
literacy, 38, 108, 200n.67, 200n.68
Lis, Catharina, 31, 53
Loo, Jacob van, *Allegory on the Distribution of Bread to the Poor*, 57
Loonen, P.L.M., 38
Lourens, P., 47, 51, 66
lower orders, 51-54
Lucas, Catherine, 155
Lucassen, Jan, 11, 15, 31, 32, 34, 37, 47, 51, 53
Manfredini, Matteo, 122
marital age:
    in Amsterdam, 99, 214n.13
    in Northwestern Europe, 99
marital prospects, 99, 109-110
marital status, 104-106
    and gender, 104, 153-154, 163-164
marriage:
    balance of power in, 117-118
    choice of partner, 115-116
    division of labor in, 117
    fatherhood, 120, 123-125
    gender ideology, 116-117
    motherhood, 120-125, 128
        and childbirth, 120-122
        and midwives, 121-122
        and mortality, 122
        and wet-nurses, 122-125, 221n.56
    parental permission, 116
    witnesses, 116
marriage pattern:
    characteristics,
        in Northwestern Europe, 98-99
        in other societies, 98-99
Marland, Hilary, 121
Marmot, Michael, 19
Marshall, Sherrin, 115, 172
Matthews Grieco, Sara F., 122, 172
Maza, Sarah C., 81
McCants, Anne E.C., 55, 154, 156, 172, 176-180
McCarthy, Mary, 182, 231n.61
McCord, Colin, 63
McGillivray, Mark, 11
McIntyre, S., 64
McLemee, Scott, 22
Megill, Allan, 200n.63
Meijer Drees, Marijke, 14, 16
Meischke, R., 71
Meldrum, Timothy, 81
men:
    and economic well-being, 109-110, 154, 162-163

    and mortality, 151
    legal status, 153-154, 164
Merian, Maria Sibylla, 147
Metsu, Gabriel, *The Sick Child*, 128
Meyers, Diana, 19
Middelkoop, Norbert, 79, 175
miasmas, 63, 205n.16
migrants, 14, 33-40
    and language, 37-40
    as "guest-workers" (*"gastarbeiders"*), 40
    earnings of, 36-40, 51-54
    experiences of, 36-40
    literacy of, 38-40
    number of, 14, 33-35
    places of origin, 34-35
    reasons for migrating, 34
    types of work done, 36-40, 51-54
Miller, Naomi J., 140
Miller, William Ian, 22
Mitchell, Juliet, 140, 145, 146
Molenaers, Clara, 146
Moody-Adams, Michele M.,11, 147, 225-226n.54
mortality (see death)
Muizelaar, Klaske, 14, 17, 43, 70, 82, 84, 86-98, 89, 97, 98, 107, 109, 120, 124-126, 142, 154, 171
Muldrew, Craig, 55
Muller, Sheila D., 158, 162
Muyssart, Abraham, 134-135
Nederveen Meerkerk, Elise van, 15, 53, 101, 118, 161
Nee, Victor, 39
Nierop, Henk van, 13, 14, 16, 29, 33, 46, 53, 231n.54
noise, 77
Noltenius, Willem, 125, 220n.52, 221n.54
Noordegraaf, Leo, 11, 20, 36, 40, 52, 53, 57, 191n.3
Noordkerk, H., 68, 87
Noordse Bos, 66-67
Norton, Mary Beth, 122
Nussbaum, Martha, 11
Nusteling, Hubert, 11, 32, 33, 48, 54, 57, 72, 73, 191n.3
Nystedt, Paul, 122
odors, 62, 70, 74
occupations, 32-34, 36-37, 40, 101-104, 121-122, 136-138, 198n.23
    and autonomy, 29, 53, 54
    and civic status, 47-54, 102
    and earnings, 30, 44-54, 57, 83, 219n.30
    and days and hours of work, 30, 53, 82, 136-137
    and social identity, 50, 101
    for citizens, 33-36, 40, 51-54, 138-139
    for non-citizens, 33-36, 40, 51-54, 178-179
O'Dea, William T., 82
Oeppen, James E., 62, 64, 99, 109, 160, 205n.22

Sanders, Catherine M., 142
Sarragan, Lysbeth, 97
Sarti, Raffaella, 83
Scanlon, Thomas, 11
Schama, Simon, 137
Schellekens, Joan, 92, 93
Schenkeveld, Maria A., 12
Schenkeveld-van Dussen, Riet, 147
Scherf, Y., 21
Schijf, Huibert, 53, 54, 137
Schipper, Mineke, 89
Schipper-van Lottum, M.G.A., 38, 88, 108, 154, 180, 181
Schmidt, Ariadne, 100, 101, 118, 161
Schmitz, Peter, 89
Schneider, Maarten, 38
Schurman, Anna Maria von, 147
Scott, James C., 22
Seba, Alberta, 55
self-esteem, 19, 40, 46, 54, 139, 226n.7
    as dimension of well-being, 19
Sen, Amartya, 11, 54, 192n.7
Sennett, Richard, 16
servants:
    backgrounds, 80
    changing employers, 91
    conflicts with employers, 83-91
        about clothes, 85-88
        about earnings and work, 84-85
        about unwanted sexual intimacy, 88-91
    deference and demeanor, 82, 83
    dependence and vulnerability, 82, 83, 90-92
    earnings, 83, 84
    in household hierarchies, 81, 83
    names, 97-98, 209-210n.3, 210n.12
    number in Amsterdam, 15, 102
    ordinance about clothing, 87-88
    preparing for the future, 91-93
    punishment for behavior, 88
    relationships with other persons,
        in the household, 81, 83-84, 87-90
        outside the household, 92
    responsibilities,
        of male servants, 81
        of female servants, 81-83
    rights, 87, 90-91
    sleeping arrangements, 70, 83, 213n.2
    stereotypes of, 87, 89, 90, 212n.31
    turnover in employment, 91
Sewel, Willem, 38
sex ratio in Amsterdam, 93, 214n.16, 216n.55
    and marital prospects, 99, 109
sexual relations:
    marital, 120
    premarital, 107
    extramarital, 90
Sharpe, James A., 48
Sharpe, Pamela, 161
Short, Roger, 122, 124, 125, 220n.44

siblings, 140-141, 146-147, 224n.48, 224-225n.50
Silverman, Phyllis S., 153, 170
Simpson, Eileen, 183
single men:
    and charity, 103, 215n.34
    attitudes toward, 105-106
    earning a living, 101, 109-110
    living arrangements, 99, 100, 110
    never-marrying, 109-110, 217n.61
    options for economic survival, 109-110
    sexual aggression of, 105-106
single women:
    and charity, 103, 215n.34
    attitudes toward, 105-106
    earning a living, 101-104, 109
    living arrangements, 99-100, 110
    never-marrying, 109-110, 217n.61
    options for economic survival, 109-110
    victims of sexual assaults and rape, 89-91, 105-106, 216n.43
Slack, Paul, 158
Smit, Jos, 45, 67
Smith, Bonnie G., 21, 121
Smits-Veldt, Mieke B., 21, 147
social distance:
    between employers and servants, 81-83, 91-92, 210n.12
    between master artisans, apprentices, and journeymen, 48, 51-52, 202n.31
    between the rich and the rest, 14, 67-68, 171, 179
Sogner, S., 80
Soltow, Lee, 11, 14, 15, 32, 43, 44, 46, 80
Soly, Hugo, 31, 53
Sorensen, Jesper B., 14
Sorgh, Hendrick Martensz, *Portrait of the Bierens Family*, 70
Spans, Jo, 174
Speck, W., 48
Speet, B., 67
Spierenburg, Pieter, 87
Spies, Paul, 45
Spon, E. and F.V., 66
Stallybrass, Peter, 86
Staring, Adolf, 80
staying alive, 11, 14, 58
    as dimension of well-being, 18
Stein, P.G., 171
Stone, Lawrence, 124
Stone-Ferrier, Linda, 175
Stroebe, Margaret S., 142, 155
Stroebe, Wolfgang, 142, 155
Switzer, H.L., 37
Taverne, Ed, 67
Taylor, Lou, 155
Teeuwen, Nicole, 15
teeth, 108
Temple, Sir William, 61-62, 69
Tesselschade, Maria, 147